PIONEER SETTLEMENT IN NORTHEAST ARGENTINA

ROBERT C. EIDT

THE UNIVERSITY OF WISCONSIN PRESS
MADISON, MILWAUKEE AND LONDON

Published 1971
The University of Wisconsin Press
Box 1379, Madison, Wisconsin 53701

The University of Wisconsin Press, Ltd.
27–29 Whitfield Street, London, W.1

First printing

Printed in the United States of America

ISBN 0–299–05920–0; LC 71–138058

To My Parents

TABLE OF CONTENTS

LIST OF ILLUSTRATIONS

LIST OF TABLES

PREFACE

The attraction of vast empty regions in Latin America has long offered a challenge for pioneer settlers who want to open new land to escape adverse political, economic, religious, ethnic, or other pressures, and for environmental scientists who attempt to direct land opening or to analyze its results. During the last few decades population pressures have intensified this attraction to Latin America's "marginal" areas, as have resurgence of the age-old desire in man to own his own acres, and improved technologies in marginal-area management which have given added hope of success. Indeed, pioneer settlement has become such a popular theme in Latin America that scores of empty regions are rapidly being occupied by individuals or groups of colonists who feel forced to leave well-established but overcrowded homelands.

There is a very current need for detailed investigations of marginal areas now undergoing settlement transformation because the scope of pioneer movements in Latin America is again intensifying, because the initial impact of pioneering sets the stage for future growth but is difficult if not impossible to identify once the landscape becomes crowded, and because there is an urgent desire to find workable colonization techniques from any period of development by which determined settlers and government officials can overcome the problems associated with modern colonization. Field research is especially needed in attractive, apparently untouched areas which have already been subjected to aboriginal or colonial land use and are being reopened by modern pioneers. It is therefore the object of this investigation, which deals with pioneer settlement achievements contrived by foreign and native colonists in northeast Argentina, to shed light on one major land opening project and the past developments with which it is closely linked in order to make clearer its role in the evolution of the modern landscape.

I am indebted to my former professor, H. J. Bruman, for first calling to my attention Misiones Province, Argentina, as an area with an unusual settlement genesis. In 1952 as a Buenos Aires Convention fellow in Colombia I travelled to Argentina to gather resource materials on Misiones but was unable to visit the Province. During a second trip, sponsored by the University of Minnesota in 1956, two weeks in Misiones excited interest in the different settlement forms being employed by government and private colonization agencies. While on a Fulbright assignment in Peru another visit of two weeks duration was made in 1960 with kind assistance from Dr. E. Indacochea, head of the U.S. Fulbright Commission, Lima, Peru. Outstanding landscape changes being wrought in Misiones by pioneer settlers of diverse origins became clearer at that time and I decided to return for a longer period as soon as circumstances permitted. Four years later the National Science Foundation awarded me a senior research grant to pursue studies of pioneer settlement not only in Europe, from which many of the colonists of Misiones emigrated, but in Misiones itself where I resided during the latter half of 1965. The National Science Foundation also made it possible for me to conduct further research on European settlement geography during 1970 just before this book went to press. Deepest gratitude is therefore extended to the Foundation and particularly to Dr. H. Hines, director of the Social Sciences Division, for his friendly encouragement.

I am also appreciative of the thoughtfulness and cooperation of Drs. W. von Zeschau and S. Simsolo, general directors of the Oficina de Tierras y Bosques, where official records, maps, and work space were provided me in Posadas, Misiones, at various times during their periods of tenure; of Dr. Osvaldo Q. de la Encina, head, Dirección de Catastro, Geodesia y Topografía, Posadas; and of Argentine pioneer settlers far too numerous to mention by name but who as individuals contributed much to this volume.

Special acknowledgment is made of the hospitality offered a total stranger by Sr. J. Wipfel of the Cooperativa Mixta de Monte Carlo, who provided me with living quarters and unstinting aid while working in Misiones; to Srs. A. Bühler, C. Jauch, and B. Wolanski, all of Monte Carlo Colony; Sr. J. Fausch of Colonia Caraguatay; and Sr. F. Moser of Eldorado.

Sr. C. Ritsche, Buenos Aires, was kind enough to take my family into his home and provide all of us with a memorable stay in Argentina. Other *porteños* (residents of Buenos Aires), including officials of the Instituto Geográfico Militar, the Universidad de Buenos Aires, the Ministerio de Agricultura y Ganadería, the Biblioteca Tornquist, the Museo Histórico Nacional, and the Central de Control Aerofotográfico, were most helpful and generous with their time.

Appreciation is particularly due my colleague Professor H. Uhlig of the University of Gießen, for many special efforts on my behalf without which parts of this book could not have been written, as well as H. Wilhelmy, University of Tübingen, for offering personal library documents and advice; and colleagues O. Berninger, E. Ehlers, R. Herrmann, R. Käubler, E. Lehmann, E. Neef, G. Niemeier, and W. Tietze, all of whom provided encouragement and companionship during numerous field investigations and discussions of European settlement forms, some of which have been transferred to Latin America.

Dr. K. Krill, dean of the Graduate School, and the Graduate Research Committee, University of Wisconsin—Milwaukee, supported this project with a generous grant. Maps were prepared by Mr. E. Seeman, whose suggestions have been much appreciated, and by the University of Wisconsin—Milwaukee Cartographic Service, under the direction of Dr. James Flannery. I am also grateful to the editors of *Economic Geography* and *Geographische Rundschau* for granting permission to use materials first published in those journals.

As in all studies of this type, valuable assistance has been offered by colleagues and close friends. Credit for this task is especially due Dr. César N. Caviedes and Professors Clinton R. Edwards and Norman R. Stewart of the Department of Geography, University of Wisconsin—Milwaukee, for reading parts of the manuscript, and Roland F. Dickey and Jane B. Knowles of the University Press, for their constructive ideas and expert editing. Responsibility for errors, however, is my own. Translations from Spanish, German, Portuguese, and Japanese are also mine. Foreign words have all been italicized the first time they appear in the text.

It would be difficult adequately to acknowledge esteemed assistance from many other individuals in Argentina, Europe, and the United States, but to all of them, including the writer's patient and helpful family, is extended warmest appreciation.

Justus Liebig-University   ROBERT C. EIDT
Gießen, Federal Republic of Germany
September, 1970.

PIONEER SETTLEMENT
IN NORTHEAST ARGENTINA

Chapter 1

INTRODUCTION

> The "science of settlement" . . . is dependent on a new condition in pioneering — that the best land has been taken in all but a few regions and the rest of it has to be occupied by departures from the commonly accepted standards of agricultural practice.
>
> Isaiah Bowman, *The Pioneer Fringe*

THE ROLE OF PIONEER SETTLEMENT

For centuries vast expanses of territory in Latin America have remained beyond the limits of meaningful settlement, and today almost half the land is still unused. This has presented challenges to various countries for broadening and strengthening their economic and cultural bases through encouragement of either spontaneous settlement or carefully organized land opening, i.e., colonization. However, pioneer settlement in these remote regions has been hindered by such obstacles as difficult soils and climates, poor health conditions, and inaccessibility.[1] Less familiar impedimenta associated with marginal areas have been inappropriate choice of settlement form, absence of bona fide land titles, inadequate or nonexistent urban facilities, and unsuitable colonists. On the other hand, from time to time pioneer groups have succeeded despite such discouraging factors; indeed, their colonies have been so outstanding that governments and private organizations continue to participate hopefully in land settlement programs. Today there is the added incentive that modern medicine, improved transportation, and new settlement techniques can overcome the basic obstacles to land opening in unused areas.

Nowhere has interest in pioneer settlement become greater during the present century than in Latin America. Overcrowding of many regions has created pressures so great that movement toward sparsely inhabited places has become advisable if not essential. Misiones Province in northeast Argentina is a case in point:

3

since passage of special colonization legislation in 1903, hundreds of thousands of pioneers have settled on densely forested land in that region.[2] In 1929 Chile began planned settlement near Santiago.[3] Since 1931 large-scale colonization has been promoted in northern Paraná and other parts of Brazil.[4] Mexico publicly announced a "drive to the sea" for settling tropical coast areas in 1941.[5] More recently, Bolivia in 1953 undertook development of the Santa Cruz lowlands.[6] Ecuador began directed settlement in 1957 in the north coast area,[7] and by enactment of colonization legislation in 1959, Colombia initiated a program east of the Andes.[8] Paraguay in 1959[9] and Peru in 1960[10] offered land to settlers along new roads extending from populated regions to the empty interior. During the 1960s Venezuela initiated official resettlement of the Llanos del Orinoco.[11] Land opening in these and still other Latin American countries, some of which have more modest plans, continues to attract both national and international support.[12]

The growing numbers of pioneer programs, many of whose techniques are highly innovative, the differences in attitude regarding foreign and native settlers, and recent massive infusions of international capital, indicate that it is already necessary to alter settlement concepts of this part of the world. Although remoteness of the pioneer areas and lack of a uniform frontier of the type once found in the United States have made it difficult to assemble detailed information about these places, the changes occurring in most of them now involve sufficiently large numbers of people and amounts of land to merit intensive study for their own sake. A major objective of this investigation, therefore, is to contribute to knowledge about one of the important areas of modern settlement in a remote part of Latin America.

Although unfavorable divergence between population growth and food production has created pressing needs for colonization programs in all of the countries mentioned, outright failure, abetted in some cases by inattention to historical settlement factors, and in others by spontaneous transfer of existing evils to new lands, must be minimized if more than stopgap economic results are to be achieved by means of pioneer settlement. It is therefore a second objective of this study to inquire into the effects of past as well as existing land opening projects in order to reveal the particular ingredients which may be relevant to successful modern settlement in this and other regions of Latin America.

Choice of the remote Misiones area for field investigation seems especially appropriate since there was intensive colonial settlement of part of the land, followed by more than a century of abandonment, and colonization again in recent times. Moreover, once the slow and painful Spanish to Republican transition ended in Argentina, modern pioneers took advantage of knowledge won during colonial experiments in Misiones, and established almost 200 agglomerated settlements and cleared 300,000 hectares (ha) of farmland in a surprisingly short period. In fact, the flow of settlers into this region mainly since the 1920s caused its population to reach an estimated half-million mark just prior to 1970. These achievements should be of importance both to those concerned with major changes in the patterns of Latin American land history, and to the increasing numbers of governmental and private agencies and individuals contemplating pioneer settlement in similar marginal areas. Despite the fact that success of pioneer settlement in Misiones has reached relatively significant proportions, this region is almost unknown in the English literature, and is a part of the great Argentine nation which few of its inhabitants have ever visited.

THE PROVINCE OF MISIONES

Misiones has about the same area as the country of Haiti and lies approximately 25 degrees south of the Equator. Rivers form all but 50 km of its borders. The rivers Alto Paraná in the west, Iguazú in the north, and Uruguay in the south also form international boundaries with Paraguay and Brazil.

Misiones has everywhere an annual rainfall of approximately 1,450 mm or more, but is subjected to short, severe periods of desiccation lasting up to three or four weeks. Annual temperatures average about 20° c, although light frosts occur almost every year. A dense subtropical forest, known locally as the *Selva Misionera*, or simply the *Selva*, virtually covers the province; yet in the southwestern extremity there is a broken savanna called the *Campo* which is reminiscent of the patches of impoverished grassland scattered over parts of the Amazon Basin.

The terrain and soils, like the climate and natural vegetation,

Fig. 1. Situation map of Misiones Province, Argentina.

emphasize the marked transitional nature of this region. Level to rolling lands in the Campo rise to hills and mountains in the Selva. The major soil type derives from the basic lava of Brazil's Paraná Plateau, the heartland of the well-known *terra roxa* coffee soil. It is relatively fertile, but easily eroded. However similarly colored although much less fertile soils derived from red sandstones are found in the Campo and in scattered parts of the Selva as well.

The transitional nature of Misiones' physical geography has posed especially difficult colonization problems. Some of these have been solved by methods originally worked out during a unique but nearly forgotten colonial settlement experiment, whereas others have been overcome by modern pioneering innovations.

JESUIT REDUCCIONES

During the Spanish period ambitious colonization efforts were made in Latin America by members of various religious orders. Between 1609 and 1707, the Jesuits established 30 viable settlements, or *reducciones*, in the frontier zone common to present-day Paraguay, Argentina, and Brazil. The 11 established in Misiones account for the name of the Province. Guaraní Indians were gathered into these reducciones and agricultural and industrial methods, worked out largely through trial and error, eventually resulted in a population of over 50,000 in or near the Campo of Misiones. During the peak of this colonization activity, appropriate settlement sites, crops, forest products, and transport systems and routes were developed throughout the zone. After 1759 in Brazil, and 1767 in Spanish areas, the entire mission colonization program collapsed because the Jesuits were forced to leave these regions. By the modern period, Misiones Province had fallen into disuse, and since its physical geography is so unlike the rest of Argentina's, it was purposely avoided by most citizens. Even so, much of the knowledge accumulated by the Jesuits was recorded and proved valuable to foreign pioneers settling in the same region over a century after the collapse of the mission program.

STATE AND FEDERAL LANDS

The question for Argentina only a few decades ago was how to proceed with land opening in this "unfamiliar" part of the national territory. Public officials first urged occupation because the War of the Triple Alliance from 1865 to 1870 made it obvious that foreigners could overrun Misiones at will, as they had done often during and even after the war.[13] National pride was at stake, and determination grew to protect the country's frontiers and prevent illegal border activities. A problem arose when the Province of Corrientes, of which Misiones was then a part, refused to give up land for federal colonization. The outcome was a government decision in 1881 to declare Misiones a separate National Territory. (Boundaries were not settled until some years later.) Corrientes received prior word of the nationalization plans, and, in a state of bitterness, decided to sell the entire zone to private interests. Only the lands formerly occupied by the Jesuit mission settlements remained unaffected because they were held in reserve. Land sales were completed in record time by dividing Misiones into enormous estates and granting them to thirty-eight purchasers.[14] Because the sales were made legally, the Argentine government felt obligated to recognize them, but it was then confronted with the same situation that most Latin American nations face today — a vital need to open new land already owned by a handful of people who insist on maintaining title to that land without using it.

As an initial recourse the federal government assumed control of the abandoned Jesuit *reducciones* and ordered their subdivision and colonization. Prior to settlement the land was surveyed by the traditional Argentine rectangular grid system which results in the *damero*, or quadrate settlement form, and in 1893 authority to issue titles was established in the territorial capital of Posadas. These actions played a critical role in early official colonization of the Campo. This small part of the territory was soon occupied and attention turned quickly to the greater problem of populating the Selva.

Three steps taken before the Selva was opened furnish examples that may be useful to modern colonization agents elsewhere in Latin America. The first was the initiation of a federal land settlement program without applying the politically difficult *método extremo*, i.e., outright expropriation. To accomplish this the Argentine Congress ordered a new title survey, in the course of which it was discovered that *latifundia* along the Alto Paraná and

Uruguay rivers did not occupy the entire Selva. Lots that had been sold by Corrientes Province were poorly demarcated and too short to meet between the rivers as originally planned. The federal government took possession of the leftover land, thus acquiring a narrow strip through the Selva in the most rugged part of the new Territory.

After gaining this foothold, the second step was actual settlement, but in spite of generous offers of land, Argentine farmers continued to avoid Misiones. For one thing the government was simultaneously attempting to colonize other parts of the country, e.g., Patagonia, the Pampa, and the Chaco, where it is flat and not so rainy. Unlike Misiones, there existed no problems of isolation from neighbors and markets by hilly forests which grew back almost as soon as they were cut down and which were infested by poisonous snakes and innumerable biting insects. Discouraged in attracting its own citizens, the Argentine government offered Misiones land at low prices to Europeans who wanted to escape the tensions of World War I. The program at first attracted dissatisfied German-speaking people from southern Brazil. Later, colonists came directly from Germany, Austria, Switzerland, Finland, Sweden, Denmark, and the Ukraine. Many were settled in new damero colonies. Others who preceded government survey teams cut *piques* (narrow machete paths) into the forest and demarcated their own small, parallel holdings on either side. The resulting settlements were similar to planned line villages called *Waldhufendörfer* developed during medieval times in forested parts of Europe.[15] The different adjustments made while creating damero and Waldhufen-like colonies have brought about important variations in pioneer settlement processes. Since these two settlement forms have been utilized in the same landscapes by people of many nationalities, there is probably no better place in Latin America to measure and compare the results of modern pioneer settlement.

Some of the first foreigners established modified *Raiffeisen* cooperatives — multifaceted types which dispensed agricultural credit and which supported most economic activity ranging from road building at the outset to the later provision of crop insurance. The cooperatives helped to assure the success of these colonization projects.

Ultimately, so many thousands of Argentine settlers joined the progressive colonies or adopted the new techniques in settlements of their own, that they now far outnumber the foreigners who opened the area.

The third step was to influence the large estate holders to subdivide and colonize their lands, following the federal government model. Gradually the *latifundistas* awakened to the settlement boom in the narrow strip of government holdings and sold large amounts of their own land to pioneers. In the private settlements, division of colonists by religion and wealth and far more extensive building of planned Waldhufen colonies have produced effects different from those of the federal government, although some of the same basic techniques have been applied. This has added flavor and experience to the newly created human landscape in the Selva.

The opening of land by foreigners has continued through the years, but at a slower pace because of the more favorable economic conditions in Europe, especially since World War II. Asiatics, particularly Japanese, began establishing colonies on private lands in the Selva in 1959. In this attempt at colonization with Oriental pioneers the same methods of land opening used by Europeans have been employed.

In recognition of continuing progress in Misiones, the former territory was made a province in 1953, and in 1956 all remaining government land was placed under its jurisdiction for settlement.[16]

The relative progress in Misiones stands as a reminder that modern pioneering can play a significant economic role in the remote interior of Latin America. There is substantial hope for eliminating the anti-economic latifundium system without creating serious political disturbances or resorting to government purchase of all land in such regions. To understand the changes that have occurred in Misiones and how its unique system of state and private colonization has evolved, the transitional and marginal physical character of the area and the antecedents of modern land tenure must be carefully investigated. Therefore the natural setting and its settlement possibilities are described more fully in chapter 2; a history of early settlement experiments which influenced subsequent trends is outlined in chapters 3 and 4, followed by an analysis of the development of modern governmental and private colonization in chapters 5, 6, and 7. A concluding chapter is a general discussion of economic growth in Misiones. This detailed analysis of past and present colonization and the development of a specific landscape by various settlement methods — a number of which have failed — will, it is hoped, not only add to our knowledge of an important but little-known area of colonization, but also provide data for evaluating the conditions of pioneer settlement elsewhere in sparsely inhabited or empty country, and increase our understanding of the role played by colonization projects in the political and economic structure of Latin American nations.

> The forces of nature . . . do not hold any magic
> power over us except when their action is outside the
> realm of experience.
>
> Alexander von Humboldt, *Kosmos*

WEATHER AND CLIMATE

Advantages.   The Province of Misiones is located in the humid subtropics of Argentina — an area popularly associated with unpleasant if not unhealthful weather conditions. Nevertheless, the climate of Misiones offers several important advantages to pioneer farmers. For example, the relatively high annual temperatures facilitate an extensive range of planting times. A long season during which it is possible to plant more than once is useful to pioneers who cannot expect to raise familiar crops and often commit errors while learning. The lengthened planting regime also makes possible a more efficient spread of the settler's limited energies throughout the year. Still another benefit accrues from the ameliorative influence of high average temperatures. The extra expense of "winterizing," or building insulated shelters, is spared, no mean saving in money and labor to the new settler. A further climatic advantage is the extent to which heavy dews influence plant growth. Dews are estimated to add 12 per cent to the yearly rainfall and help preserve soil and plant moisture during most brief periods of drought.[1] In addition, the dews act as a protective device against light frosts which characterize the semitropics, thus contributing to the extended growing season.

The abundant rainfall in Misiones provides readily available fresh water. Depending on the survey system, settlers even on small holdings often have streams which furnish a convenient water supply. If streams are not present, as is frequently the case after damero surveys, colonists must dig or drill for water. Fortunately wells do not have to be more than 10 to 15 meters deep in most of Misiones, and water for personal needs is easily obtained if rock formations do not interfere with drilling.

Although annual precipitation is relatively heavy, a further benefit to pioneers derives from the combination of rainfall variability and the hilly nature of the Misiones landscape: there is very little malaria, a malady distressingly prevalent in the more level parts of semitropical and tropical Latin America where greater amounts of stagnant water provide natural mosquito breeding grounds.

Misiones also has a climate which offers psychological advantages to settlers. Night temperatures are low enough to make blankets a year-around sleeping requirement. This phenomenon is in itself a pleasant surprise to Europeans and others who arrive thinking of the Misiones region as a "green hell." The climate has helped create an extremely pleasant landscape in terms of the variety of surface forms and of the dense green natural vegetation which contrasts vividly with deep red soils. These, to be sure, are aspects which cannot be measured easily, but they are present and create a genuine attraction which settlers in the area are quick to appreciate and comment on.

Notwithstanding these advantages, climatic variations do occur, and since they are apt to be more critical in the lower latitudes, it becomes necessary for pioneers to be exceptionally well informed about the nature of weather extremes. Knowledge of these phenomena in Misiones is often sufficient to suggest certain agricultural remedies. Recorded statistical excesses are therefore dealt with in the paragraphs that follow.

Problems. According to the Köppen system of classification, the climate of Misiones is transitional between tropical and mesothermal, with humid to sub-humid rainfall conditions. The annual precipitation averages 1,500 mm in the Campo and 1,800 mm in the Selva (Fig. 2). Average data, however, shroud precipitation extremes which occur in Misiones. Throughout the area there are two periods of exceptionally heavy rains: March through May, and September through November. Rainfall during the wettest month, generally April, may reach peaks of 180 mm in the Campo lowlands and 500 mm in the Selva uplands. Downpours of 25 mm per hour are not uncommon during the "rainy season"; the maximum recorded precipitation is for Loreto, which received 150 mm within two hours on May 9, 1928.[2] Accurate data for the remote interior are lacking, but even greater intensities are suggested. Such out-bursts not only make soil erosion a grave problem, especially in areas where normal methods of plowing and cultivation are em-ployed, but may cause plant damage by root rot and loss of leaves and fruit.

There is no true dry season in Misiones, only a notable lessening of precipitation during the intervals between heavy rains. The longer less-rainy interval is in summer (December through Feb-ruary) and may extend up to four months in a narrow belt along the Paraná River valley. A somewhat shorter, more intensive period occurs from June through August. However, every several years completely rainless periods lasting up to thirty days also occur.[3] Curiously, these totally dry periods appear most often during the wettest seasons and bring real drought to the Province. Some for-est trees lose their foliage, and new orchard plantings are frequently damaged. Sandy soils become desiccated when even moderate winds prevail. In fact, the longer the ground is exposed to drying, the lower the soil permeability becomes because of cementation, and the greater the erosion danger from accentuated runoff during the next heavy rain. This phenomenon is acute in the Selva where precipitation averages are some 300 mm higher than in the Campo. However, damage is more widespread in Campo settlements be-cause of the generally open nature of the land.

Significant precipitation variations also occur on a yearly basis in Misiones, as is demonstrated by the figures in Table 1. These fluctuations cause unreliable harvests and make more difficult the prediction of yields.[4]

TABLE 1

Rainfall Variability Statistics, Misiones

Station	Years of Observation	Annual Variation (mm)
Posadas	28	910–2,549
Apóstoles	3	1,057–2,170
Pindapoy	19	832–2,294
Barra de Concepción	4	1,230–2,344
Bonpland	22	1,030–2,645

Source: Glieb Grüner, *La erosión en Misiones*, 2nd ed. (Buenos Aires, 1955), p. 45.

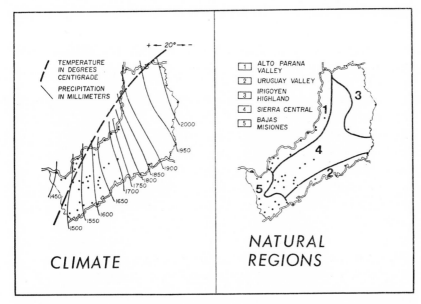

Fig. 2. Physical features of Misiones (dots represent place names shown on Fig. 3).
Sources: Misiones Province, *Planeamiento de la Provincia de Misiones* (Buenos Aires, 1961), vol. 2; Misiones Province, *Informe edafológico* (Buenos Aires, 1964); Misiones Province, *Informe sobre los recursos forestales* (Buenos Aires, 1964); Misiones Province, *Informe geológico* (Buenos Aires, 1964); other government publications.

diabase and melaphyre belonging to the *Planalto do Paraná* of Brazil whose southwest extremity extends into Argentina. It is believed that the lava formed in southern Brazil during several Mesozoic effusions of varying extent.[9] Although the geologic components in Misiones are not entirely the same as those in Brazil, the predominant upper layers of iron-rich lava and some intercalated, metamorphosed sandstones are both present and retain the same nomenclature in Argentina, i.e., *Serra Geral* and *São Bento*, respectively.[10]

The diabase and melaphyre stem from a basic lava whose outward forms and mineral composition have been altered by tectonic and climatic activities. Since the primary lava source was in Brazil, the resulting formations decline from 1,200 meters above sea level in the Serra Geral to 800 meters at the Argentine border and only 100 meters in southwestern Misiones where they disappear beneath the surface between Posadas and Apóstoles. In the

latter instance much of this westward sloping surface has been
eroded into compact successions of hills, the highest about half-
way between the Alto Paraná and Uruguay rivers. These hills
form a sharp, but discontinuous water divide which parallels the
length of the Province from San José to San Pedro (Fig. 2). Although this *divortium aquarum* is called the *Sierra Central*, it is
not a true mountain range, but only a higher erosional remnant of
the old, tilted platform. The Sierra rises from the 200 meter isohypse and is readily distinguished from the surrounding gentle,
rolling landscape with its local relief of some 35 meters. On higher
slopes along the water divide, erosion has left only piles of talus
and jagged rock outcrops. At the uppermost levels majestic table-
lands which have resisted erosion still stand (Pl. 1). Twisting
stream channels plunge down both sides of the Sierra Central
toward the bordering Alto Paraná and Uruguay rivers. Interfluves
are reasonably level and large enough to be used for centers of
colonization such as those of Leandro N. Alem, Oberá, and Campo
Grande (Fig. 3).

A landscape which is made of gently rolling hills lies in two
strips on either side of the Sierra Central (Fig. 3). Both strips extend inland approximately 20 km from the bordering rivers before
reaching the edge of the Sierra. They have an average elevation
of 100 meters and are characterized by occasional flat-topped
hills underlain by Serra Geral formations. Both strips are crossed
in numerous places by the twisting streams which drain the area.
These two narrow foothill regions are reminiscent of lower parts
of the German Erzgebirge south of Dresden and of the northern
Schwarzwald. Both foothill regions have elongated valley and
ridge settlement forms which correspond to their German counterparts. The bordering fringes of Misiones were, indeed, colonized by numbers of people from the same two areas in Germany.

A broad upland, the Altiplano de Irigoyen, begins at the end of
the Sierra Central near San Pedro and continues northeastward
until it reaches the Brazilian border opposite Bernardo de Irigoyen (Fig. 3). There it sends out two main branches: one southwest, and one which proceeds almost to the Iguazú Falls at the
northwest edge of the Province. Its various segments in Misiones
give the Altiplano the topographic shape of a volcanic island with
its apex at Bernardo de Irigoyen. This section of Misiones is part

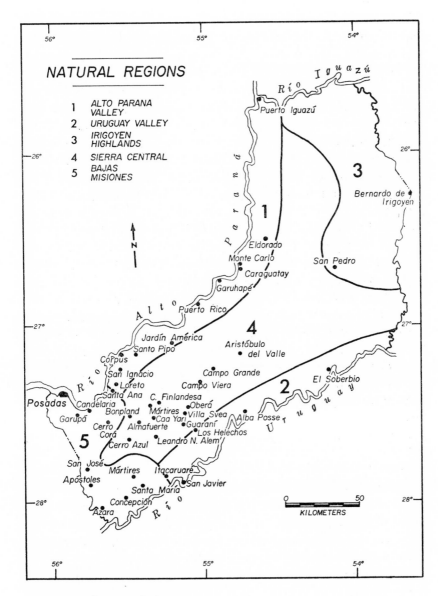

Fig. 3. Natural regions of Misiones.

of the higher core area of the Brazilian Shield and lies almost entirely above the 500-meter level. It is characterized by gently rolling land from out of which rise the highest peaks in Misiones. One of these, in the vicinity of Bernardo de Irigoyen, reaches approximately 800 meters. The whole northern half of the Altiplano appears so high and steep when viewed from the south that early settlers coined the much used term *Sierra de la Victoria* for the so-called range. The Altiplano is covered by a dense network of streams which flow out in nearly every direction from the highest parts (Fig. 2). Climatically, the area has much to offer, although remoteness has kept it from being heavily settled.

In southwestern Misiones between the Alto Paraná and Uruguay rivers, and west of a transecting line drawn from Santa Ana via San José to Itacaruaré, the Misiones landscape is in an advanced erosional stage of rolling hills and isolated peaks interspersed with perfectly level areas. Argentineans earlier referred to this nearly flat region as *Bajas Misiones* (Fig. 3).[11] It is crossed by non-entrenched meandering rivers such as the Zaimán and Pindapoy. Low terraces formed from unequal removal of the successive layers of lava are present. The whole area rises gently toward the east where it merges with the two strips of rolling land on either side of the Sierra Central. In the transition zone the two are not always easily distinguished, but the strips of land are higher (100 meters) and are generally marked by a greater density of steeper slopes. Fig. 3 shows the Campo almost cut in two by the Sierra Central. This lower, less hilly area of southwestern Misiones was a major attraction to early settlers.

RIOS AND ARROYOS

Misiones is characterized by three special drainage features: the Province is completely surrounded by rivers except for only 50 km of its borders; there is a congestion of water systems within this region of continuously heavy rainfall; and the hydrologic network has been affected by tectonic activity.

Tectonic movements during the Mesozoic and Cenozoic eras produced general uplifts which affected Misiones drainage by causing incision of earlier stream patterns as well as splintering of the old landscape in this part of Latin America into higher and lower areas. The result is marked entrenchment of river channels everywhere except in the Campo and a tendency for major rivers to follow tectonically determined courses. The largest and longest of these is that of the Alto Paraná which originates in the highlands of Brazil and flows westward to become the international boundary between Argentina and Paraguay. Its channel along the Misiones border is deep and navigable. However, upstream from Santa Ana the Alto Paraná tributaries are deprived of accordant junctions — a feature which has resulted in the inland movement of rapids on the tributaries and, hence, their frequent lack of navigability in Misiones.

The overall gradient of the Alto Paraná is impressive: 41 meters in the 342 km between Puerto Iguazú and Posadas. The river appears to rush downward, sometimes through spaces less than 500 meters wide, to where it first enters a real lowland channel near Santa Ana. Along most of its length the banks are almost vertical and rise between 50 and 100 meters above the water. Nevertheless, flooding occurs and special installations are required for port construction along the Alto Paraná. However, the river has no rapids or falls along the Misiones border and until the 1950s, when heavy trucking to Buenos Aires began, it remained the principal shipping route for goods produced upstream from Posadas.

The Iguazú River originates in the Serra Geral of the southern Brazilian Highland, flowing west to the Alto Paraná. Over the last 50 km of its course it forms the international border of northern Misiones between Argentina and Brazil. The Iguazú is a tributary river without a conformal base level. It catapults over the main escarpment of the Planalto do Paraná in a spectacular waterfall some 20 km from its junction with the Alto Paraná. Above the *Garganta del Diablo*, as the narrow drop area is called, the Iguazú gives no hint of the impending plunge. This scenic region is one of America's greatest underdeveloped sources of hydroelectric energy and provides an ever increasing attraction to settlers and tourists.

In northeastern Misiones, uplift of the Planalto do Paraná caused entrenchment of numerous meandering rivers on the Altiplano de Irigoyen. Picturesque falls and rapids have been formed on these water courses. The rivers flow in a radial pattern from the high ground near Bernardo de Irigoyen to the lower areas, the San Antonio and the Pepirí Guazú forming the northeastern border with

Brazil. A survey line 18.75 km in length connecting the headwaters of these two rivers is one of Misiones' two land boundaries. The rivers flowing west from Bernardo de Irigoyen toward the Alto Paraná are the longest in the Province. The Piray Miní and the Piray Guazú, for example, which form the north and south boundaries of Eldorado Colony, journey 125 km to the Alto Paraná. Because of the great changes in elevation over short distances — 500 meters along the Piray Guazú — there is a widespread availability of potential hydroelectric energy for the installation of small generators, a feature which one day should encourage settlement in this remote part of Misiones. The greatest disadvantage of such a drainage system is its erosive quality. Decomposed diabase is easily washed away, a fact that demands special understanding of soil use for effective settlement.

The principal runoff channel of southeastern Misiones, i.e., the Uruguay River (325 km), also forms part of the Argentine border with Brazil. Like its counterparts in the Altiplano de Irigoyen, the Uruguay shows both old age and youth. The river achieved maturity in an earlier erosion cycle. Meanders are numerous in its upper stretches, while the main channel has many falls and rapids. Meandering tributaries are now entrenched so that the whole system appears hillier and more complex than that of the Alto Paraná. The steep, twisting banks dominated by rounded hills create a sense of domesticity on the upper Uruguay; colonists familiar with the rolling hills of the middle Rhine view the upper Uruguay River with nostalgia. Downstream from San Javier the Uruguay widens and straightens and navigation improves. More placid tributaries from Bajas Misiones encourage the construction of landing facilities. However, the Uruguay River is regularly navigable only at high water, and its use has been limited primarily to transporting logs along the Misiones border. Because of the isolation and the poor navigation facilities, settlement along the Uruguay has always been retarded.

The Itaembé and the Chimiray, both called *arroyos* (permanent streams in this part of Latin America), form part of the southwestern provincial border. They are of little economic importance to settlers. Between their headwaters a survey line 30 km long has been drawn which makes up the second and only other land border of the Province.

The similarity of Misiones to other large river-islands of the Latin American interior is striking. It is to be noted that settlement in all these places is favored by better transportation facilities and greater ease of communication because of the typically long, narrow shapes of the islands and their thick network of rivers.

MINERAL RESOURCES

Minerals have been found in the Province of Misiones, but usually not in sufficient concentrations to be considered valuable. A part of the ground structure contains limonite, a sedimentary rock known locally as *tacurú*.[12] The deposits occur where ferrous oxides have been concentrated; with a lowering of the water table, the oxides change to the ferric (limonite) variety. Tacurú has between 20 and 40 per cent iron, but exists only in thin, separate patches whose areal extents vary between 8 and 25 ha. Although their exploitable potential is limited, they are widely distributed throughout the Province and have been of some use to settlers. In 1965 construction was begun of a small iron mill near Posadas to utilize tacurú. In southwestern Misiones a second mineral — amygdaloidal deposits of copper varying in size from a few millimeters to 20 cm or more — is found in the diabase. During colonial times copper was laboriously exploited by the Jesuit mission Indians near Corpus, Candelaria, and San Javier.[13] The metal once attracted settlers, although its mineral value soon proved commercially unimportant. At the western edge of the province near Monte Carlo a poor quality of coal (57 per cent carbon) was unearthed in 1953, but the deposit is too small to be utilized profitably.[14] At present, only local areas of red valley clay and São Bento sandstone are extracted in Misiones by primitive means. It is evident that mineral deposits have not played an important role in the settlement of the region.

SELVA, CAMPO, AND TIERRAS COLORADAS

Selva. The natural vegetation of Misiones is derived from extensions of two major physiognomic types whose centers lie outside the region: the dense subtropical Selva traces a convex path from south central Brazil across most of Misiones and eastern Paraguay, and a park landscape referred to as the *parque correntino paraguayo* arcs from the Mesopotamian region of Argentina across the southwestern tip of Misiones to southern Paraguay and the Chaco. This southwestern park landscape exists only in Bajas Misiones and is widely known as the Campo. The division of the two vegetation types follows a line drawn between Santa Ana and Itacaruaré — a line which has gradually moved eastward as a result of land clearing by modern settlers.

The dense Selva east of the line contains many subtropical trees, and a profusion of ferns, epiphytes, and lianas. One authority places the average number of tree species at 69 per ha in the region.[15] Other estimates for the Province run as high as 150 per ha.[16] Both soft and hardwood types are extracted by the lumber industry and their value in virgin areas is sufficient to pay for clearing the land. The diagnostic importance of plant types to settlers and colonization agencies is manifold. Commercially valuable lumber trees, for example, indicate good soils. Some trees, such as *ubajai* (*Eugenia edulis*), approximately 10 meters high, indicate poorly drained soils. The presence of one valuable type, Paraná Pine (*Araucaria angustifolia*), warns of elevations at or above 500 meters — or the zone in which severe frost is more prevalent. Several tree types are used for extracting resins and dyes. A number of other native plants furnish materials for basket and hat weaving and for the manufacture of rope and even clothing. Some varieties are reputed to have medicinal qualities and are commonly used in cases of anemia, fevers, heart problems, and snake poison.[17]

The configuration and distribution of these forest plants vary with changes of slope, soil depth, and climate. Extending 10 to 15 meters from the edge of the true Selva to the banks of main rivers occur dense growths of *tacuará* (*Guadua* sp.), *tacuarembó* (*Chusquea ramosissima*) or *tacuapí* (*Merostachys Claussenii*). Mixed with tree ferns, lianas, epiphytes, and other vegetation, these plants are important in the control of erosion and flooding along the rivers, and settlers have found it dangerous to remove them promiscuously.

In widely separated forest areas there are grass covered openings known as *campiñas*. These openings result from thin or loose soils or rock outcrops at or near surface level which produce conditions too dry for tree growth. Tall members of the *Cephalo-*

cereus genus are occasionally found in such places. Several of these mid-forest openings, such as Campo Grande, Campo Viera, and San Pedro are old settlement sites in Misiones.[18]

Campo. In sharp contrast to the luxuriant vegetation of the eastern area, west of the Santa Ana–Itacaruaré line the Campo supports only open grasslands, i.e., campos, or *sabanas* if there are scattered *Piptadenia macrocarpa* — trees under 10 meters in height. This terrain encouraged the establishment of ranches and farms that now cover the Campo interior and was instrumental in attracting the earliest settlements in the Province.

The configuration and distribution of native Campo plant life vary principally with different drainage patterns, since elevation and climatic changes are less marked in this section of Misiones. In areas where summer drying is more pronounced because of impervious surface layers, or high soil porosity, three types of grassland, each dominated by a single species, are distinguishable on the basis of grazing utility: *barba de bode,* or *flechilla* (*Aristida pallens* Cav.), *espartillo* (*Elyonuris tripsacoides*), *paja de arrancar* (*Andropogon nutans* L.).[19] The three grasses often appear in association with the genera *Paspalum, Eragrostis, Panicum,* and *Axonopus*; but one usually excludes the others. Barba de bode is distributed mainly south of a line drawn between Apóstoles and Concepión. Espartillo is found primarily in the intermediate elevations north of the Apóstoles-Concepción line, but not in the highest parts of the Campo or on cutover land along the Campo-Selva border. Here paja de arrancar predominates.

In poorly drained areas within the Campo, the dominant natural vegetation is aquatic (*Ciperaceae, Graminaceae, Juncaceae* and *Bromiliaceae*). This growth is limited to the narrow confines of *bañados,* or flood zones along streams. The fodder makes inferior forage material, but sometimes is a valuable reserve for winter and drought periods.[20]

Improper use of the Campo has resulted in serious erosion problems and in the creation of an overlay of rachitic grasses, perennial shrubs, and only occasional clumps of trees, known locally as *capones.* Least disturbed are the gallery forests. The barren aspects of the Campo gullies and thin, unprotected soils have been relieved since 1960 by extensive eucalyptus plantings. How-

ever, land damage still remains as a warning of what conditions
in the rest of Misiones would be if erosion continued unchecked.

Tierras Coloradas. The alarming degree of erosion found in
parts of northeastern Argentina is attributable in large part to the
soil type of the area. Over 80 per cent of the Province is covered
by blood-red, decomposed bedrock popularly called *tierra colorada.* This soil varies in depth from a few centimeters to over 30
meters and has been weathered and leached to a deep red, fine-
textured material. Two subtypes are recognized: the "lateritics"
or unstratified deposits of chemically weathered and eroded lava;
and the "basic effusives" formed *in situ* (Fig. 2). In the forest the uppermost layer of soil consists of several centimeters of
friable organic material derived from tree litter and leaf mold.
Except for sandy areas the second horizon has a high percentage
of sesquioxide clay compounds through which movement of water
is relatively good. Beneath this layer is rotting bedrock. The thin
layer of humus is easily removed by rain splash on sloping land.
The rest of the soil tends to dry rapidly and hardens in the process
once organic surface material has been removed. When this happens, the land becomes more difficult to work and agricultural
losses occur from gullying, wind erosion, and fertility decline.

Good orchard crops demand rather deep tierra colorada. Many
settlers have learned that a neighbor's yerba mate orchard may
be far more productive because he purchased a forest holding
where soils were deeper than the three-meter minimum required
for this crop. Some purchased forest lots where the dense vegetation hides almost pure rock outcrops. There is little real soil in
these places, and when covered by trees they are difficult to dis-
tinguish by inexperienced settlers. During the 1920s and 1930s
simple economics forced pioneers to abandon such holdings.
Later it was learned that the rock material is relatively soft, and,
although it is frequently several meters deep, it responds fairly
well to continued machine plowing on level land. Preparation of
this soil, however, is a tedious operation, and can only be performed with adequate capital and modern equipment. Table 3
illustrates the chemistry of Selva and Campo soils.

Although frequently the same color, Campo and Selva soil similarity ends there. Campo soils have little organic material such
as one finds in the rainforest. Lacking a uniform supply of humus,

Campo soils have become strongly acid. Important crops, such as alfalfa[21] for the livestock industry, and yerba mate as a cash crop, cannot be grown well without appropriate fertilization. Unhappily, the scientific treatment of Campo soils is not simple. The familiar middle-latitude method of broadcast fertilizers does not work, primarily because of the rainfall intensity. As a result, these factors aggravate both the livestock production and the cash crop problems in Misiones.

TABLE 3

Soil Characteristics, Misiones

Place	Slope	Vegetation	Horizons		
		SELVA			
El Alcázar	20%	Forest			
			A1.1	A1.2	B
		Depth (cm)	0.8–10	10–34	34–80
		Sand (%)	61.6	49.3	29.4
		Lime	33.5	36.2	18.0
		Clay	4.9	14.5	52.6
		C	2.5	1.4	0.8
		N	0.38	0.31	0.11
		pH	5.0	5.2	6.2
		CAMPO			
Apóstoles	12%	*Capuera*			
			A1.1	A1.2	A/C
		Depth (cm)	4.5	15–40	45–60
		Sand %	61.1	63.7	70.2
		Lime	28.7	12.5	13.1
		Clay	10.2	23.8	16.7
		C	1.6	0.38	—
		N	0.18	0.16	—
		pH	4.7	4.9	5.1

Source: Misiones Province, *Informe edafológico* (Buenos Aires, 1964), pp. 165 (Selva), 132–35 (Campo).

Another Campo problem resulting from the lack of humus is the lowered permeability. When exposed by plowing, this soil loses porosity and puddles easily; increased runoff is inevitable. Thus, what little organic material that may have formed is lost and the soil dries out completely. In fact, the dry soil tends to become indurated, and, if puddled thoroughly, tends to "case harden" like a true laterite. The soil is then extremely difficult to work even with powerful machinery. A rain at this stage so fouls tractor wheels that operation of the machine is impossible. The mud adheres to disc blades as well, rendering them completely useless. By plowing at the proper times and depths such features can be overcome, but they are often used as an excuse not to mechanize and explain the frequent resort to hand labor found on "modern" Campo farms.

Sandy areas in both the Campo and Selva of Misiones have played important settlement roles. Fortunately such soils do not occur in more than 10 per cent of the Province. They are indicated by the presence of *urunday* (*Astronium Balansae*) and are apparently concentrated in Bajas Misiones. Some of these soils are cemented with limonite and at first sight appear similar to the rest of the tierra colorada. Sandstone-derived soils are less fertile, dry out and harden more quickly, and are even less resistant to erosion. These soils gully quickly and, once broken down, support only a poor quality *capuera* (second-growth vegetation) with xerophytic traits. The rich appearance of sandy soils has led unwary pioneers to think the land more fertile than it is.

Although rainfall is sufficient to support a denser plant growth in the Campo, rapid soil drainage lowers precipitation effectiveness and exposure of less permeable sandstone rocks promotes accelerated runoff. The net effect is that soil desiccation is rapid during short periods of intense sunlight or wind, and cementation is quickly renewed. Thus plant growth is retarded and roots may suffer from exposure. Such is the case in a densely settled 45 km belt of sandy soils paralleling the Alto Paraná from Candelaria to Corpus, and in another belt extending intermittently across the Province from San Ignacio to San Javier (Fig. 2). There are also patches of sandy soils in Mártires and Apóstoles. Soils derived from metamorphosed sandstones are found in L.N. Alem and in dispersed areas throughout the Selva. Their rapid deterioration is similar to that of old Campo soils at the Jesuit mission sites. Swift soil depletion in both zones has prompted a continuous stream of second-generation settlers to new areas in the forested interior of Misiones.

The presence of long gravel lenses from old river beds has occasionally disappointed settlers in forested areas. These lenses remain hidden until the land is cleared, whereupon rocks and stones interfere with planting and plowing. Such formations spell economic hardship for the colonists and have resulted in lowered colonization stability.

In spite of the problems discussed above, all soils in Misiones respond well to modern fertilization techniques developed in the tropics. New techniques stress that soils should be worked sparingly, that plants should be individually drill fertilized, and that commercial crops thrive best if their physiognomy approximates native plant types in a given region. Orchards with cover crops such as *Vicia villosa* and *Medicago hispida*, which reseed themselves easily, are thus recommended. Otherwise, soils and fertilizers wash away, yields of the second harvest usually decline by half, and the land is systematically abandoned, equalling the most primitive agricultural practices.

NATURAL REGIONS OF MISIONES

Maps depicting the distribution of physical geographical factors, or geofactors, such as climate, drainage, elevation, natural vegetation, and soil, show that a number of the lines separating subdivisions of these items would overlap if all the illustrative maps were carefully superimposed. These overlapping lines indicate transitional zones on either side of which are areas of different physical character. Correspondingly, areas within the boundary lines have uniform physical features. Superimposing the maps facilitates drawing conclusions about the location of the natural regional boundaries, boundaries which are essential to the understanding and direction of settlement practices. Each area with uniform physical characteristics may suggest a specific land clearing and use system, crop types, holding sizes, village forms, and transport networks. The five physical regions of Misiones shown on Fig. 3 are derived from such a boundary selection process. Their individual personalities may be summarized briefly as follows:

The Alto Paraná Valley. This is a region of moderately rolling land which tilts gently upward from Santa Ana to Puerto Iguazú and extends from the Alto Paraná, where its edge is close to 100 meters above the water, approximately 20 km inland. Its eastern boundary is the 200-meter isohypse. Dozens of entrenched tributaries cross it, most of which flood several times a year making overland transportation difficult and expensive. Except near the rivers, the region is covered with dense subtropical forest. The lateritic soils are primarily derived from old lava, but are mixed with a similar appearing but less desirable sandy type. The climate of the area is characterized by high average annual temperatures (20°C), heavy yearly precipitation (everywhere over 1,400 mm), two "dry" seasons, and light frosts. A nearly frost-free zone exists next to the river and dense fogs occur almost daily up to 5 km inland from the banks. The Alto Paraná is navigable the year around and has long served as a major transportation link with Posadas, the provincial capital, and with the outside world.

The Uruguay Valley. This region is similar to the Alto Paraná Valley, although the width is not so great (approximately 15 km). The narrow strip along the river starts from San Javier and rises gradually to the confluence of the Uruguay and the Pepirí Guazú. Although native plant life and soils are like those in the Paraná Valley, landforms differ. Numerous rapids and entrenched meanders present a more complex physical landscape. Hillslopes are steeper, but not higher, and twisting tributaries enter the main channel. Neither the Uruguay River nor its tributaries can be used successfully for transporting large quantities of agricultural or industrial products, a feature which has retarded colonization in this region.

The Irigoyen Highland. This is a remote altiplano in the north of Misiones with borders from San Pedro to the Falls of Iguazú and eastward to the edge of the Province. The elevation is above 500 meters, lower limit of sizeable stands of Paraná Pine. Extensive level surfaces occur, although the area is a sharply hilly zone. There is a nearly radial drainage pattern represented by rejuvenated, meandering streams. Soils are good and deep in places, rocky or nonexistent in others. A cooler climate exists in the highest part of this region but due to good air drainage, temperatures are not so extreme at some of its middle levels as they may be in lower parts of Misiones. Hydroelectric and erosive potential are great, but inaccessibility has preserved the area from extensive settlement.

The Sierra Central. This is not a true mountain range, but rather the remains of more resistant, hence higher, parts of the ancient lava platform covering Misiones. The Sierra is the divortium aquarum between the Alto Paraná and Uruguay rivers and rises through the middle of the Province from the southwest near San José to San Pedro in the northeast. Its most distinguishing features are its elevation above 200 meters above sea level, its steep hillslopes interspersed with tilting flat expanses of land, the discontinuous, often flat-topped crestline, and the intensity of erosion by streams flowing down both its slopes. Soils are lateritic, vary in thickness, and are frequently rocky. Heavy rainfall (over 1,600 mm) and frost in the highest parts or where air drainage is not pronounced, characterize the climate. The Sierra is covered by dense subtropical forest vegetation. Grassland openings are present in a few areas (campiñas) and have long served as settlement sites.

Bajas Misiones. This area has a number of homogeneous qualities which differentiate it from other Misiones regions. The gently rolling to level topography is below 200 meters in elevation. The rivers often meander, have left ox-bow remnants, produced swampy land, and have no deeply entrenched confluences with either the Alto Paraná or the Uruguay. Campo vegetation is distinctly open with trees appearing in clumps or in gallery forests. Soils are frequently thinner than anywhere else in level parts of Misiones. Longer dry periods, followed by torrential rains, and improper agricultural methods have contributed to modern erosion problems. Because of its favorable topographic features and its location, Bajas Misiones, nearly identical with the so-called Campo, was the first part of the Province to be settled.

Chapter 3

COLONIAL LAND OPENING

IN MISIONES: THE BEGINNING

OF EUROPEAN SETTLEMENT

> Each age finds it necessary to reconsider at least
> some portion of the past, from points of view fur-
> nished by new conditions which reveal the influence
> and significance of forces not adequately known
> by . . . previous generations.
>
> Frederick Jackson Turner
> *The Frontier in American History*

FIRST ARRIVALS

The first European to appear in the picturesque but remote
Misiones area was Sebastian Cabot who had been employed in
1525 by Carlos V to open trade between Spain and the Spice
Islands.[1] Cabot took an expedition to the mouth of the Paraná
River, and, contrary to orders, sailed upstream in search of the
rumored "White King,"a supposedly wealthy native ruler in the
interior.[2] At the mouth of the Carcarañá River close to Rosario,
Cabot built in 1527 a fort which he christened *Sancti Spiritus*.
The following year he continued exploration along the Paraná
until stopped by low water not far from the present capital of
Misiones. He then returned to the Paraguay and sailed a short
distance up that river before being discouraged by belligerent
natives. While in the area, Cabot acquired a certain amount of
silver which caused him to name the large river system he had
discovered the *Río de la Plata*.[3] He later sent some of the silver
to Spain where it excited much interest as the first shipment of
this metal from the New World and gave added publicity to the
Río de la Plata region. Cabot continued his explorations, but in
1529 nearly all the inhabitants left at his settlement were killed
by Indians and the site had to be abandoned.[4]

Another voyage to the region was made a few years later under the leadership of Pedro de Mendoza.[5] Mendoza sailed from Spain to the Paraná River estuary, the only segment of the Paraná which is still called Río de la Plata, and in 1536 built a fort on the right bank at the mouth of the Riachuelo tributary. The settlement was named *Nuestra Señora Santa María del Buen Aire,* now Buenos Aires. Within months after its founding the colony withstood the first of a long series of demoralizing attacks by Pampa Indians.[6]

Mendoza, who had not forgotten rumors of the "White King," sent an exploratory group up the Paraná-Paraguay rivers. In 1537 the survivors of this group established at Asunción the first permanent Spanish settlement in this part of South America.[7] The colony was located only 300 km northwest of the present boundary of Misiones Province. A site on a bend of the east bank of the Paraguay River was selected for Asunción not only because of the better drained land but because the Indians were considered more peaceful than the nomadic hunters across the river. In fact, the Spanish had discovered the partially sedentary Guaraní who had already developed primitive agriculture and were relatively numerous. The Guaraní helped build the fortifications at Asunción and the Spanish were so pleased over the Indian situation that in 1541 they ordered the beleaguered Buenos Aires abandoned and moved all survivors far upriver to the new settlement.[8]

Misiones was approached from still another direction late in 1541 by Alvar Núñez Cabeza de Vaca.[9] This explorer began an overland march from the Brazilian coast near the island of Santa Catarina. He reached the Iguazú Falls in 1542 and continued down the Alto Paraná River past Misiones.[10] The same year Cabeza de Vaca joined other settlers at Asunción where he took over as governor and gained recognition for rebuilding the city after a serious fire, as well as for his fair dealings with the Indians.[11]

During the next forty years settlers in Asunción kept the Paraná-Paraguay river system open to shipping and gradually probed south and east toward the densely forested region of Misiones. One of the earliest satellite settlements was Ontiveros, founded in 1543 by gold miners on the Piquirí River, an Alto Paraná tributary some 200 km northeast of Misiones. Ciudad Real was constructed at the mouth of the same river in 1557 after settlers had left Ontiveros.[12] Movement of people from Asunción toward the coast began in 1573 with the founding of Santa Fe, and was completed with the resettlement of Buenos Aires in 1580. Concepción (1585) and Corrientes (1588) were then built near the important confluence of the Paraná and Paraguay rivers, less than 300 km west of Misiones.

The settlements mentioned above were all located along navigable rivers. In spite of the accessibility to water transportation, distances were long and the colonies could not be supplied permanently with provisions from Spain or from Buenos Aires. Pioneers were thus compelled to produce subsistence crops. This was done by making new and unpopular demands of the Indians. Indian rebellion became so common that the Spaniards were forced to resort to arms to keep peace in the area and to maintain a steady supply of laborers for the basic necessities of life.[13] Indian problems unquestionably prevented any widespread settlement near the riverine colonies. Native settlement of Misiones began instead.

Conflicts between the Spanish and Guaraní natives close to Asunción, and between the Spanish and other tribes such as the Caingang farther south caused many of the Indians to move east from those more settled areas.[14] The densely forested region in Misiones became a haven for Indian escapees and was generally avoided by the Spanish except for necessary traffic along the Alto Paraná. An armed expedition of Governor Hernandarias (Hernando Arias de Saavedra) went from Asunción to the Misiones region in 1603, but failed to subjugate the Indians. Spanish-Indian relations reached a low ebb after this failure of the military, and the Crown adopted a policy of appeasement toward the natives.

CROWN POLICY CHANGES

Since it was considered desirable to bring the region southeast of Asunción within the Spanish orbit, it was first necessary to make the area safe for settlement. Private and military attempts having failed, the Crown turned for help to the Society of Jesus. The appearance of Jesuits is not surprising in view of the Crown's desire to halt mistreatment of the Indians, to bring about their conversion as rapidly as possible, and to recognize attempts of the Jesuits to become based in the interior of South America as the Franciscans had become in Peru and other places (Fig. 4).[15]

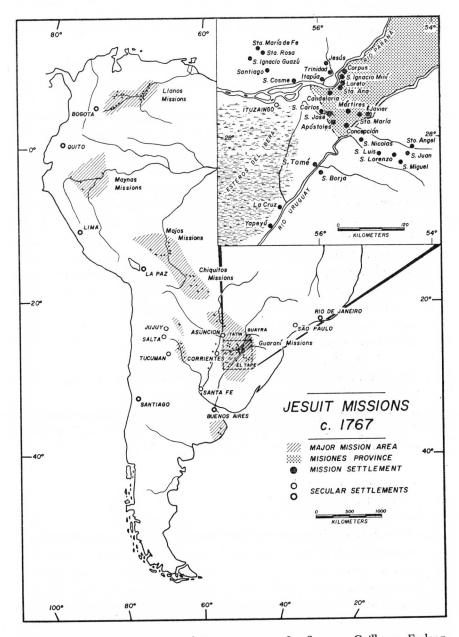

Fig. 4. The 30 Jesuit missions of Paraguay, ca. 1767. *Sources*: Guillermo Furlong, *Misiones y sus pueblos de Guaraníes* (Buenos Aires, 1962); Oskar Schmieder, *Die Neue Welt, 1. Teil. Mittel- und Südamerika* (Heidelberg, 1962); Pablo Pastells and F. Mateos, *Historia de la Compañía de Jesús en la Provincia del Paraguay* (Madrid, 1956–59), vols. 6–8.

Requests by the Jesuits to work in Asunción were granted by the Crown in 1607. Permission was given two years later for the extension of operations east of the Paraguay River.[16] This expansion of Jesuit activities materially influenced the course of modern settlement in Misiones.

In late 1609 Jesuit fathers traveled southeast from Asunción and built the first permanent mission at San Ignacio Guazú, only 125 km northwest of the present Misiones border. Other missions followed in Guayrá, north of the Iguazú River. In 1615, Itapúa was built at Posadas, subsequently to be moved across the river to Encarnación. The first permanent mission in what is now Misiones was constructed at Concepción (1619) near the Uruguay River. The Jesuits crossed Misiones in 1626 and established San Nicolas in the district known as El Tape, or Río Uruguay–El Tape, located in the present state of Rio Grande do Sul, Brazil. Within forty years, nine other missions were founded between the Alto Paraná and Uruguay rivers (Fig. 4). Corpus, first established in 1622, appears to have been moved to Misiones in 1647. It was shifted to its present position in 1701.[17]

Not long after the Jesuits began work east of the Paraguay River, they were given complete control over the Indians. In an attempt to improve the lot of the natives, the Crown ordered an official investigation of Guaraní affairs by the *visitador* (field investigator for the Crown), Francisco de Alfaro from Peru. The *ordenanzas* which resulted in 1611 placed a tax on the use of Indians by the Spanish. A special decree made the *encomienda* (a land grant which included Indian labor) illegal for converted Indians and named the Jesuits as solely responsible for civilizing the natives.[18] The latter task was to be accomplished at reducciones built near the land where Indians had worked for *encomenderos* (recipients of encomiendas) or at their native places.[19] Spaniards, half-castes, and Negroes were not to be allowed in the reducciones and Indians were no longer to be forced to collect wild yerba mate leaves, from which an increasingly popular beverage was made. The Spanish, who needed Indian labor for construction, agriculture, and collection of yerba mate, found their sources of aboriginal help disappearing to the missions. Since the Indians were offered a refuge by the Jesuits, an extremely favorable atmosphere for growth of religious settlements resulted. However, such Jesuit action brought about the Order's downfall in this area by creating lasting resentment toward itself. Private settlers held the priests responsible for the text of the ordenanzas, and drove the Jesuits from the city as soon as the visitador had left Asunción.[20] Even the governor of Asunción took control of mission settlements in Guayrá on the pretext that they were ready for civilian administration. As a result 40,000 Indians were divided among the conquistadors.[21] The *mamelucos*, or free Portuguese from São Paulo, also realized the value of the expanding religious settlements as ideal sources of cheap labor. Slave raids, or *malocas*, were even carried out with encouragement from the governors of Paraguay, especially from 1619 to 1631. Civilian officials thus attempted to extend their authority over the Jesuits. Malocas became devastating. The Guayrá missions first came under attack, and, according to early reports, from 1628 to 1631 nine missions there were destroyed and 60,000 Indians taken prisoner by Paulista raiders.[22] Of the 100,000 mission Indians living in Guayrá only 12,000 escaped and fled toward isolated forests of Misiones which already were a refuge for Indians who had evaded the Spanish raids from Asunción. Some 4,000 finally arrived and with these the Jesuits established in 1632 the two missions of Loreto and San Ignacio along the Alto Paraná.[23]

Even prior to the loss of Guayrá in 1631, the Jesuits had chosen a safer area between Guayrá and the Paraguay River, designated Itatín, for the construction of four missions. In 1632 three of these were destroyed by the mamelucos and further progress was halted.[24] The clergy and their remaining charges then decided to move south to the refuge between the Alto Paraná and Uruguay rivers.

Trouble with El Tape natives and malocas in that area made continued resettlement necessary during the 1630s. Although Jesuit Indians were armed and offered resistance, a gradual evacuation took place northward toward the haven of the upper Uruguay River.[25]

It is evident that Paulista raiders north, east, and south of Misiones, and Asunción authorities and other conquistadors to the west forced the Jesuits and Indians into the region where the Alto Paraná and Uruguay rivers converge within 75 km of each other. Subsequently, many new missions were built and this refuge became the center of Jesuit activities.

The construction of new religious settlements in the narrow

zone between the rivers reached its apogee from 1629 to 1639. San Javier was built on the right bank of the Uruguay in 1629. Loreto and San Ignacio followed three years later, as noted above.[26] Santa María la Mayor was constructed near the Uruguay in 1633 and received refugees from El Tape.[27] Apóstoles (1638) and Mártires (1639) were also built in the vicinity of the Uruguay. Santa Ana and San José were located south of Loreto in 1660. Candelaria, later the capital of all the missions, was established nearby in 1665. Other mission settlements were erected outside this narrow Meso-potamian zone until in 1707 the total number east of the Paraguay River stabilized at thirty. Collectively, they became known as the *Misiones del Paraguay* (Fig. 4).[28]

Malocas were revived by the Portuguese in the area between 1639 and 1641 but the slave raiders were soundly beaten by the armed Indians and a period of mission prosperity began which lasted nearly a century.[29]

JESUIT PLANNING

The Jesuit missions were the result of a well-planned coloniza-tion effort. The General of the Order, Claudio Aquaviva (1581–1618), disapproved of the scattered field activities of individual priests and initiated a plan under which the clergy concentrated in centers where the natives could be protected in large numbers.[30] Padre Diego de Torres Bollo was transferred from Peru in 1607 to the post of Provincial for Chile and Paraguay and had the task of establishing the system in the Guaraní region. Torres had al-ready learned much about working with natives and had observed the techniques adopted by Franciscans in Peru since the time of Pizarro. Moreover, some of his most efficient administrative help in the new area came from A. Ruiz de Montoya, a Jesuit who had been born and raised in Peru.

Under the mission settlement system Indian colonists lived and worked at centralized, planned villages. Each of these had a church, housing for the priests and their charges, and a large garden. Most of the work, including subsistence farming, was performed near this main group of buildings. However, the large commercial farm fields and grazing lands which formed the basis of their economy lay outside the village. Generally, such an estab-lishment was referred to by the clergy as a *misión*. During the initial stages of development when church work was just beginning with the aborigines, the mission settlement was classified as a *reducción*. This term was derived from a seventeenth-century Spanish phrase regarding Indian conversion: *se reducían a cruz y campana* (they brought themselves to cross and bell, i.e., to religious settlements).[31] Properly speaking, the *reducción* was the site of conversion, although as soon as all the Indians in a place were Christianized, the settlement was classified as a *doctrina* and became a regular Indian parish.[32]

The site of the earliest *reducciones* was usually chosen by trial and error. Because some were moved more than once the historical record is confused. Settlements had to be moved because of floods, fog, and "sickly conditions," as was the case for example at Corpus.[33] By the time the stations in what is now Argentina became permanent, however, the Jesuits had accumulated an impressive amount of field experience in location logistics. The mission sites reflect this experience not only by their general success during Jesuit times, but by their frequent presence today in the midst of thriving settlements. They were and are almost invariably associated with cooler micro-climates, well-drained land, permanent streams, access to main rivers, and ease of defense.

MISSION SETTLEMENTS

The physical organization of the Jesuit missions was in some respects similar to that of the usual Spanish village. Both were planned settlements. In the latter case, the *Ordenanzas de Poblaciones* of the *Código de Indias* prescribed to the last detail construction of a square central plaza and the orientation, appearance, function, and distribution of its buildings. Streets extended at right angles from the corners of the plaza according to the rectangular grid system of surveying which the Spanish had borrowed from the Romans.[34] The grid network was not only applied to the typical Spanish village, but extended to the farm lots beyond. The *cabildo* administrative plan, whereby a ruling council was supposed to be elected but was usually appointed by the Spanish authorities, was followed.

The Jesuit settlements were also regularly constructed around a central square, but this area was partially enclosed by the thick walls of the buildings, and frequently part of the settlement was

surrounded by a deep trench or a dirt rampart for defense purposes.[35] The appearance and main functions of the plaza and its
buildings were different in these settlements too. The religious
theme dominated life and was prescribed in as much detail as
the secular order in the Spanish villages. The church, priests'
quarters and religious classrooms were prominent buildings.[36] The
main edifices were permanent structures built from red São Bento
sandstone taken mainly from outcrops at San Ignacio, Apóstoles,
and Santa María.[37] Native hardwoods were employed to build
veranda-style houses which were roofed with tiles made from
local red clay. This practical house structure is still common in
Misiones and adjacent Paraguay.[38] Iron obtained from the tacurú
deposits was used in construction work and for making utensils.
Copper items, such as bowls and church bells, were common. Some
of the metal was taken from amygdaloidal deposits in the Uruguay Valley at the Cerro del Monje northeast of San Javier, in
the Paraná Valley at Corpus, and in Bajas Misiones at the Arroyo
San Juan between Candelaria and Santa Ana.[39] Visitors reported
that mission homes were superior to those found in either Asunción or Buenos Aires during the same period.[40]

The diagrams in Fig. 5 compare sizes and building distribution
for the secular and religious types of settlement, although only
the latter appeared in Misiones.

The number of people living in the missions varied from time
to time, but, according to census data, the total for the thirty
reached a maximum of 138,934 in 1731.[41] Usually only two priests
were present at each settlement.[42] These figures yield an average
of approximately 4,630 inhabitants per station, which indicates
that there were probably as many as 50,000 Indian settlers in the
eleven missions of northeastern Argentina during the most flour-
ishing period. This was by far the most important colonization
center in eastern South America.

AGRICULTURE AND INDUSTRY

The Jesuits developed a mission economy which not only sus-
tained the charges under their tutelage, but permitted bountiful
commercial relations with other parts of South America. Their
agricultural undertakings, which were the foundations of the

economy, were extensive, diversified, and thoroughly managed. During the time of planting from April to August, for example, certain days were prescribed by the priests for plowing. The announcement was passed from the major to the lesser officials and on plowing days all nonessential tasks were suspended.[43] At this time every Indian settler was given a pair of oxen. Indians who could not plow awaited their turn. Meanwhile, they busied themselves with "removing the excess forest . . . [and] . . . cleaning the fields . . . ."[44]

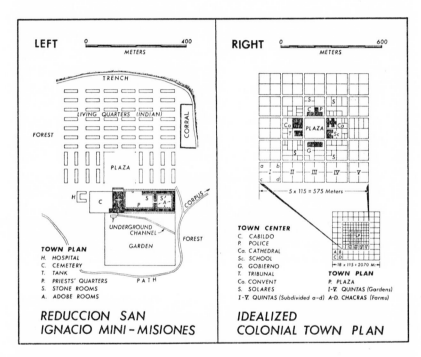

Fig. 5. Spanish colonial settlement types: *left*, religious (Misiones); *right*, civil (general). *Sources*: (left) Raimundo Fernández Ramos, *Apuntes históricos sobre Misiones: Posadas, Territorio de Misiones* (Madrid, 1929) opp. p. 50; (right) H. Wilhelmy, *Südamerika im Spiegel seiner Städte* (Hamburg, 1952), p. 85.

Each settler had his own plot of approximately 2 ha where subsistence crops were raised;[45] but native farm practices were so careless that Indians had to be told when to plant and harvest.[46] In general, natives worked four days a week on their own lands, or

Abambaés, but had to work two days on communal holdings called *Tupambaés.*[47] If the Indians were inefficient or would not tend their own crops, they had to perform extra duty in the communal fields where horticulture and plantation farming were carried on.[48]

Vegetable gardening flourished in the main settlement area immediately behind the principal buildings (Fig. 5). Crops were raised experimentally until it was determined which were appropriate, what the best planting and harvest dates were, and what method of farming achieved the highest yields. Carrots, tomatoes, beans, peas, radishes, and even *bayrische Rüben* (Bavarian beets) brought from Munich, were described in published reports.[49]

The Jesuits determined that citrus was most appropriate to the area.[50] Oranges were found to do especially well and were raised in large orchards to provide a steady source of food. Wild orange trees may still be seen in use around the ruins of the San Ignacio mission and in other parts of the Misiones forest.

Yerba mate became the most important plantation crop raised outside the mission compound.[51] At first the leaves of this tree were gathered wild from the surrounding forests. The leaves were then carefully dried and ground so that a kind of tea could be made from them. Gradually, this developed into a lucrative business because the Jesuits were able to sell the excess product in Asunción where it was much in demand, and later in Santa Fe and Buenos Aires.[52] One of the biggest markets developed in Alto Perú, where Indian laborers in the mines of Potosí requested the drink. Therefore, each village devoted fifty or more men to yerba mate collecting.[53] They remained two or three months in the forest and on return had to contribute one *arroba* (11.5 kg) each for the payment of royal taxes. By 1760 the thirty missions alone used approximately 30,000 arrobas yearly, and another 10,000–12,000 arrobas were exported.[54] Yerba mate became a pillar of the economy, and average annual harvests approximated 1,300 arrobas per mission. An annual production of 40,000 arrobas was needed to maintain an economy involving a required yearly crown tribute of 25,116 pesos, as well as financing imports of salt, raw iron, steel, tools, wine, and other items.[55]

Since yerba mate trees were in greater and greater demand, the Indians were sent on long trips to discover new sources. Sometimes workers travelled almost 200 km, to the Iguazú Falls area, for example, until every important wild yerba mate stand or *yerbal* in Misiones was exploited.[56] Competition with the Spanish from Asunción reached the point where Indians were in danger of being forced into the secular yerba mate business if caught.

Increasing economic importance of yerba mate and the growing risk of losing the Indians who collected the wild leaves, led the Jesuits to clear land and raise yerba mate efficiently on their own plantations — a system which disappeared when the Jesuits left, but which was copied again after 1900. Eventually the Jesuits monopolized the yerba mate business with their more productive farm methods.

Land was first cleared with axes imported by the Jesuits.[57] Tree trunks were burned and the land then hack- or hand-farmed until stumps and roots rotted. After four or five years light wooden plows fitted with sharpening hatchets were adequate, since the underlying soils were either too sandy or clay-filled to be disturbed by deeper plowing. Harrows were employed to break clods, according to early records.[58]

Usually tobacco and maize were planted on freshly cleared land.[59] Maize could be planted nearly the year around and numerous sheds were built to store the crop.[60] *Batatas* (sweet potatoes) and melons were also raised. Manioc was found to be an especially useful crop because it could be grown on poorer soils and the tubers could be left in the ground until needed — a practice adopted by later settlers and still used in Misiones.[61] Sugar cane was produced in the Paraná Valley and elsewhere in Bajas Misiones.[62] Cotton and yerba mate were planted on land where several maize and tobacco harvests had been made.[63] Appropriate spacing of yerba mate plants was developed and undoubtedly the Jesuits discovered that warmer north slopes produced higher yields, just as is realized today. A native, perennial, tree-type cotton was used up to seven years or longer in Misiones. It was pruned regularly but the plants probably suffered from excessive rainfall, occasional drought, and low temperatures, just as more modern varieties do.[64] Cotton was grown on large, cleared fields which were somewhat higher and well-drained "like the cornfields of of Bavaria," and "accessible to winds."[65]

As most crops made heavy demands on the soil, and fertilizer was not always available because livestock were not integrated with agriculture under the Spanish system, fields generally had to be rotated after two or three years.[66] Thus new land was constantly needed until the first field could be replanted. According to one report, this occurred from six to twelve years after land opening, depending on soils and crops.[67] These planting and plowing methods are still being followed in Misiones.

Livestock raising was another important part of the economy. Most of the animals were kept on ranches in the open grasslands of northern Argentina, Uruguay and southern Brazil, although some were maintained at the missions. Hernández records the number of livestock pertaining to the eleven mission settlements as 381,304 in 1768.[68] Among these were 250,650 cows and bulls, of which almost half were listed as farm cows (Table 4). Sepp reports that the reducción that did not have three to four thousand horses was considered poor.[69] One aspect of ranching which differed from the usual Spanish concept was that the Jesuits appeared to give considerable attention to breeding livestock, as may be inferred from the recorded herd classifications in Table 4. Indeed, some of these north-European-trained Jesuits must have been animal husbandry experts.

In addition to the agricultural undertakings of the mission priests, a major effort was made to balance the economy with industry. Some writers even claimed that the Guaraní reducciones represented the only really industrialized landscape in colonial South America.[70] As in agriculture, many of the priests had received industrial training in European countries. Teaching the Indians industrial self-sufficiency was but a natural outgrowth of such leadership. The esteem with which Germans were held in both agriculture and industry is seen in the publication of a special Crown decree in September of 1734 specifying that 25 per cent of the missionaries could be German.[71] Handicraft production developed quickly under these circumstances and in each mission were to be found weavers, tailors, shoemakers, bakers, carpenters, cabinet makers, stone workers, gold and silver smiths, and even organ and clock makers and painters.[72] The first printing press in this part of Latin America was built under the direction of J. B. Neumann, who produced *Martirologio Romano* on it in 1700. Another religious book was published in the Guaraní language by I. Nieremberg and A. Ruiz de Montoya in 1705.[73]

TABLE 4

Cattle Records at the Missions, 1768

Mission	Corraled Cows	Wild Bulls & Cows	Mules	Oxen	Sheep & Goats	Horses
Candelaria	13,662	860	501	1,788	4,648	4,088
Santa Ana	—	33,796	3,053	3,331	6,564	2,814
Loreto	—	30,000	63	500	1,259	2,196
San Ignacio	—	33,925	628	1,025	7,991	445
Corpus	—	12,292	1,396	—	4,079	2,320
Sta. María	—	12,000	716	320	7,475	438
Apóstoles	43,811	5,120	492	2,383	22,673	3,465
Mártires	7,741	136	227	2,950	10,840	435
Concepión	10,000	—	445	—	11,215	2,607
San José	33,112	—	740	1,900	5,700	3,916
San Javier	8,389	5,806	253	—	1,966	809
Totals	116,715	133,935	8,514	14,197	84,410	23,533
All Animals	381,304					

Source: Pablo Hernández, *Misions del Paraguay: Organización social de las doctrinas de la Compañía de Jesús,* 2 vols. (Barcelona, 1913), 1:544.

(The reconstructed press on exhibit at the Museo Histórico Nacional in Buenos Aires is believed to be one used in Misiones by the Jesuits.) Later the Crown authorized arming the Indians with the result that weapons and even uniforms for soldiers were manufactured at the missiones. All these activities but one were carried on in special workshops: weaving alone was performed at home by the Indian women.[74]

The mission products destined for sale were assembled and displayed in *ramadas*, i.e., public guest houses near the mission, which were visited by tradesmen from Santa Fe and Buenos Aires. Orders were taken and manufactured items later shipped to these markets on small river boats which the Jesuits had begun to employ.[75] The primary exports were yerba mate, cotton, sugar, tobacco, hay, rugs, honey and wax, hides and livestock, fuel wood, furniture and other wood products.[76]

LAND OPENING PROCESSES

Since the economy of the mission system was based primarily on agriculture, on limited ranching around the mission sites, and on the use of forest products, a good deal of land had to be cleared in the vicinity of the reducciones. Forests disappeared where crops were planted, sometimes over large areas. From an account of production at one of the stations in Misiones, probably that of San José, the land use for 1757 can be estimated as follows: 15,000 kg, or 1,300 arrobas, of yerba mate were produced, requiring approximately 25 ha; 12,000 kg, or 1,050 arrobas, of cotton were produced, requiring approximately 60 ha; 60–70 *fanegas* (about 1.60 bu) of wheat required approximately 2 ha; 20,000 head of livestock required approximately 10,000 ha.[77]

From these data we may assume that the land devoted to communal farming in San José amounted to approximately 100 ha for crops. There were approximately 3,400 Indians at San José in 1754, and, as mentioned previously, each family generally raised crops on some 2 ha, so another 1,360 ha must be added to the total, assuming 5 members per family. One mission, then, involved 11,460 ha — crops, 1,460 ha, and livestock production, 10,000.[78] Furthermore, most crops were raised for only two or three years on freshly deforested areas.[79] Assuming that the originally cleared 1,460 ha could have been reused 15 years after the initial rotation, 8,300 ha would have been needed for crops alone at San José in a three-year rotation system. Even yerba mate plantations were probably moved every twenty years, just as they are today when yields begin to decline in eroded zones. Cattle were then grazed on abandoned clearings, a system which is still carried on in Misiones if fresh water is available. Since the Jesuits did everything possible to bring about use of the plow which produced higher yields than hack-farming, deforestation was thorough. Finally, the use of wood for fuel and industry established a constant need for forest products. As a result, cleared land was one of the earmarks of Jesuit settlements.[80]

The eleven missions in Misiones were concentrated in the southwestern 15 per cent of the Province, or mainly in the Campo. In a little over a century and a half a good deal of the forest covering this part of the modern Province was removed. A total of approximately 1,000 square km of cleared land for the eleven missions could account for the destruction of almost 50 per cent of the virgin trees during this period of occupancy, even if the Campo had been originally half forest. Moreover, loss of natural vegetation by primitive agriculture and overgrazing triggered accelerated erosion that eventually led to the disappearance of much of the easily removable tierra colorada soil, which may never have been deep in southwest Misiones. In the vicinity of Loreto, for example, severe gullying attributed to the Jesuit cultivations may still be observed, although the area is now forested.[81] Soil and climatic factors apparently reached a critical point in the Campo region, and made it a marginal zone for forest vegetation. Harsh use of the land therefore prevented reestablishment of natural tree growth in much of the area, and Campo conditions were extended. Thus agriculture gradually became impoverished so that the worst parts of this open country became a dangerous trap to all subsequent settlers.

DECLINE OF THE MISSIONS

The strength of the mission economy began to weaken after the middle of the eighteenth century. Although reduction in agricultural yields probably was a contributing factor, this was not the only cause. The great smallpox epidemics which killed thousands of Indians, especially in 1764–65, and renewed Portuguese malocas were among other factors contributing to the steady decline of the missions.[82] The negative attitude of private colonists toward the Jesuits was of growing importance in Spanish governing circles and weakened the status of the Jesuits at court. People complained that the Jesuits did not teach the Indians the "language of Cervantes," and that too many "foreign" priests administered the natives.[83] The old argument that the Spanish economic system depended on Indian labor but that the Crown had acted contrary to its own interests by turning the Indians over to the Jesuits carried more and more weight with the years. Besides, as the overall Spanish economy began to crumble, the Crown brought wrath on itself by having prevented industry and trade from growing in its own colonies while permitting the Jesuits and Indians to carry out both in theirs. Such arguments weakened the royal consideration and protection once afforded the missions and hastened their downfall.

The Portuguese also were influential in this decline by proposing to give up their settlement of Colonia opposite Buenos Aires in exchange for the seven doctrinas of El Tape (Fig. 4).[84] The intensive smuggling through Colonia made the Spanish determined to control both sides of the Paraná estuary. Simultaneously the possibility of exerting greater authority over the missions by dividing them found increasing favor among Spanish officials. The terms for the exchange were agreed upon by both parties at the signing of the *Tratado de Permuta* in 1750.[85] The Treaty stipulated that El Tape mission Indians would resettle in the refuge zone between the Uruguay and Alto Paraná rivers. Instead, some 30,000 Indians resisted any intrusion by either Spanish or Portuguese. During a three-year war known as the *Guerra Guaranítica* thousands of Indians died fighting, others resettled elsewhere, and many fled to the forests.[86] In 1761 the Treaty was annulled by Carlos III, but the Portuguese, who had expelled the Jesuits from Brazil two years earlier, continued their war and not until 1763 were the mission lands recaptured by the Spanish.[87] By this time the seven doctrinas of El Tape were in ruins. The Jesuits, who had been driven to extremes by the contradictions within the Spanish system on the one hand, and by malocas and influential propaganda on the other, lost favor rapidly. Finally, in 1767, the government of Spain issued an order terminating Jesuit control of the missions.

HISTORICAL AND ECONOMIC SIGNIFICANCE OF THE MISSIONS

The establishment of the Jesuit reducciones in the area of Bajas Misiones has influenced modern settlement in this region both directly and indirectly. The great success of mission settlements was responsible for the decision to continue them after the Jesuits were banned in 1767. However, the official division of these settlements among Franciscans, Dominicans, and Mercedarians destroyed the continuity of the old system.[88] Each new administrator was confused over the exact extent of his jurisdiction and before an understanding was possible, the missions rapidly deteriorated into Crown "reservations." The trouble with the reservation idea was that its purpose was less to help the natives than to keep them under surveillance. Natives were sufficiently discouraged under the new regime that they escaped to the Sierra Central where they joined raiding bands. Still others chose the relatively greater security of Spanish communities in neighboring provinces.

The rapid decline of the native population in the missions was of much significance to later settlement of the open Campo region, since it was precisely there that the missions had proved most successful, and had made the land safe from Indian attacks. On the other hand, the forest locations into which the Indians retreated after 1767 became unsafe for European settlement for over one hundred years. This was particularly true in the Selva of Misiones, which again became an Indian stronghold comparable to that of highland Peru, where large numbers of Incas operated after the Conquest. A major difference between the two areas is that in Misiones the natives were far less numerous and had been subjected to civilizing forces for over a century and a half. They failed in their sudden attempt to survive by themselves in the Selva. Those who became dangerous were eliminated by military campaigns, since they were located too near a major political frontier to be allowed to interfere with settlement.[89] The disappearance of the Indians has meant that they have had little direct effect on the Europeanization of Misiones.

As mentioned earlier, the ultimate location of each mission was the result of a combination of successful planning and experience. Many of the same working relationships established between physical and human features at these sites proved very functional for the pioneer settlements which followed and were copied by them. It is not surprising, therefore, that, even in ruins, some of the imposing Jesuit structures served to attract colonists both because of the indications of previous success at a given place and because of readily available building materials. Often cisterns and aqueducts could be used, as they were in Apóstoles until the early 1900s.[90] Descendants of the Jesuit orange plantations continue even today to supply settlers with fresh fruit. Thus, the old Jesuit sites gradually became surrounded by new communities, some of which have prospered as is the case, for example, in San Ignacio, where the old mission has been partially restored and is now a major tourist attraction. In all, nine of the eleven missions were so well located that they became modern townsites in Misiones. Five are near the Alto Paraná — Corpus, Loreto, San Ignacio, Santa Ana, and Candelaria — San José is in the extreme southwest of the Province, and San Javier and Concepción are near the right bank of the Uruguay. The remaining mission, Apóstoles, is now the heart of the Campo's second largest urban community which has, like the others, kept the original Jesuit name. No remains of Mártires and Concepción exist.[91] The mission of Mártires was thoroughly destroyed during the War of the Triple Alliance (1865–70) and forests have reclaimed the site.[92]

The most important influence of the Jesuits in Misiones has been the adoption of their agricultural methods. The yerba mate plantations were not only of immediate use to later colonists, but the certain evidence that this plant could be cultivated inspired modern settlers to experiment until the Jesuit "secret" for speeding the normally slow germination rate of yerba mate was learned. If, as is popularly assumed in Misiones, the Jesuits kept knowledge of the process such a well-guarded secret that the thousands of mission Indians never learned it, then it is understandable why rediscovering the technique took so long. On the contrary, a more plausible explanation is that the hard-working Jesuits had no secret at all, but utilized their immense labor source to transplant forest trees to missions fields. Also, the colonists learned, if wild seeds were gathered just after ripening they were easily divested of pulp and germinated more rapidly, a simple technique quite probably known to the Jesuits. However, not until the nineteenth century was it learned that soaking the seeds in a lime solution so softened the hard outer shell that the germination period could be reduced to only a few weeks. Jesuit tree-spacing and other cultivation practices were likewise copied and later slowly modified. Unfortunately, adoption of these methods brought about more rapid soil depletion the second time around. That special techniques were needed in such areas was not recognized in the early modern period, partly because of the strong Jesuit influence. The Jesuit tobacco, manioc, orange, and yerba mate plantings remained the four basic cash crops of Misiones until the 1930s. In ranching the major Jesuit contribution was the so-called Jesuit grass (*Axonopus compresus*, or *gramilla*), still common in Misiones.

Not all the Jesuit agricultural achievements have influenced the economic evolution of Misiones. One wonders why, for example, subsequent pioneers have not recognized that cotton was one of the major Jesuit crops. Wool has replaced cotton as the basic fiber manufactured in Argentina, even as it did during Jesuit times at their own reducciones in Tucumán, for instance. But in Tucumán there were relatively few Indians available, and, as cotton requires much more labor than does sheep ranching, the latter was a more logical choice. On the other hand, the missions of northeastern Argentina were distinguished by large numbers of Indians whose labor was readily available to the Jesuits. Consequently, sheep raising was somewhat deemphasized (see Table 4), and, despite an imperfect climate, cotton raising was another Jesuit success. In modern times cotton has proved to be uneconomical in Misiones since low cost labor now is unavailable. In addition, sheep and new varieties of cotton plants are now raised more profitably in other parts of the nation.

Another former Jesuit activity which continues to puzzle modern pioneers in Misiones is mining, an industry believed to be of great potential because of colonial successes, but no longer pursued except for working small deposits of iron ore near Posadas. Copper, even though in tiny and scattered deposits, was used by the Jesuits for utensils. These items have been collected over the centuries and knowledge that they were made in the missions gave rise to the mining legend. This legend later influenced important naturalists who wrote about Misiones, such as R. Hernández, R. Lista, Martin de Moussy, and others. Their nineteenth-century publications were in some cases overly enthusiastic reports to potential colonists about the riches to be won from mining in the Province.[93] The rumors of copper attracted at least one interested German settler to Santa Ana in 1833. He sank a shaft but failed in his attempt to find commercial quantities of the metal.[94] Only under the Jesuit system, which was based on a well-organized labor supply, could the small deposits in Misiones be commercially profitable. Yet even after the economy of the individual modern pioneer proved inadequate to exploit such mineral findings, the legend did not die. Because of this, and the fact that the Jesuits also manufactured some iron at the missions, there are few if any twentieth-century pioneers in Misiones who are not hopeful of the possibilities of exploiting minerals. After two centuries these hopes have largely failed to materialize, although they have been revived by construction of a foundry in Posadas in 1964 to use local deposits of tacurú, and by metasomatic deposits of copper reputed to be near some of the old mission sites.

The sixteenth-century transportation methods developed in the forest were also continued by the Jesuit's successors. The techniques were directly related to the development of the yerba mate economy, and were started by the Spanish in Asunción. Since the isolated yerba mate stands occurred in the midst of the Selva, the most practical way to get to them was by cutting straight narrow paths through the forest from the major navigable rivers or from the campiñas, or natural forest openings. Usually these paths (piques) were just wide enough for Indians to travel fully loaded with yerba mate sacks, but when stands were sufficiently large, trails were broadened into roadways (*picadas*) for mules, which were linked in tandem by a central rope — a practice still used on the picadas of northern Misiones. Since there was constant traffic from one Jesuit mission to another, and since the yerba mate had to be removed from the missions to Candelaria on the Paraná before shipment to Santa Fe, Buenos Aires, or Peru, the Jesuits developed the long forest trails and roadways in Misiones wherever necessary. This is one of the main reasons why they also bred mules at each settlement. Although neither river valleys nor interfluves are long or easy to follow in Misiones, the rolling hills presented no major obstacles to movement except in the high parts of the Sierra Central. Modern settlers have continued the pique and picada system for reaching new yerba mate stands, lumber areas, or pioneer settlements. The colonial technique was a significant factor in the introduction of the line settlement form by today's pioneers.

The Jesuits were thorough enough to maintain good records of their activities. The relatively numerous reports of plant experimentation and of various aspects of climate, natural vegetation, soils, native life, and other features recorded by men like A. Sepp, A. Böhm, B. Nusdorfer, J. de Escandón, F. J. de Charlevoix, A. Ruiz de Montoya, and L. Muratori were all published in German, and some in French and Italian during the eighteenth century. They left valuable general and specific information and propaganda for the use of later settlers. The economic data which were compiled facilitated reconstruction of farm methods and routes of transportation as well as calculations about potential commercial agricultural and industrial profits from the region and have been much quoted during the modern colonization period. These data illustrate why Argentine officials were later convinced that this entirely "foreign" part of their nation, the only densely forested subtropical region in Argentina, could be made productive again. The amount of incentive generated from reading the Jesuit records cannot be measured, but it unquestionably gave modern settlers an awareness of the value of innovation, and instituted much needed self-confidence, an element which sometimes by itself can spell the difference between success and failure of a pioneer settlement in difficult country.

After the Argentine, Paraguayan, and Brazilian wars over control of the mission centers there were still sufficient Indians in Misiones to argue successfully for the creation of a separate political state. Indeed, because the Jesuit missions had supported a population of 50,000 in only the smallest part of Misiones and because of the land settlement policies developed for the missions during the early Republican period, the separate political entity called the Territory of Misiones came into being. Even when the rest of Misiones fell into private hands during the Republican period, the former Jesuit holdings in Bajas Misiones continued to be claimed by the federal government and were therefore considered part of the public domain. As a direct consequence of this policy, the national government was later able to initiate one of its most successful public colonization programs in the former Jesuit province, and to extend this program into the Sierra Central. Thus, it was the missions and their Indians, both of which succumbed, that saved the region for statehood, and for the modern federal colonization program which in turn strongly influenced private colonization attempts along the Alto Paraná and Uruguay rivers.

However, in spite of the ultimate success of the government program, a long period of administrative confusion occurred following the departure of the Jesuits from Latin America. This confusion, which reshaped government settlement policies, brought about an extended period of uncertain federal decisions, initial colonization failures, and even the depopulation of Misiones. In fact, the area reverted to the wilderness it once had been prior to the arrival of the Spanish before modern pressures stimulated another attempt to integrate Misiones with the economy of Buenos Aires.

Chapter 4

CORRIENTES PROVINCE AND
THE DEVELOPMENT OF
LATIFUNDISMO IN MISIONES

> One of the most extraordinary features of South
> American life is the persistence of frontier conditions
> through the centuries since the Conquest.
>
> Isaiah Bowman, *The Pioneer Fringe*

CROWN ADMINISTRATIVE CONFUSION

Some months after the departure of the Jesuits in 1767, Crown attempts to replace the efficient clerical administration failed badly. At first two governors were appointed for the 3 missions: one, with a residence in Candelaria, was in charge of the 13 so-called pueblos northwest of the Sierra Central; the other, with a residence in El Tape, had control over the 17 pueblos south of the divortium aquarum. The inadequacies of this form of government brought about reunion of the two administrations in 1771 with one capital at Candelaria.[1] At this time five departments were created (Concepción, Yapeyú, San Miguel, San Ignacio, and Candelaria) which were administered by lieutenant governors who had authority over every aspect of life. In practice the plan did not function well because each pueblo was led by an *administrador* whose decisions rarely agreed with those of the lieutenant governor.[2] Furthermore, the 80 Jesuits who had managed religious life in the missions were replaced by only 56 Franciscans, Dominicans, and Mercedarians, none of whom were given clear control over the Indians.[3] Typically, these replacements were untrained and transient.[4] The resulting confusion among the Jesuit-trained native artisans forced many of them to move to Asunción, Corrientes, Santa Fe, and Buenos Aires. The exodus further weakened the pueblo structure, as did the frequent cattle and Indian raids by the Portuguese.[5]

Other administrative changes produced division of southeastern Latin America into eight *Intendencias* and four *Provincias* in 1782. In this manner the Province of Misiones, bordering the new Intendencia of Paraguay, was formed in the area of the old reducciones. Ensuing conflicts between the two over control of the mission pueblos and with the city of Corrientes, which claimed land in the mission area, grew so serious that settlers and Indians continued to leave.

Statistics for the former Jesuit pueblos reveal a 25 per cent decline in population between 1767 and 1795; only 10,000 Indians and a few hundred Europeans were left in the eleven reducciones of the modern Province of Misiones by this time.[6]

In 1800 some 300 Indian chiefs who remained in the mission pueblos were released from work on the Tupambaés. This created disturbances among the other Indians who felt they had been discriminated against. In addition, the removal of the most capable from pueblo lands left a leadership vacuum.[7] At the same time, an *Informe*, or official report, proposed closing the missions and liberating all the Indians.[8] Production declined and the mission structure crumbled even further.

Taking advantage of the general disorder, Portuguese troops overran El Tape in 1801. The Spanish were finally prompted to encourage settlement in the remaining twenty-three mission pueblos to avoid further losses of the frontier region. One plan of action described in a *Cédula Real* dated May 17, 1803, specified that even Indians were to be given land grants of "a league to every [mission] quarter, as there is plenty of land for everything . . ." and expressed the Crown feeling for what had been occurring by recommending that "great caution . . . be taken so that . . . the Spanish may not acquire any lands [in the native areas] . . . as experience has shown them as always ending by seizing all or the greater part of the land in the possession of the Indians . . . ."[9]

Another early nineteenth-century attempt to encourage settlement in the old mission region was made by enactment of a Royal Tobacco Tax. After the Jesuit departure there was a shortage of tobacco in the Spanish settlements of Río de la Plata so a voluntary head tax of 25 arrobas of tobacco was inaugurated which could be paid in lieu of military service and payment of public

taxes. In 1805, 1,683 individuals from the twenty-three missions
were reported paying these tobacco taxes.[10]

Indians were also urged to raise tobacco. However, their lot
was always endangered by the arrival of private settlers and by
the menace of raiders. Ironically, natives were armed for their
own protection after the fashion of the Jesuits and organized by
a military leader appointed to the mission region in 1806.[11] Had
trouble with Spain not begun shortly afterward, more might have
been done to save the Indians of Misiones. Unfortunately for the
mission pueblos, forces from Asunción occupied Candelaria, Santa
Ana, San Ignacio, Loreto, and Corpus in 1810. General M. Belgrano was sent north from Buenos Aires to the disputed area and
succeeded in liberating these pueblos.[12] In Candelaria, December,
1810, he published his famous *Reglamento para los Pueblos Mi-
sionarios*, which is considered to be the first attempt at making
an independent constitution in Argentina.[13]

Belgrano crossed the Alto Paraná and was defeated in Encarnación. Paraguayan troops reoccupied Corpus, San Ignacio, Loreto, Santa Ana, and Candelaria, or the missions north of the
Sierra Central *divortium aquarum*. Paraguay declared itself and
the occupied territory independent of Buenos Aires and a treaty
was signed between the two in 1811 which gave only the southern
ten of the old mission pueblos to Argentina.[14] However, the pueblos north of the divide had decided earlier in favor of Buenos
Aires and discontent raged over the truce line. The compromise
solution that the Alto Paraná form the boundary with Paraguay
gained strong support in Argentina.

Settlers in the mission pueblos were still in disagreement in
1814 whether administrative leadership should be in Buenos Aires
or in their own area. The struggle led to creation of the provinces
of Entre Ríos and Corrientes the same year.[15] Corrientes was assigned the land within the present Province of Misiones, plus eastern acreage later lost to Brazil. Although Corrientes was the political capital, as a compromise to the Indians a military capital was
established in Candelaria. Within only a few months the Indian
militia under leadership of the Guaraní Andresito forced the Paraguayans out of the missions south of the Alto Paraná.[16] His successful forces then attacked the Portuguese and drove them from
El Tape. However, in 1817, the Portuguese and Paraguayans

united and advanced on two fronts. The invaders were finally driven off, but the fighting made a shambles of the former Jesuit reducciones between the Alto Paraná and Uruguay rivers and all but eliminated their Indian populations.[17]

BOUNDARY PROBLEMS

A formal border between Misiones and Corrientes was established in 1819 with the participation of remaining Indian leaders who had fought hard to free their settlements.[18] The sixteen missions between the Alto Paraná and Uruguay rivers became part of Misiones. Even so, Corrientes insisted on occupying land it had once held eastward to the Uruguay and north across Misiones, approximately along the present border. Constant disputes with Brazil made it impossible to clarify the eastern limits of the modern Province of Misiones until much later.

Unfortunately for the few settlers still in the mission pueblos, confusion over the administration of Misiones had invited a state of lawlessness. Between battles and conflicting political decisions, veterans and "liberated" Indians raided settlers within the provincial borders as well as in Corrientes. Things deteriorated so badly that in 1822 action was undertaken by Corrientes to stop the troublemakers from gaining complete control of Misiones. Many Indian raiders were captured and sent with their families to cities such as Corrientes to become servants. There they slowly mixed with the rest of the population.[19] During this hectic period the Paraguayans, who had earlier begun to trade with their Portuguese ally along a route from Encarnación south through Bajas Misiones to Santo Tomé, reoccupied Candelaria to keep the passageway open and to prevent renovation of the Jesuit yerba mate plantations.

The inability of Buenos Aires to control Misiones encouraged the Portuguese to take military action against Argentina in 1827, and, although this war brought about the creation of Uruguay, the old pueblos of El Tape in the land south of the Uruguay River remained under the jurisdiction of the Portuguese. In the interim, settlers in Misiones are reputed to have sought protection from Indian raiders, and had again received assistance from Corrientes.[20] A military expedition defeated the bulk of the rebellious natives in the battle of San Pedro and brought survivors west to Corrientes proper. The zeal with which Correntinos came to the aid of the remote settlers was no doubt inspired by the opportunity to control yerba mate plantations and forests which represented not only a source of great income in danger of being overrun by Paraguayan or Brazilian factions, but potential competition in the case of a separated Misiones. In 1830 Corrientes took over administration of Misiones without interference from Entre Ríos or Buenos Aires and two years later forced the Paraguayans out of Candelaria. This finally permitted control of trade with Brazil and a chance to obtain salt as well as a shorter overland route to the Atlantic. Part of the old trade route between Paraguay and Brazil was employed for this purpose — across Bajas Misiones to Santo Tomé on the Uruguay, down this river to Monte Caseros and then eastward across El Tape to the coast.[21] By this route traders could avoid the heavily forested regions of Misiones and adjacent Brazil, an advantage which explains why Brazil clung so tenaciously to the El Tape mission area during the colonial period.

Trade developed more slowly than might have been expected in Bajas Misiones because Corrientes Province insisted on protecting its own industries with heavy tariffs. In 1822, the exportation of hides and the importation of wheat and flour were prohibited. In 1833 the importation of yerba mate was prohibited, but this negative action helped make the old mission area somewhat more attractive to settlers.[22] The move was designed to supplement a government decree of November 9, 1832, which attempted to establish an official yerba mate industry in Misiones. This decree invited all Argentines to exploit yerba mate and wood in the forests of the old missions (Art. 1), although a Corrientes license had to be obtained; people could only use rifles which had been registered and specially marked in the Misiones area (Art. 2); and yerba mate tree roots could not be cut (Art. 9). Yerba mate duties were to be paid at Tranqueras de Loreto (between the Laguna del Iberá and the Paraná River west of Misiones) (Art. 12), and the yerba mate plantations of the ruined pueblos were to remain in the hands of the government of Corrientes (Art. 17) (Fig. 4).[23] A relatively peaceful period which followed the decree lasted only until 1841 when Corrientes's autonomy was threatened by the dictator Rosas from Buenos Aires. Forced by this threat into a defensive treaty with Paraguay, Corrientes had to agree to divide the missions between the Alto Paraná and Uruguay rivers along the divortium aquarum. Thereafter a thriving trade developed between Brazil and Paraguay during which the latter built warehouses at San José, Misiones, opposite Encarnación. However, in 1843 Rosas, ever distrustful of Corrientes, gave Entre Ríos Province control of Misiones until final disposition could be made in Buenos Aires.

MISIONES AND WAR WITH PARAGUAY

The impracticality of control of Misiones from Entre Ríos was evident at once. Rosas finally maneuvered until he broke the Corrientes-Paraguayan friendship treaty and in 1845 threatened Paraguay until that nation declared war against Argentina. Rosas had overextended his supply lines and three years later Paraguayan troops were able to occupy without opposition the missions south of the Alto Paraná. By this time Buenos Aires was vigorously objecting to Rosas's policies and he was overthrown in 1852. The new authorities drafted the Republic's important Constitution of 1853, which was designed to promote settlement in Argentina and which is still in effect. During this confused period Corrientes reassumed control of the former mission land along the west side of the Uruguay River. Paraguay finally recognized Argentine sovereignty up to the Río Alto Paraná in 1852, but did not remove her troops from the old mission ruins south of the border.[24] Continued internal political difficulties prevented Argentina from taking action until 1865 when the belligerence of Paraguay's President López caused Brazil, Uruguay, and Argentina to unite against the Paraguayans in the War of the Triple Alliance (1865–70). As part of the preparation for battle, López's soldiers fortified San José (later called Trincheras de San José) at the narrows in the Alto Paraná opposite Encarnación. After the war the city of Posadas developed at this strategic site.[25]

During the War of the Triple Alliance Paraguayan troops moved south and captured the missions of Concepción, Santa María, and Mártires, from which they removed yerba mate and whatever was still worth taking from the old ruins. Only the most isolated settlers were not uprooted by the fighting. One of these was an Italian who had opened a pique to the Uruguay River along which he exploited yerba mate.[26] In the northeast, Brazilian troops crossed the Misiones border and began exploiting yerbales at Campiñas de América and San Pedro during their attempt to reach Paraguay overland. San Pedro became a center of early Argentine colonization efforts because of fear of the Brazilian occupation.[27] By 1870 Brazilians had retired from Misiones so Argentina was left in possession of the land up to the Alto Paraná. Corrientes Province, convinced of the need for controlling Misiones and worried about national colonization interests there, was determined to fill the vacuum left by the war and decided to colonize the region as rapidly as possible.

PROVINCIAL ATTEMPTS TO ENCOURAGE SETTLEMENT

One of the primary stimuli for colonization of the provinces of Argentina came from the federal government. Since 1852 Buenos Aires had grown economically and militarily stronger and had exerted ever more influence over the separate provinces. The Constitution of 1853 had instructed the authorities to encourage immigration according to Argentinean political theorist Juan Bautista Alberdi's dictum "to govern is to populate," and guaranteed civil rights to foreigners.[28] The establishment of the first successful immigrant colonies of Esperanza (1856), San Carlos (1859), and San Gerónimo (1858), with Germans, Swiss, and others in Santa Fe Province; of Baradero (1857), with Germans and Swiss in Buenos Aires Province; and of San José (1857) and Villa Urquiza (1858), with German and Swiss settlers in Entre Ríos, began a long period of state- and federally-assisted foreign colonization. After 1860, when Argentina revised the Constitution of 1853 to include all the provinces and became a nation in fact, the federal government intensified its encouragement of foreign colonies. In the succeeding decade the question of limits with Paraguay in the Chaco and in Misiones, and with Chile in Patagonia, demonstrated the urgent need for effective settlement of land around the nation's fringes. These circumstances were responsible for passage of the major federal colonization Law 817 of 1876.[29]

The spirit of colonization was felt in the Province of Corrientes, which adopted plans to direct settlement in the remote area of Misiones. By this means Corrientes commerce and trade were to be protected and further Brazilian and Paraguayan invasions stopped. Besides, the demand for yerba mate from this region was increasing steadily and augured well for the future of colonists. Preliminary steps were taken to issue land to settlers in Bajas Misiones as early as 1860. The *Mesa Topográfica y de Estadística* of Corrientes recorded property grants to individuals at the following sites between 1860 and 1865: 1860, Santa María, 1; 1861, San Javier, 1; 1862, Itacaruaré, 1; 1862, Garruchos, 1; 1863, Concepción, 2; 1864, Santa María, 1.[30]

Nevertheless, three things defeated Corrientes's attempt to attract colonists to Misiones. The first was overzealous taxation. On April 4, 1861, the legislature established the unrealistic tax of two *reales metálicos* for each arroba of yerba mate extracted.[31] Second, hostilities broke out with Paraguay before settlement could get under way. Third, it was well known that the dense tropical forests of Misiones were impassable except under the harshest circumstances, and that it was a long, difficult route from inhabited parts of Corrientes to Bajas Misiones. On April 6, 1863, the Department of Interior of the government of Corrientes reported that there were only two useful paths by which Misiones could be reached.[32] One of these was overland along the margin of the Alto Paraná. The river itself defied transportation past Ituzaingó because of the 15 km/hr rapids at Apipé.[33] However, even the shoreline route was complicated by the Laguna del Iberá which often flooded and extended to the Alto Paraná itself (Fig. 4). The other route to Misiones was south and east of the Laguna, more or less along the Uruguay River. However, the latter river was navigable only for boats that drew less than one meter in the high water season.[34] One German settler who was far upstream on the Uruguay River was described as being completely isolated from the rest of Argentina except for the difficult river connection.[35]

YERBA MATE AND COLONIZATION LEGISLATION

Because of poor transportation a law was passed on July 13, 1863, calling for construction of piques needed "to facilitate the extraction of yerba mate in Misiones from the convenient points of Corrientes Province . . . ."[36] As compensation for trail opening, individuals willing to work at this remote and arduous task were allowed to charge a use fee and could receive a land grant of 5 square leagues (10,000 ha) as long as the land was outside the yerba mate areas reserved by the state.

Several other positive attempts to develop a permanent Misiones yerba mate industry and to promote colonization were made at this time by Corrientes. On January 7, 1864, the *Reglamento para los Yerbales* made a permit necessary to collect yerba mate. The harvest time was limited to the months of April through August. Common practice had long been to start the harvest in January, which made the cutting season so extensive that wild trees could not be used again for many years. Furthermore, unrestricted pruning was so severe that trees were killed or damaged and the whole operation was therefore regulated. By official decree, once cut, trees could not be used again for four years.[37] This was the first detailed official attempt by Corrientes to control yerba mate exploitation since the more primitive legislation of 1830.

On March 2, 1864, the high taxes on yerba mate were lowered to one-half real.[38] Ten days later the legislature decreed that the yerba mate industry was destined to become one of the principal sources of wealth for the Province of Corrientes and that forests should be made available to anyone willing to work in them. The decree reserved all lands not yet disposed of by sale or rent between the Sierra Central and the Uruguay River east of San Javier for the "maintenance of animals suitable for the transport of yerba mate . . . and for the establishment of both yerba mate and lumber processing centers" (Art. 1).[39] Land grants were to be given which would average one-half square league (1,000 ha), but could be larger or smaller, depending on their importance and on the local topography (Art. 2). Commercial cattle and sheep breeding were prohibited and no more than 300 head of livestock were allowed (Art. 3), probably to prevent competition with Corrientes proper. *Ejidos*, or holdings, of one-half square league were reserved in the ruined Jesuit villages for farms (Art. 8).

Handfuls of farmers and ranchers occupied parts of southwestern Misiones near the Jesuit ruins of the Uruguay, since land north of the divortium aquarum was still in dispute. Although the region was heavily forested in places, vast open areas played an attractive role during this phase of settlement. The openings were covered with lush grasses such as *Andropogon* sp. and *Pani-*

cum sp., as well as tender herbage of the genera *Paspalum* and *Axonopus*. The tall grasses made excellent breeding grounds for mules, the preferred yerba mate cargo animal. They could graze even on *tacuarembó* leaves if necessary. Horses on the other hand contracted *mal de cadera* and died. Whether this was a disease known to the Jesuits is not clear, but it had become serious by the nineteenth century.[40] Even if overgrazing brought on swift erosion, there was plenty of land available for everyone. The scattered openings simplified travel throughout the region, while the abandoned mission compounds testified to the feasibility of settlement and provided both yerba mate plantings and useful building materials.[41] Extracted forest products were sent to the Uruguay River for shipment out of the region. Although some enthusiasm for settlement was inspired, the Uruguay caused great inconvenience as yerba "rotted in the warehouses" owing to the irregularity of water travel.[42] Reliable shipping facilities existed only during the high water period, so settlers gradually concentrated on lumbering rather than on yerba gathering in this region. Logs could at least be stored and then floated downstream at high water just as is still being done. Some commercial agriculture began with manioc, a crop so hardy that it requires little attention. Between 1864 and 1872 four manioc mills were built at Concepción; one was constructed at San Javier in 1876. A few of the farmers began to raise sugar cane and between 1871 and 1876 three small mills or *trapiches* were built at Concepión and two at San Javier.[43]

LAND GRANTS AND ECONOMIC GROWTH

Once Paraguayan occupation forces left the region north of the Sierra Central water divide, settlers began to occupy the old northern mission pueblos. In fact, they even began to leave good ground near the Uruguay because of the limited navigability of that river.[44] In 1869 the legislature of Corrientes Province made Trincheras de San José the administrative center of a new Department of Candelaria, i.e., all land between the Sierra Central and the Paraná, indicating both concern for the presence of Brazilian troops there and recognition of the always navigable Paraná. The latter notion was confirmed in 1870 by J. Irigoyen who published a report that the Alto Paraná was 3–4 meters deep even during the low water period.[45] A year later the area of Trincheras de San José was surveyed, and in 1872 the site was made a municipality, which indicates a population of at least 1,000.[46]

It is important to note that the continued paucity of official land grants already demonstrated a serious titling deficiency, a trait that resulted from the desire to maintain strict control over yerba mate resources during colonization. For example, only the following settlements were titled in Misiones between 1865 and 1872: 1868, Concepción, 1; 1869, Santa María, 2; 1870, Santa María, 1; 1872, Mártires, 1.[47]

After 1872 Trincheras de San José began to assume importance as a trade center. Yerba mate was shipped mainly from Paraguay and several Buenos Aires firms located branch offices in the town to handle the business.[48] In 1872 alone, 10 yerba mate mills were built in the vicinity of Candelaria; 4 more were added the next year.[49] Between 1874 and 1876, 5 mills were constructed in San Ignacio. During the same decade over 20 yerba mills were built in Santa Ana.[50] Agriculture received an impetus from the renewed settlement and maize, sugar cane, and manioc became major commercial crops. The following corn flour mills were built near Candelaria: 1873, 1; 1874, 2; 1875, 3; 1876, 2; 1877, 1. Sugar processing centers were also built, 1 each in 1874 and 1876. In 1873 a manioc flour mill was constructed in the Candelaria area; in 1876 one went up in San Ignacio.[51] Modern steamboats opened the Alto Paraná beyond the rapids of Apipé. The increased activity resulted in a new and detailed *Reglamento para los Yerbales* (November 20, 1876), especially designed to control yerba mate collecting in San Javier, Santa Ana, and Corpus, as well as any possible new areas of exploitation, i.e., yerbales.[52] The changes introduced at this time not only affected the wild yerba mate industry but caused restricted settlement activities until the establishment of plantations after the turn of the century.

According to the new law yerbales were divided into four parts (Art. 1).[53] Each year one quarter section of a yerbal was used for cutting and then prohibited from further exploitation for the three following years (Art. 2). Newly discovered yerbales belonged to the finder during the first year, and then were subjected to the regulations. Anyone desiring to cut yerba mate had to acquire a permit either in San Javier or in Santa Ana (Art. 4). Cutting was restricted to the period between March 1st and July 30th (Art. 5). Groups of yerba mate cutters were allowed 60 square *cuadras* of land (a *campamento*), each cutter within the group receiving 6 of these units. Cutters were not allowed to damage the trees in any way. Campamentos were always characterized by the presence of one main structure known as the *noque*, a yerba mate storage facility. Noques were 7 to 10 meters long by 6 meters wide, had peaked roofs, and were raised some cms above ground level. Roofs and walls were thatched with tacuará leaves.[54] The law required that a clearing be established in the vicinity of the noque for a *ranchería* or temporary settlement. However, only huts could be erected for laborers; permanent habitations were absolutely forbidden (Art. 16). Although movements of personnel and campamentos were permitted, they were strictly controlled.

As a consequence of the concern for yerba mate protection, the yerbales did not become sites of permanent settlement as might otherwise have been the case. Cutters were supposed to return eventually to the rehabilitated mission pueblos which served as yerba mate markets, or to other officially approved sites (Art. 22). As new yerbales were opened in the more remote interior, they eventually attracted families away from the old mission ruins. Campamentos both large and small started as squatter settlements without free status, and, since no land titles were ever granted in them, they became rural slums. Because of these restrictions, neither Misiones yerbales nor bona fide settlements were rapidly developed, and most of the yerba mate exported from this area actually came from Paraguay.

Unhappily, the Paraguayan source of yerba mate, located upstream on the Alto Paraná at Tacurú Purú, was soon closed to all but one firm by the Paraguayan government. This created an economic depression in Misiones.[55] Moreover, high *patentes*, or taxes, imposed by both provincial and federal legislatures which saw new sources of revenue developing, hastened the general decline.[56] The case of Santa Ana is typical. Only one yerba mill was left at the time of Hernandez's visit at the beginning of the 1880s.[57] Of the 600 mules used for transporting yerba mate during the preceding decade he reported fewer than 150 still in service. The same was true along the Uruguay where Peyret wrote that San Ignacio had only one yerba processing center left by 1881.[58] The depression brought a shift of emphasis along the Alto Paraná to lumbering, which long-term isolation had already produced on the Río Uruguay.

Fortunately, by 1875 interest in the potential of Misiones' yerbales had awakened; an official expedition was organized to make investigations inland from the Alto Paraná and to defeat the last of the belligerent Indians deep in the Sierra Central.[59] An important side effect of the expedition was the opening of a picada (or crude roadway) from Trincheras de San José to San Pedro. The picada passed through Campo Grande and Yerbal Nuevo, both of which were richly endowed yerba mate areas. These, along with the stands at San Pedro, were made available just as Paraguayan trade was officially closed. The situation in Misiones was made to order for an intensified colonization program.

PROVINCIAL COLONIZATION FAILURES

Official recognition of Misiones as a part of Argentina was postponed until 1876, well after the defeat of Paraguay. However, the War of the Triple Alliance had made the government uneasy about the precarious nature of this international frontier area. In 1869 Alberdi had proposed restoration and settlement of the old Province of Misiones. On October 15, 1875, federal authorities promoted colonization by a law granting up to 100 ha of land in alternate sections in remote parts of the nation. Transportation costs of colonists were to be paid to these regions. Concern over this law prompted Corrientes Province to pass the Ley de Pueblos Agrícolas on November 6, 1875, ordering surveys for the establishment of agricultural colonies and their pueblos in the old mission areas.[60] This action spurred a tendency to separate the concepts of yerba mate exploitation and colonization — a separation partially abetted by the location of the former mission settlements in the Campo and by the remoteness of wild yerba mate stands in the Selva. No thought was given to the successful Jesuit method of combining the two operations, since it was felt that yerba mate was extremely difficult to plant successfully and that sooner or later the remaining interior yerbales would be opened to exploitation.

The Corrientes plan specified that each pueblo agrícola was to include farm lots and urban area and measure 6 km on a side. Urban areas were reserved in the center of each pueblo where

100 blocks, each 100 meters square and separated by 25-meter-wide streets, were to be laid out. The town blocks were further subdivided by law into *solares* 50 meters square. One road around this urban area divided the solares from the surrounding farms. The latter were to be 500 meters square (25 ha square) and to be separated by roads 30 meters wide. Article 7 of the law made it mandatory to survey by a grid net of straight lines, a system which had been successfully used in Esperanza and other early colonies of the Pampa (Fig. 5).[61] Town solares were to be sold for 25 pesos, one-fifth in cash and the rest in four annual payments. Rural lots were listed at 40 pesos to be paid for in four annual amounts after the first year of residence. The former had to be populated and fenced within one year after sale, the later settled and cultivated within two years following the contract. All properties were tax free for two years.

Marcos Avellaneda. The law contributed to the foundation of one colony in Misiones in 1876. On October 10, an Italian named Caesar Augusto del Vasco was granted a concession near Corpus not to exceed 5 square leagues and with a front along the Alto Paraná between the arroyos Iguaguy and Santo Pipó. The immediate objective of the concession was to settle the area with 300 families within three years (Art. 1).[62] Three-fourths of the families could be foreigners. Vasco paid for all surveying costs. The Province of Corrientes agreed to build a primary school after 50 families arrived. Vasco named his colony Marcos Avellaneda, and, within a few months, attracted Volga Germans and some French families.[63] Unfortunately the colony was two days overland from markets and there was only infrequent river transportation available. In addition, the river captains, knowing there was no legal protection for settlers, charged exorbitant rates.[64] Finally, when the Alto Paraná flooded and destroyed property several months after the colony's founding, the project failed to survive.[65] Some of the families resettled on higher ground near Santa Ana where government holdings were made available, and no more arrived at Marcos Avellaneda. The failure made a major contribution to the choice of settlement locations when the federal government began its colonization program in Misiones a short time later.

Sociedad Anónima de Colonización. After this failure, the federal government awarded a colonization contract (February 27,

1877) to Otto Rosse, a north German immigrant, for settling 800 square km of land along the Río Uruguay.[66] It appears that the legality of the contract was based on the federal colonization Law 817 of 1876, which gave the nation authority to grant colonization concessions anywhere in lands not previously surveyed (Art. 104).[67] The area in question was to follow the river below San Javier for 20 km and to extend inland an equal distance. Rosse's *Sociedad Anónima de Colonización del Alto Uruguay* was supposed to bring a minimum of 250 families within four years and sell each family group of three men at least 50 ha of land. The news travelled swiftly to Corrientes Province where it was greeted without enthusiasm. Bitterness developed over the usurpation of provincial territory by the federal government. In April, several Corrientes citizens protested formally by stating that the land in question had already been granted to others. It was further requested that negotiations with Rosse be suspended on grounds that borders of the Province had never been clearly established. Before the matter got any farther Rosse was found impaled on a tree near his property with the official documents still in his possession.[68] He was the victim of the kind of dispute that flares when jurisdiction and possession of a policeless frontier region are at stake. The clash between Corrientes and Buenos Aires over Misiones began a long lasting quarrel which undermined the relationship between federal and provincial authorities in Argentina.[69]

Firmat, Napp, and Wilcken.   Forced by the turn of events to take swift action, Corrientes asserted its authority by attempting again to colonize Misiones. Because of the new national colonization law of 1876 it was necessary to proceed according to the federal requirements. This was done on November 15, 1877, when the Province contracted with the firm of I. Firmat, R. Napp, and G. Wilcken of Buenos Aires to establish colonies in Misiones. By this contract the firm received: 500 square km at the confluence of the Ríos Iguazú and Alto Paraná; 100 square km at the confluence of the Ríos Pirú Guazú and Alto Paraná; 100 square km at the confluence of the Ríos Paranay Guazú and Alto Paraná; 100 square km at the confluence of the Ríos Caranguayí and Alto Paraná. All yerbales were retained by the Province of Corrientes (Art. 12).[70] Although a generous amount of land was granted, the Company never followed through with the project.

The Vasco, Rosse, and I. Firmat failures received much publicity in Argentina and had the cumulative effect of giving a bad
name to the idea of colonizing Misiones. Even though it became
increasingly difficult for Corrientes to do anything with this area,
fear of losing it to the federal authorities forced the Province to
keep trying.

Santa Ana. A new farm colony was founded at Santa Ana on
August 4, 1877, with a surface area of 2 square leagues (10,000 ha).
By legislation all previous residents of the old Jesuit pueblo as
well as poor people in the area were granted a free solar for farming.[71] On October 2, 1877, the Province created nine more farm
colonies in Misiones, most of which were at former mission sites
(Table 5).[72] These were surveyed within approximately two years
and, like Santa Ana, attracted small numbers of settlers, mainly

TABLE 5

Farm Colonies Created by Corrientes Province in
Misiones by Law of Oct. 2, 1877

Name	Area	Location
Corpus	10,000 ha	Old mission pueblo
San Ignacio	10,000 ha	Old mission pueblo
Candelaria	3,984 ha	East of property of D. Felizario front-ing on the Alto Paraná
San José	10,000 ha	Old mission pueblo
Apóstoles	10,000 ha	Old mission pueblo
Concepción		Bordering the Uruguay River between the arroyos Concepción and Capibari, and 2 leagues inland
Mártires	10,000 ha	Old mission pueblo
San Javier	—	Bordering the Uruguay River between the arroyos Acaregua and Pindati, and 2 leagues inland
Garruchos	—	Bordering the Uruguay River between arroyos Garaby and Chimaray, and 2 leagues inland

Source: Corrientes Province, *Recopilación completa de códigos, leyes y
decretos reglamentarios vigentes de la Provincia de Corrientes,* 2 vols. (Corrientes, 1904), 2:25.

squatters from the local area and German-Brazilians from Rio Grande do Sul.[73]

Farm Colonies Program.   In spite of Corrientes's attempts at colonization, discussions in Buenos Aires began to take place over the possibilities of federal intervention in Misiones. No less a dignitary than Bartolomé Mitre, former president of the Republic, argued that federalization of the Misiones frontier region was desirable.[74] Partly because of national hints that Misiones should be removed from incompetent provincial control, Corrientes hastily passed several new land laws designed to increase its own authority as well as to profit by the sale of property in Misiones. On January 1, 1878, a second Department called San Javier was created which encompassed all the land in Misiones south of the Sierra Central. Concepción was made the capital.[75] On September 17, the name of Trincheras de San José was changed to Posadas to emphasize the fact that the man, Gervasio A. de Posadas, originally responsible for creating the Province of Corrientes in 1814 had included the entire area of Misiones. On October 30, 1878, an imaginary line was drawn between Corpus and San Javier separating Selva from Campo, i.e., from Bajas Misiones.[76] On the east side of the line the more remote property of the Selva was offered for sale for 2,000 to 2,500 pesos per square league, so long as it did not contain yerbales which the Province zealously continued to protect for its own interests. West of the line, Campo land outside the farm colonies could be bought for 3,000 to 5,000 pesos. Strictly open Campo land, or grassland, was considered to possess fewer natural resources and wherever it occurred in large amounts land was sold at only 2,000 pesos per square league. One year later the legislature permitted sale of up to 100 square leagues of land at a 50 per cent price reduction for cash payment. The law was limited to eight months but was extended for a second term in order to sell the remaining land.[77] In January, 1880, half a century of legislation was annulled when even the yerbales were offered for sale. A new line was drawn separating farm land from woodland and yerbales. The line began at the mouth of the arroyo Santa Ana, continued to its headwaters, followed the base of the Sierra Central to a point west of Mártires and then proceeded to the pueblo of San Javier, following the natural division between Campo and Selva (Fig. 2). New agricultural colonies with a maximum size of 27,000 ha were to be developed in the Campo. One hundred ha per colony were reserved for a pueblo unless the area included an old mission center which could be used for urbanization. Rural land prices were 1–2 pesos per ha. Forests and yerbales in the Selva were to be sold for 40–80 centavos per ha. Land could also be rented for four years at 5 per cent of the value annually. An official was commissioned in Santa Ana and another in San Javier to explore land, draw maps, and write reports on natural resources. Low taxes of 25 centavos per arroba of yerba mate and 50 centavos for wood over 5 meters long (35 centavos for wood under 5 meters) were imposed. It is a tribute to the official yerba mate protection policy of many years standing that not a single ha containing the plant was offered for sale under this law, nor were the people of Corrientes willing to force the issue. On February 3, 1881, Corrientes officials authorized colonization of any part of the Misiones area under the supervision of National Colonization Law 817 of 1876. Two days later 80 square leagues of land were made available for the establishment of sugar mills, three of which were to be located along the Alto Paraná and five along the Uruguay.[78] Surveys were to be carried out within three months after signing for a concession.

LATIFUNDISMO AND FEDERALIZATION OF LANDS

On July 5, 1881, Argentine President Julio A. Roca made the first formal proposal to nationalize Misiones. He stated:

In that vast extension [of land] which in another time was an active center of work and of culture, today there are no churches or schools; not a single new industry has been introduced; one cannot find the smallest nucleus of stable population which can exert itself and spread over the land it occupies; the greatest potential wealth remains inevitably lost in this manner, and the natural products of a land so fertile are entirely abandoned to isolated efforts which if they satisfy individual gain cannot intend or do anything in favor of the general interest.

. . . .

It is necessary to consider, furthermore, that we are not dealing with a piece of land hidden in the interior of the nation. Misiones is on the frontier of our territory; it is in immediate contact with the land of other nations and thereby deserves double attention by the government.[79]

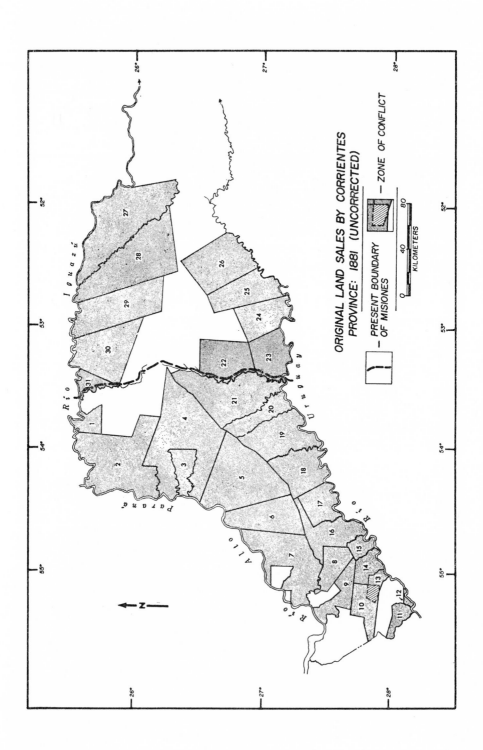

ORIGINAL LAND SALES BY CORRIENTES
PROVINCE: 1881 (UNCORRECTED)

— PRESENT BOUNDARY
OF MISIONES

— ZONE OF CONFLICT

KILOMETERS

0   40   80

It was a period for making concessions. Buenos Aires Province had just ceded land for the capital district and Salta Province was urging federalization of the Chaco. Furthermore, the precedent set in the United States of dividing frontier regions into separate political entities influenced Argentine legislation, much as United States land survey laws had done earlier. The trend was against Corrientes, so the Province hastily began to implement a law of June 22, 1881, in order to get the last possible cash benefits from the sale of public land in Misiones. By this law all remaining land was offered at 500–750 pesos cash per square league, in holdings up to 25 square leagues. Article 5 of this law stipulated that bona fide surveys were to be made by owners of holdings within ten years of purchase dates.[80] By enforcing this and other similar important articles of the law, the federal government was later able to acquire sufficient land for colonization in a narrow longitudinal strip throughout the middle of Misiones (compare Figs. 6 and 7).

Another law was rushed to completion on November 4, 1881, whereby the two departments of Misiones (Candelaria and San Javier) could sell any remaining land to finance the construction and repair of public buildings.[81]

The long series of laws permitting land sales resulted in the subdivision of all public property in Misiones by the end of 1881. Incredible as it may seem, holdings were so large that almost the entire area of Misiones fell into the hands of only thirty-eight individuals.[82] Moreover, the sales were made without the bene-

Fig. 6 (*facing page*). Misiones: original land sales by Corientes Province, 1881, uncorrected. 1. C. Boggio, 6 leagues; 2. Martín Errecaborde y Cía, 100 leagues; 3. Francisco Comas, 25 leagues; 4. Bernardo Acosta Chavarría y Cía, 125 leagues; 5. Martín Errecaborde y Cía, 73 leagues; 6. Gallán, 41 leagues; 7. Eladio Guesalaga, 25 leagues; 8. Desiderio Rossetti, 32 leagues; 9. Andres Rolán, 32 leagues; 10. Alaralde Adolfo Dávila, 27 leagues; 11. Justino Grané, 15 leagues; 12. Doctor Balestra, 3 leagues; 13. Getting (?); 14. Martín Errecaborde y Cía, (?); 15. Manuel Cutchi, 25 leagues; 16. Manuel Herrera, 20 leagues; 17. Rosa Cásares de Chaine, 15 leagues; 18. Santiago Regenal, 20 leagues; 19. Don Manuel Giménez, 25 leagues; 21. Olegario V. Andrade, 25 leagues; 22. Dolores Cásares, 25 leagues; 23. Antonio Cásares, 25 leagues; 24. Esquivel Galarza, 25 leagues; 25. J. A. Campora, 25 leagues; 26. Olegario V. Andrade, 25 leagues; 27. Emanuel J. Montenegro, 25 leagues; 28. Pablo M. Yarsi, 25 leagues; 29. Francisco P. Rolón, 25 leagues; 30. Claudio Rolón, 25 leagues; 31. Pincarello, 7 leagues. *Source*: original map published by Corrientes Province, now on file at the Oficina de Tierras y Bosques, Posadas.

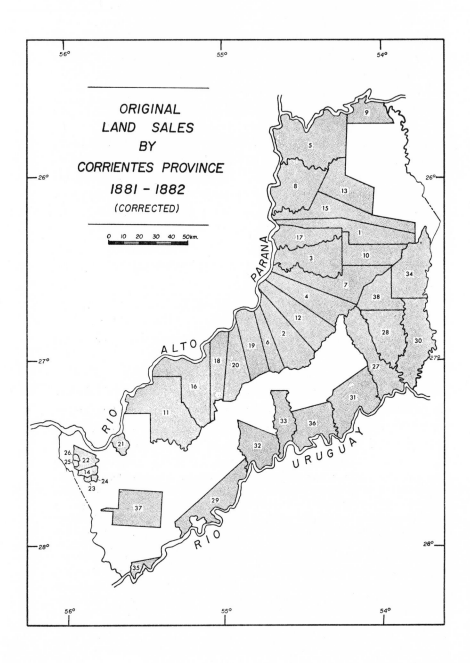

ORIGINAL
LAND SALES
BY
CORRIENTES PROVINCE
1881 - 1882
(CORRECTED)

0 10 20 30 40 50km.

fit of proper surveys—a fact made possible by the lack of an adequate titling policy in Corrientes (Figs. 6 and 7).

On December 22, 1881, preparations for federalizing Misiones were completed and the area was declared a national Territory.[83] Its western border was established along the Pindapoy and Chimiray arroyos with a line drawn between their headwaters so that Misiones kept the former Jesuit pueblo of San Carlos, although Corrientes was granted the agricultural pueblo of Garruchos founded in 1877. The eastern border remained a problem because of disputes with Brazil. Much to the embarrassment of the federal government, which wanted Misiones in order to colonize this frontier area as soon as possible, Corrientes Province had suddenly turned over to private purchasers an enormous zone of unoccupied latifundium holdings in which the nation supposedly owned no land but for which it had collective responsibility. The country was thus faced with the same problem Latin American nations must solve today wherever there is urgent need for effective use of empty lands. The method by which the federal govern-

Fig. 7 (*facing page*). Misiones: original land sales by Corrientes Province, 1881–82, corrected. 1. E. Guesalaga, 25 leagues, Aug. 9, 1881; 2. Froilán Pérez, 25 leagues, Aug. 8, 1881; 3. Francisco Comas, 25 leagues, Oct. 27, 1881; 4. Antonio Rodríguez, 25 leagues, Aug. 8, 1881; 5. Rafael Gallino, 50 leagues, Oct. 20, 1881; 6. Lino Andrade, 25 leagues, Aug. 9, 1881; 7. Emilio Gallino, 25 leagues, Aug. 10, 1881; 8. Ana Gallino de Fernández, 25 leagues, Sept. 21, 1881; 9. Luis Pizzariello, 7 leagues, Oct. 11, 1881; 1. Rodolfo Molina, 25 leagues, Aug. 8, 1881; 11. Ruperto Fuentes, 25 leagues, Aug. 8, 1881; 12. Rodolof Alurralde, 25 leagues, Aug. 8, 1881; 13. Luis A. Díaz, 25 leagues, Dec. 16, 1881; 14. Gervacio Gómez, 5992 ha, Aug. 10, 1881; 15. Cristóbal Cajal, 25 leagues, Aug. 8, 1881; 16. Pedro Z. de Vergara, 25 leagues, Aug. 8, 1881; 17. María O. de Ferreyra, 25 leagues, Nov. 26, 1881; 18. Miguel Malarín, 25 leagues, Aug. 8, 1881; 19. Dionisio Alvarez, 25 leagues, Aug. 8, 1881; 20. José E. Casco, 25 leagues, Aug. 9, 1881; Manuel Herrera, 3 leagues, Aug. 19, 1881; 22. Francisco Insaurralde, 34,614 ha, 46 a, 97 square cm, Aug. 25, 1882; 23. Roque Galarza, 2204 ha, 01a, 95 ca, Aug. 17, 1881; 24. Mauricio Chapo, 1181 ha, 62a, 26 ca, April 22, 1882; 25. Rómulo Massera, 1455 ha, 03a, 92 ca, July 11, 1881; 26. José Bossano, 1700 ha, 70 a, 21 ca, Nov. 25, 1882; 27. Olegario V. Andrade, 25 leagues, Dec. 19, 1881; 28. Antonio Cásares, 25 leagues, Dec. 13, 1881; 29. Manuel Cutchi, 25 leagues, Dec. 18, 1881; 30. Exequiel Galarza, 25 leagues, Sept. 22, 1881; 31. Mauricio C. Garay, 25 leagues, Aug. 26, 1881; 32. Manuel Herrera, 20 leagues, Aug. 9, 1881; 33. Rosa Cásares de Chaine, 15 leagues, Nov. 5, 1881; 34. José A. Cámpora, 25 leagues, Nov. 19, 1881; 35. Rafael Casarino, 3 leagues, Oct. 12, 1881; 36. Santiago Requeral, 20 leagues, Dec. 18, 1881; 37. Luisa Fernández de Aturralde, 25 leagues, Oct. 17, 1881; 38. Evaristo Corrales, 25 leagues, Dec. 18, 1881. *Source*: Province of Corrientes, Exp. 56.778/47 (1881–1882) now on file at Oficina de Tierras y Bosques, Posadas, Misiones.

ment of Argentina proceeded to change the large estate economy of Misiones is of potential importance to the rest of Latin America and is given detailed attention in the following chapter.

POPULATION AND SETTLEMENT CHANGE

Population Estimates. By 1881 decline of the yerba mate business, various colonization failures and scandals, and a confused land tenure situation had drawn Misiones into economic turmoil which made population and settlement progress virtually impossible. Enterprising settlers chose to leave Misiones and those who remained were uneducated people raised in the area or in the forests of adjacent Paraguay and Brazil. Hernández, who visited the region at the time of federalization, recorded that the remaining families, with only a few exceptions, consisted of bad social elements scattered among the ruins of the old Jesuit pueblos. They lived on wild oranges, by raising a little maize or manioc in the most primitive ways, and by spending a good deal of time fishing. Small numbers of people gathered near river coves where fish were trapped by the natural lowering of water made high by heavy rains. These groups worked together to beat the water to force fish into traps of interwoven branches. Intermittent work was also carried out in yerbales and lumber camps. Most settlers were obsessed with the idea that they could get rich by finding their own wild yerba mate stands and constantly wandered through the Selva. Peyret describes them as forest nomads who had the "fever of unfulfilled desires for imaginary riches."[84] They gradually grew weak and sick from malnutrition. The same author reports that by 1873 the first cases of *chucho*, or malaria, appeared and became a plague to the population.[85] The disease caused untold hardship along the Paraná when large numbers of pioneers from Europe began arriving just after the turn of the century. Hernández states that there was no real language spoken by these nomadic people but rather a crude mixture of Spanish, Portuguese, and Guaraní, and that of these Spanish was the least used. He describes some Guayaquí Indians who could not even communicate with words.[86] There was no specific physiognomic type, but rather a mixture of "Indian, Paraguayan, Correntino and Brazilian." They wrapped themselves in long white sheets, and, if "seen from a distance crossing deserted valleys on foot with a

a monotonous gait, alone and silent, these indecisive figures, without contours, color or grace, their cloaks agitated by the breeze,
appear[ed] to float between the green of earth and the blue
of sky."[87]

The numbers of people who had settled in Misiones were as
uncertain as their character. The first census taken in Argentina
was in 1869; calculations made for the present area of Misiones
indicate that there were 2,000 inhabitants then. This figure does
not include groups of several hundred Brazilians who had settled
in various yerbales, especially those of San Javier, Paggi, Campo
Grande, and San Pedro, or the forest Indians. From various later
estimates of the population, it can be inferred that the number
of inhabitants had grown to about 9,000 by the time of federalization. One estimate calculated about 7,050 people, divided as follows: San Ignacio, 60 families, 300 people; Corpus, 100 families,
500 people; Candelaria, 50 families, 250 people; Santa Ana and
Loreto each, 200 families, 1,000 people; and Posadas, 800 families, 4,000 people.[88] Assuming from other evidence that the three
towns of Apóstoles, Concepción, and San Javier, which were not
included in the estimate, averaged 500 inhabitants each at this
time, 1,500 more people must be added to the figure 7,050, producing a total very close to that in another estimate, which assumed a population of 9,000 divided as follows: 4,700 Argentineans, 3,200 Brazilians, 200 Indians, and 900 of unknown origin.[89]

Although 9,000 people could have made a respectable colonization base in Misiones, the problem was that this population
was nomadic, scattered, and ineffectual, and that authentic land
opening had not been permitted.

Type of Settlement. Two factors are largely responsible for
the type of settlement in Misiones up to the time of territorialization. The first is the confusion sown by administrative instability
during the late colonial and early republican periods. The original
tug of war between Asunción and Buenos Aires resulted in both
a splintering of the northern missions and border difficulties on
the Alto Paraná. Brazilian concern about holding on to valuable
trade routes led that country to persist until it won the southern
missions in El Tape. Finally, the stress and strain between Corrientes and Buenos Aires over the remains of the once large region caused another division, leaving the capital and only one

important cluster of missions in the area now known as Misiones. Had these changes transpired within even a half a century, there might have been a long enough period of stability to allow a broader base of permanent settlement. Instead, over a century of political uncertainty magnified by the series of colonization failures in Misiones had left no enthusiasm for living in the region.

The yerba mate economy developed in the former Jesuit region must also share some of the responsibility for permanent settlement failures in Misiones. With the arrival of the Spaniards in Asunción, the demand for the yerba mate beverage grew overnight. Already the favorite dish of the natives, Spanish employers quickly accepted the pleasant drink as their own, and the importance of yerba mate culture in the economy of the area became a recognized fact. As the demand for the product spread to the more distant Upper Peru and Pampa regions, the future of the industry was even more assured. Although the Jesuits approached the problems of production more scientifically than all the others and created large commercial yerba mate plantations, after their departure the people who renewed the same economy without Indian labor reverted to exploiting wild stands. The latter were sufficiently great to satisfy early demands but by 1830, when Corrientes made the first attempt to regulate cutting, destruction of the Misiones resources was becoming severe. Concern over losing the valuable trees forced officials of Corrientes to develop even more intensive legislation to protect them, culminating with the Reglamento of 1876. This Reglamento was so thorough that it served as the model for exploitation used by the new Territory of Misiones until the federal government passed even more detailed regulations in 1894.

Difficult as it is to change an exploitation pattern once officially sanctioned, it is still not easy to understand why Corrientes failed to respond to the pressure of declining resources by starting agricultural colonies for raising yerba mate. True, the Province was more interested in exploitation than colonization at first, but it was equally clear that the wild resource would not last and that the Jesuits had based a more lucrative economy on planted yerba mate trees in only a small and more easily accessible part of Misiones. Instead of following the Jesuit lead of combining colonization and yerba mate agriculture successfully, Corrientes sponsored the development of more and more distant yerbales while at the same time it strictly forbade permanent settlement in them. Curiously, the only attempt made to organize colonies was in the Campo at the sites of old reducciones, but these were too far from the yerbales. Furthermore, there never was sufficient money in the provincial treasury to carry through both the exhaustive tasks of separate colonization and of highly regulated yerba mate exploitation far from the colonized areas. On the other hand, there would have been much less need to police the yerbales had land been granted specifically for planting or transplanting yerba mate in stable farm communities, or, for that matter, had the forest surrounding wild yerba mate stands been removed and the remaining yerba mate trees been divided among established colonists.

Although the protection of natural resources is a laudable goal, it can be pursued with such intensity that other more valuable and necessary developments may be obscured. Failure to consider that a sizeable population in the immediate area was needed to exploit the tropical forest brought on five major problems which have strongly influenced the character of modern settlement. First, the intensive conservation policy led to a de-emphasis of the land titling program which the Corrientes Mesa Topográfica y de Estadística had begun. Lack of titles made farm colonists insecure and those with initiative left for other places in Argentina where they could acquire their own land. Second, the yerba mate policy created a sizeable squatter society which had little or no interest in the land it occupied. Third, under these circumstances it was impossible for the yerba mate business to give support to the development of farm colonization. Such colonization would have produced a reliable supply of commercial agriculture products for the yerba mate workers; instead there was only emphasis of unstable subsistence farming, hunting, and fishing in the scattered parts of the forest where the small groups of yerba mate workers were temporarily permitted to live. Fourth, for the same reason, expansion of the food processing industries (manioc, maize, and sugar cane) and of road building was hampered. The Corrientes government was interested in exploiting isolated yerbales, and therefore merely continued the colonial practice of opening crude trails to these places. Fifth, the futility of taking seriously the offer of developing free or inexpensive land in the old mission pueblos when heads of families had to spend many months at distant points of the Selva was brought about as a direct reflection of lack of understanding by officials who were too far removed from the region their legislation was supposed to serve.

The effects of the location and narrow shape of Misiones made the area easily accessible to foreigners from neighboring countries. Thus, since proper settlement did not occur, the frontiers were not respected, much smuggling transpired, and there arose a population of questionable character which inevitably attracted less desirable people to the area. By the time of federalization, some 1,800 yerba mate producing families had chosen to live an isolated, scattered, impermanent existence far from any contact with civilizing influences. In fact, by 1881 the Argentine public had begun to think of Misiones as a sort of international *refugium peccatorum* — quite a contrast with the thriving centers of Indian agriculture and industry that had supported some 50,000 people in the Campo during Jesuit times.

CHAPTER 5

PUBLIC LANDS AND
GOVERNMENT COLONIZATION

> Thousands of immigrants, hundreds of whom are
> admirably equipped for the life of the pioneer, are
> on tiptoe to start as soon as word comes to them in
> trustworthy ways that by strenuous labor a man may
> with certainty win land of his own.
>
> Mark Jefferson, *Peopling the Argentine Pampa*

FEDERAL LAND POLICIES

After the frustrating failures of mid-century settlement attempts, the latter years of the nineteenth century witnessed a renewed determination on the part of the government to colonize
Misiones, not only to rectify the undesirable population and land
tenure developments, but to bolster national defense in the area.
On March 16, 1882, the federal government therefore designated
Corpus as capital of the new Territory.[1] Rudecindo Roca was appointed governor, although he refused to live in Corpus, the isolation of which had already brought failure to the private colony
of Avellaneda. He chose instead to reside outside the Territory
in the city of Posadas, Corrientes, and then succeeded in the difficult tasks of convincing the Corrientes legislature to give up the
valuable city to its former stepchild, and of having the federal
government transfer the capital of Misiones from Corpus to Posadas. These changes were sanctioned by Corrientes on August 26,
1882, and by Buenos Aires on July 30, 1884.[2] In shifting the boundary of Misiones from the Arroyo Pindapoy westward to the Itaembé
to include Posadas, the former mission pueblo of San Carlos had to
be bisected and was, therefore, entirely turned over to Corrientes
Province by the *agrimensor*, or surveyor. This eliminated the largest natural area of open land held by the new Territory and so
inhibited ranching in Misiones that the Province has always had
to import meat.

The federal government specified colonization procedures for Misiones on October 24, 1882 (Law 1,265), stipulating that federal holdings had to be surveyed prior to settlement. The federal holdings, or tierras fiscales, were limited to the small area of the former reducciones (except for Mártires, which had fallen into private hands) and some lots in the Posadas area. These lands were divided into secciones of 10,000 ha, or parts of secciones. They in turn were subdivided into 100-ha lotes, each of which possessed four square 25-ha holdings.[3] Individuals were allowed to purchase surveyed land for two pesos per ha and could acquire between 25 and 100 ha. Article 5 of Law 1,265 took into account former disasters such as that of Colonia Avellaneda and required that lands close to populated zones be sold first. The national government had no experience in the yerba mate business and simply followed the policies of Corrientes by making reserve lands out of all official yerbales.

In spite of the colonization impulse caused by new land policies in Misiones, positive results of the federal program were as slow to come as they had been under the Corrientes regime, a fact which clearly indicated the significance of poor communications and slowness of surveying and titling—both problems which had been inherited from the Corrientes regime. On February 20, 1883, the government decided to speed up settlement by nationalizing the colonies of Santa Ana and Candelaria. They were mapped relatively quickly by Rafael Hernández, a well-known government surveyor, and subdivided into square 25-ha lots to produce the so-called damero settlement form (Figs. 8 and 9).[4] The federal government succeeded in attracting handfuls of foreign colonists to this surveyed land—60 Brazilian families were reported in Santa Ana by 1885[5]—but it was evident from the start that greater numbers of settlers were needed, and that urban facilities were required to attract them. Therefore, two colony towns were created by law on October 27, 1891.[6] Each was 400 ha in area and subdivided into blocks of 100 × 100 meters. Each block was further subdivided into 6 town lots. Two town lots per block were reserved for public buildings and the education of colonists. The overall size of the colony at Santa Ana was expanded to a full "16 square leagues" (approximately 32,000 ha). Holdings of 100 ha for agriculture and 1,000 for ranching were authorized in

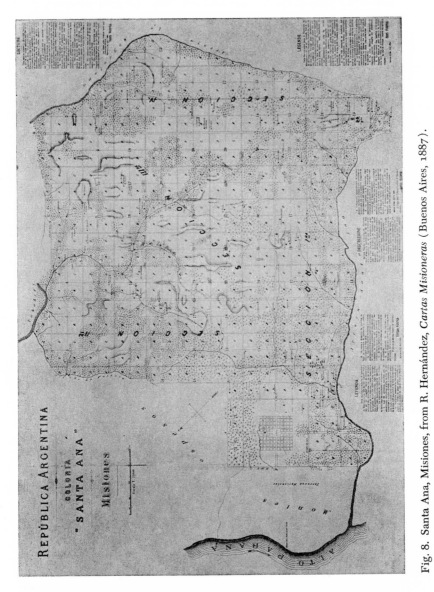

Fig. 8. Santa Ana, Misiones, from R. Hernández, *Cartas Misioneras* (Buenos Aires, 1887).

these places. The latter regulation proved to have little overall stimulus on cattle raising since water was not always available and much of the settled terrain was rough and forested. Moreover, colonists did not have the money or the desire to initiate livestock competition with Corrientes Province. Land was quoted at 4 pesos per rural ha; town lots sold for 10 pesos. Payments were to be made in eight years for rural holdings, in three years for urban. Colonists were enticed to pay cash with a 10 per cent discount — a Corrientes-initiated policy which is still practiced in private and public land transactions. Titles were supposed to be granted after one year of cultivation.

In reality, titling problems occurred because to secure final papers a lot had to be paid for in full, and one-fourth of each rural holding was to be under cultivation the first year, conditions with which few native settlers complied. Another major disadvantage to the settler was that land owners were prohibited from exploiting forests for commercial purposes until they received titles, a provision which was an obvious reflection of the long-standing Corrientes yerba mate policy. Thus the settler was caught in the pincers of contradictory government regulations: pay up and cultivate, or no title; but do not sell trees with which to pay debts while clearing land for required cultivation. In practice these obstructions proved so great that no definitive titles were granted by the authorities in Buenos Aires. This encouraged illegal settlement, and unwary Argentine and foreign colonists armed with provisional papers from the capital often arrived in Misiones only to find their land occupied by squatters.[7] Consequently the number of real settlers grew slowly and by 1900 over half the available lots in Santa Ana and Candelaria were still officially unoccupied.

Another major cause for delayed colonization was the damero settlement form which was not in harmony with the hilly landscape of Misiones: 85 per cent of the holdings in Candelaria and some 45 per cent of those in Santa Ana had no permanent surface water; 9 per cent were excessively steep.[8] It did not occur to the authorities to question the appropriateness of the settlement form then in use; rather, it was decided that if colonization were to continue more land would have to be acquired.

Further *ensanchamiento*, or expansion, at Santa Ana or Candelaria was out of the question because federal land was wanting

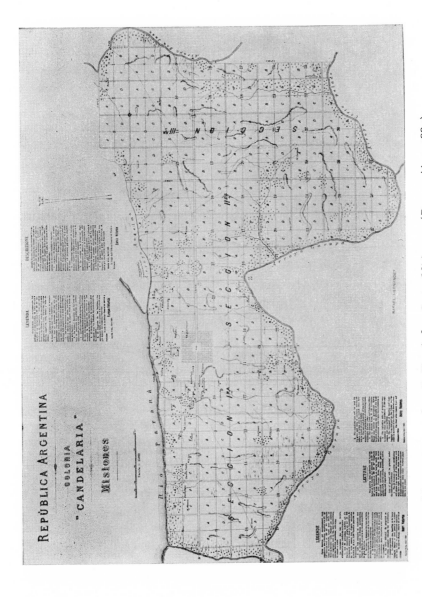

Fig. 9. Candelaria, Misiones, from R. Hernández, *Cartas Misioneras* (Buenos Aires, 1887).

in both places. As a result, the government took measures to increase its supply of property elsewhere.

On November 21, 1891, the Colonization Law of 1876 was formally modified so that people with settlement concessions who had not fulfilled their obligations had to return to the government one-half their concession, and invest on each section of 10,000 ha or fraction greater than 5,000 ha, 8,000 pesos for industry if land was less than 50 km from navigable rivers or ports or rail stations, 6,000 pesos if 50 km–100 km from these points, and 4,000 if over 100 km. Three years were given to accomplish the investment and to erect a building whose value in pesos was not below 2,500, 2,000, or 1,500, respectively.[9] The spirit of conservation for Argentina's only subtropical rainforest region was so strong that capital invested in lumbering did not count toward fulfillment of these obligations. Indeed, forest exploitation was prohibited until concession holders had complied with the new orders. Land had to be privately surveyed within fifteen months of the date of the law. By 1895, 220,000 ha were obtained by the federal government from four owners who had not fulfilled the above requirements. They were D. Rosetti (80,000 ha), A. Rolón (80,000 ha), J. Grané (40,000 ha) and P. Christopherson (20,000 ha).[10]

All other large land concessions made before federalization were cancelled on February 20, 1894, if owners had not complied with requirements of the Corrientes law of June 22, 1881.[11] This law specified that holders must survey their own land within ten years of the date of the concession. In several cases this provision was not carried out and such lands were declared *caducas*, i.e., they were returned to the nation as public property. By 1896 these included the lands used for the colonies of Cerro Corá (10,000 ha), Apóstoles (10,000 ha), and Bonpland (18,000 ha).

Because Misiones was actually wider than the authorities of Corrientes had realized when the 25-league concessions were sold prior to federalization of the area, the federal government could take a third step which added a major amount of land to the fiscal holdings. Most of the concessions ran inland from the Alto Paraná and Uruguay rivers and were not large enough to meet at the water divide in the center of the Territory as originally planned. The government learned from rapid initial surveys of the Territory that a narrow strip along the crest of the Sierra

Central between 300 and 500 square leagues in area could not be claimed by concession holders. Although exact limits of this new federal terrain were only gradually determined and are still incompletely known, the wealthy yerba mate stands of Yerbal Viejo, Yerbal Nuevo, and San Pedro were correctly assumed to be part of the official holdings.[12] These yerbales had much attraction for potential settlers, although the federal government maintained its attitude against cutting timber for sale before titles were granted. This time, however, the effect was not to slow down colonization, but merely to make it "illegal," from the viewpoint of Buenos Aires.

FOREIGN COLONIZATION

Knowledge of the additions to federal property spread rapidly and contributed to renewed interest in settling Misiones. Fortunately this attention coincided with a period of improving financial conditions in Argentina, especially from 1892 to 1896. During this period (1895) the long disputed eastern border of Misiones was fixed to the advantage of Brazil so that the Argentine government promoted colonization in the newly defined lands with more energy than ever.[13] Although a new governor of Misiones, Juan Balester, made the mistake of paving the way for latifundium holdings on federal lands in the Campo, he achieved considerable colonization gains which enabled his successor to push the process into the take-off, or self-perpetuating stage – a feat which would not have been possible without the prior acquisition of the strip of federal lands through the middle of the Territory. Balester's solution to colonization was to remove the major barrier to progress in Misiones by changing the old faulty provisional land concession policy to one with a practical titling method under the federal program. Although the authorities at the Oficina de Tierras in Buenos Aires had tried settlements at Candelaria and Santa Ana in 1883, not a single property title had been granted in the succeeding ten years.[14] The same was true of the other old mission areas, with the sole exception of Concepción. Here the inhabitants numbered more than 1,000 and, according to Law 2,735 of September 29, 1890, claimed the right to form a *municipio*, or municipality, which possessed authority to issue land titles. This measure attracted numerous farmers to the site and made for such rapid growth that Concepción became second to Posadas in total population and first in the Territory for farm production by 1895.[15] Thus, it was evident that land titles were a decisive factor in attracting settlers. Balester then applied the same technique to Posadas, San Javier, Apóstoles, San Ignacio, Corpus, San José, Candelaria, and Santa Ana. On February 20, 1894, he was even able to add to federal property by means of reclaiming unsurveyed concessions where squatters had taken over a holding of Graciano Ferrero y Cía.[16] There he established the new colony of Cerro Corá, which was the first federal settlement outside the old Jesuit missions. Because of its large population, the urban center of Cerro Corá became a municipio within a year. Additionally, in 1895, the colony of Bonpland was surveyed on new federal land between the large estate holdings of R. Fuentes and F. Beiró (Fig. 10).[17] Both were typical of the damero settlements in this landscape: some 40 per cent of the holdings were without surface water and about 10 per cent were too steep to be efficiently farmed;[18] but momentarily there was plenty of land.

In order to speed up the process of titling in Misiones, a federal Oficina Topográfica was created in Posadas so that all land registration and survey approval could be completed in the Territory. A land title office was also created to expedite the paper work involved. For the first time, the malfunctioning procedure of having authorities in Buenos Aires issue provisional titles for unsurveyed land which they had never seen was superceded by a method which granted forty-seven local titles in 1894 alone.[19] Once again, the tobacco market was the basis for some economic hope and on October 3, 1895, the federal government decreed that all Misiones holdings must be between 25 and 100 ha in size, with those of 50, 75, and 100 ha required to have 4, 6, and 8 ha, respectively, of tobacco.[20]

Outside the official borders of Cerro Corá and Apóstoles, and in the colonies of Sierra de San José, Santa María, Mártires, and Itacaruaré, settlers awaited anxiously the day their populations would reach 1,000. So deeply impressed by this progress was the government surveyor-author J. Queirel, that in 1895 he advised private owners of the 25-league estates in Misiones to assign 2 or 3 leagues each for colonization, after the style of the Dávila

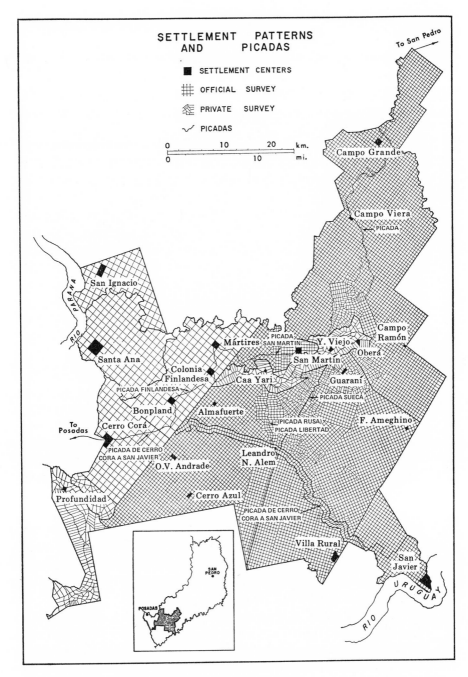

Fig. 10. Settlement patterns and picadas (compare with Fig. 11). *Source*: Plano de ubicación, Buenos Aires, 1933.

Company in San José.[21] Latifundistas had already taken to renting holdings near federal lands at high prices because of the success of the government settlement programs. It was, however, still too early for any further action by the *terratenientes*, or estate holders, of Misiones.[22]

Because of improved settlement conditions in Argentina during this period, Europeans who had been invited to pioneer in southern Brazil now began to view Misiones with favor. Brazil maintained an aloof attitude toward its foreign colonists at this time whereas the Argentine government was willing to sell titled land at modest prices and to pay transportation expenses to remote parts of the country. Volga Germans, such as those who had gone to Colonia Avellaneda, German-Brazilians fleeing from serious political disturbances which afflicted Paraná and Rio Grande do Sul during the last years of the century,[23] and Poles from eastern Galicia who were discontented with life in Brazil began to leave for Argentina. Now, at long last, Misiones reaped the benefit of its large supply of public lands near southern Brazil.

Between 1893 and 1895 some 12,000 landless German-Brazilians and others crossed the Uruguay River and obtained holdings in Misiones.[24] Although many of them left within the next several years as strife ceased in southern Brazil, the sure titling policy, ample land, and proximity to their old homes produced the first relatively positive colonization results in the Territory. The populations of Cerro Corá, San Javier, San Ignacio, Corpus, and Apóstoles all doubled; reported increases were even greater in Candelaria, Santa Ana, and San José.[25]

The more favorable turn of events is well illustrated by what happened south of Posadas. In August, 1897, a group of fourteen Galician families arrived in Posadas and were sold federal land acquired by reclamation of unsurveyed concessions around the old Jesuit mission of Apóstoles. The colonists were given free lots by the government in order to make the area attractive to others. Thus the first Poles wrote enthusiastically to relatives and friends so that within a short time others came and took land. By 1900 over 1,800 colonists had settled in Apóstoles, most of whom were Poles, and some of whom were Ukranians and Brazilians.[26] So many continued to arrive that federal land had to be found for another colony. This was done by declaring an estate south of Apóstoles public property because of an unfulfilled colonization contract, and by surveying the new farm colony of Azara in 1901.[27] Within several years this colony was also full, and, since there were no more government lands available, Poles, Ukranians, and Brazilians began to take formerly rejected lots in the earlier settlements of San José, Cerro Corá, and Corpus (Fig. 19).

The foreign colonists who received holdings in the old Jesuit pueblos and in the new settlements of Bonpland, Cerro Corá, and Azara are listed by number and nationality in Table 6.

TABLE 6

Foreign Colonists in Misiones, 1903

Nationality	Families	Cultivated ha	Av. Cultivated ha per Family
Polish	810	6,171	7.6
Brazilian	502	2,544	5.1
Argentine	311	1,424	4.6
Paraguayan	116	458	3.9
Italian	72	584	8.1
Russian	70	363	5.2
German	59	322	5.4
Spanish	38	240	6.3
French	30	195	6.5
Swedish	15	46	3.1
Oriental	10	54	5.4
Swiss	6	55	9.8
Arabic	2	6	3.2
Danish	1	3	3.0
English	1	2	2.0
Greek	1	3	3.0
N. American	1	5	5.0
Totals and Averages	2,045	12,475	5.1

Source: Pedro J. Yssouribehere, *Investigación agrícola en el Territorio de Misiones* (Buenos Aires, 1904), p. 200.

At the same time, small settlements at Campo Grande, San Pedro, and Manuel Belgrano were inhabited by Brazilians who began to collect wild yerba mate. Production in these three colonies was restricted mainly to yerba mate, whereas in the others,

TABLE 7

Number of ha in all Misiones Colonies, 1903

Colony	Fami-lies	Maize	Man-ioc	Beans	Sugar Cane	Tobac-co	Pea-nuts	Vege-tables	Cot-ton	Rice
Apóstoles	539	2,839	—	269	81	10	80	455	208	171
Azara	351	1,356	—	264	54	1	22	389	129	72
Cerro Corá	219	543	—	105	110	105	24	120	1	35
Santa Ana	179	183	78	53	38	60	—	—	—	—
Concepción	172	450	445	181	51	12	31	2	2	227
Bonpland	111	258	49	105	30	71	—	—	—	6
Corpus	104	181	75	140	32	4	52	82	—	—
San Ignacio	100	210	30	15	8	3	19	—	—	2
San Pedro	91	505	28	112	—	—	—	38	—	—
San José	76	218	—	61	98	1	5	76	2	8
San Javier	68	152	32	44	27	22	4	9	—	8
Candelaria	35	49	—	9	2	4	—	28	—	—
Total	2,045	6,944	737	1,358	531	293	237	1,199	342	529

Total 12,170 ha

Source: Pedro J. Yssouribehere, *Investigación agrícola en el Territorio de Misiones* (Buenos Aires, 1904), pp. 72–73.

tobacco, rice, manioc, maize, and sugar cane were raised. Table 7 illustrates colony acreages as of 1903.

Unfortunately, most of the colonists in Misiones were not trained in tropical and semitropical agriculture and proceeded to clear land without regard for soil improvement. The fact that Jesuit reducciones had already extended Campo conditions and caused removal of topsoils was not considered. Since as many as one-third of the holdings in Apóstoles, Corpus, and Cerro Corá lacked level land, good soils, and water, land use was severely restricted or even impossible.[28] This initial colonization set a pattern which caused so much land damage that a great deal of the Campo area was later officially declared an emergency "Poor Zone" and was permanently ruined for all normal farming.[29]

Still another serious problem arose because of the undisciplined sale of titles by the individual municipalities. After populations reached the magic number of 1,000 and titling became a local task, people with savings began to purchase groups of lots so that a problem of latifundismo appeared on these government lands. Large holdings, some of which reached 70–80 square leagues, were purchased but never settled and their sizeable forested areas kept many colonists isolated from markets. Untended cattle on clearings in these estates were allowed to roam freely and to destroy the plantings of scattered settlers.[30]

Finally, incompetent surveying caused boundary problems whose documentation crowds the archives of the Posadas Oficina de Tierras y Bosques and plagues the corresponding areas even today.

With the first small wave of colonization, significant changes in the human landscape appeared in Misiones. The so-called *carro polaco*, a four-wheeled wooden wagon introduced by the Galicians and German-Brazilians, immediately replaced the more cumbersome two-wheeled *carretas* of the Argentine colonial period. This new vehicle was more maneuverable and was often used with horses instead of oxen. It also required the widening of narrow forest piques into picadas and resulted in a better road system. By 1900 there were some 200 of the wagons and they were already being manufactured in the area.[31] The Ukrainians are known for their introduction of the *breke*, or brake, a lighter, four-wheeled vehicle now known in the Campo as the *carro ruso*. The Polish settlers invested a great deal of money in building churches and cemeteries, some of which are still among the finest in Misiones and always earmark Galician settlements. Cemeteries are maintained at some distance from their associated hamlets and are surprisingly pleasant in every respect. Unfortunately these Campo settlements made progress slowly; in fact even Apóstoles and Azara remained small and backward and incurred much criticism in the press and popular books of the period.[32]

Attention to the growing criticism of federal colonization results in southern Misiones was diverted by two important events in 1903: passage of a new national land law; major alteration in the damero settlement form.

THE LAND ACT OF 1903

The new federal land law was passed on January 8, 1903. It was the result of: the concern over vulnerability of areas like Misiones which were exposed to illegal border activity; the problem of latifundismo which began to receive much national attention around the turn of the century; the need for new forest and yerba mate exploitation legislation; the desirability of continuing government land surveys (with hope of acquiring more land from the latifundistas in the case of Misiones); and the necessity of revamping the old colonization law of 1876.

The Land Act of 1903 (No. 4,176) had as its basic goal the establishment of new colonies on federal lands wherever this was appropriate.[33] The government hoped that the formation of new settlements in Misiones would help to guard the important international frontier zone from possible repetition of a wave of invaders with less peaceful motives than those who had swept westward from Brazil a few years earlier, as well as from the dangers of increased contraband in a region so difficult to police. The exploitation of forests was legalized by offering concessions of up to 10,000 ha for 10 years and 10 per cent of the value of the timber removed from the port of shipment. The way was simultaneously opened for the exploitation of yerba mate on timber concessions and vice versa. In the latter instance holdings issued were to be between 25 and 100 ha.[34] Taxes of 50 centavos per 10 kilos of wild yerba mate gathered on private lands were reduced to 30 centavos as a gesture toward encouraging development of the large, empty estates which made up most of Misiones. Federal lands were still not completely surveyed and the new law specified that the task should be carried out before the initiation of settlement. Several weaknesses in the old colonization legislation were corrected as well: the tendency to formulate law after law without regard to existing legislation, by simply abrogating all previous conflicting laws (a change, incidentally, which still needs to be made in some Latin American countries in order to facilitate modern land opening); the oversimplified division of all lands into either agricultural (*tierras de pan llevar*) or pastoral (*tierras pastoriles*), by the formulation of different types of colonization zones such as pueblos (urban settlements), *colonias agrícolas* (agricultural colonies), *colonias ganaderas* (ranch settlements), and *colonias mixtas* (mixed colonies), according to a long list of land types; and the failure of the titling program, by specifying that titles would henceforth be authorized by the federal government at periodic intervals to people who complied with government requirements. This ended the local issue of titles, much to the dismay of pioneer settlers. Some attempt to attract colonists anew was offered by authorizing the gift of 20 per cent of the land to the first arrivals at these new settlements. Payments

by later colonists did not have to be made until the end of the
second year and then were divided into six annual increments.

MODERN DAMERO SETTLEMENTS

The Land Law of 1903 brought with it a general wave of pioneering enthusiasm in Argentina. One of the first results was the
employment of government officials to survey several new farm
colonies, some of which were established at once in Misiones. The
damero settlement form which had been used throughout Argentina in the colonized parts of Patagonia, the Pampa, and the Chaco
was already officially adopted and had been introduced in Misiones. This form was, in fact, simple to lay out since Argentine
land was generally level and treeless.[35] Roads were never a problem — it was only necessary to leave a little land between town
and farm lots at appropriate intervals and no construction work
was required. The water table was usually high, the ground was not
rocky, and wells could be easily dug. All this changed, however,
when the surveyors began to work in Misiones. Here the land
was very hilly and rock outcrops were common. Further, almost
the entire area was covered with dense forests. It was inevitable
that settlers in places like Santa Ana, Cerro Corá, and Azara became disillusioned because so many lots possessed only rocky
land or steep slopes. Besides, even though the southern part of
Misiones received some 1,500 mm of annual rainfall, the lots
which did not have permanent streams suffered from a water
shortage. Wells were difficult or impossible to dig in many places
because bedrock was at or near the surface. European settlers,
who were accustomed to mixed farming, could not have livestock
because of this lack of water. To farm without livestock meant
to farm in the primitive way of all peoples who do not have the
plow, i.e., with a digging stick or hoe. The results ultimately attracted a poor quality settler and emphasized the fact that land
opening as such was not being achieved. Only small amounts of
forest were cleared for the primitive farming system: 1903 statistics reveal that the average farm lot had only 5 ha of cultivated
land, a characteristic which is true today of similar primitive farm
settlements in parts of Paraguay, Brazil, and northeast Argentina.[36] Inevitably there was little or no enthusiasm for crop rotation except by the most optimistic Europeans, and yields de-

creased steadily as soils wore out and became severely gullied.

When the federal government ordered new colonies surveyed in 1903, the authorities ignored the problems inherent in the damero form of settlement and its extension was ordered without change for the hilly landscape of Misiones. This action may be partly attributed to long lapses of time between periods of colonization activity, to the insignificant extent of settlement in Misiones by 1903, to the lack of experience of government surveyors, who were not colonization planners, and to the fact that it was a mistake to try and direct a major settlement program at conference tables over 1,000 km from Misiones. By a stroke of good fortune the damero system was halted, but then only for the shortest time.

In 1903 the government chose as a new surveyor a French settler in Misiones who was not only familiar with local problems but who had professional land survey training in Europe. F. Fouilland was first commissioned to cut a picada from Cerro Corá to San Javier in order to open communications between the Alto Paraná and Uruguay rivers. The instructions to Fouilland stated that boundary markers were to be placed along the picada at 500 meter intervals, a plain indication that the authorities of the *Dirección General de Tierras* in Buenos Aires envisioned a transfer of the damero system to the region of the Selva. (Fig. 10).[37]

WALDHUFEN-LIKE SETTLEMENTS: TYPE A

Fouilland was also ordered (1903) to survey an elongated piece of federal land in the vicinity of Profundidad. His instructions were to lay out the usual damero settlement with square lots, and to reserve a small zone for future urban facilities. After a reconnaissance of the narrow, hilly area, Fouilland concluded that if square lots were marked out as ordered many would have "not a single hectare of exploitable land."[38] He therefore asked to change the damero system and was granted permission by the bureaucratically minded Buenos Aires office on the grounds that Law 4,167 required colonists to cultivate 20 per cent of their lots in order to win a title. In other words, since many damero lots in Profundidad were unexploitable, the damero system would actually have been illegal.[39] Fouilland then decided to cut a N-S picada down the center of the slender strip of public land and to survey narrow lots along this path (see Profundidad, Fig. 10). Each lot would thus have immediate access to the road and would receive reasonably fair amounts of land with similar degrees of slope from the road to the interior. He did not locate each lot so that it had access to running water, a feat which could have been accomplished. However, because the shape of the public area prompted liberal use of river boundaries, approximately 75 percent of the holdings possessed surface water. As a result the colonists immediately brought cattle to their farms. Most had 10 to 15 cows; two were reported with 100 each in 1906.[40] That colonists approved the change in settlement form is indicated by the rapid purchase of all lots as well as by the introduction of cattle. Sixty years later nearly everyone had a permanent title and no federal land was left. In stark contrast, the older neighboring damero colony of Cerro Corá still had a sizeable amount of uncleared public land at this time and only a few of the isolated settlers had bothered to acquire permanent titles (see Fig. 11). It is evident that the change of settlement form brought about the first major improvement in colonization on government lands since that of local titling a few years earlier. The fact that improvement may be attributed directly to the employment of a new settlement form illustrates that even when titles are available for the asking, other ingredients are of major importance in the success of colonization.

Profundidad colony had what may be called a Waldhufen-like settlement form since it was not a true Waldhufendorf, the German term for a forest settlement which by chance it approximated in appearance. The Waldhufendorf, briefly, is a planned forest (*Wald*) line settlement in which colonists live on their own long, parallel strips of land (*Hofstreifen*), all of which extend upslope from a particular valley bottom toward the adjacent interfluve, or vice versa. A problem of interpretation arises from the fact that the settlement term Waldhufendorf implies the presence of a village because of the suffix *dorf*. Unfortunately the word Dorf may be used in German to describe agglomerated settlements (including Waldhufendörfer) whether or not central-place or internal-trade and socio-religious–service functions have ever developed. That is to say, either hamlet or village may be meant by the term, and only field work or maps will reveal what actually

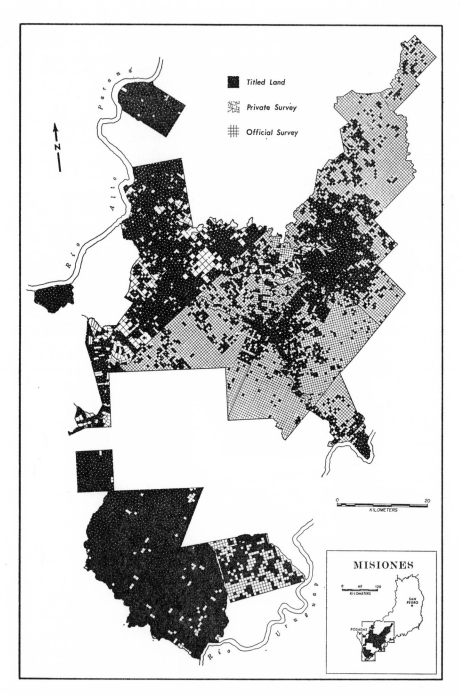

Fig. 11. Federal settlements and titled land. *Sources*: Plano de ubicación, Buenos Aires, 1933; Oficina de Tierras y Bosques, Posadas, 1965.

exists if descriptions are not detailed. In order to avoid possible ambiguity, the word Waldhufendorf will therefore be employed in this and subsequent chapters only for forest long-lot farm settlements in which linear village functions have developed, especially after a considerable period of growth. The term *Waldhufenweiler* (Waldhufen hamlet) will be used specifically for German-style forest long-lot farm settlements in which only a few lower order or no central-place functions have developed (see Fig. 17, p. 160). The expression Waldhufen settlement will be employed in a generic sense to refer to both Waldhufenweiler and Waldhufendörfer. More authentic Waldhufen settlement forms were eventually introduced in Misiones by private colonization companies and a detailed discussion of their characteristics will be found in the next chapter. Because the settlement form of Profundidad represents one of three Waldhufen-like varieties in Misiones, it will be designated as a long-lot road settlement, or, for brevity, Type A.

Three more Type A settlement forms were planned by Fouilland immediately following the work at Profundidad. In 1904 the government acquired the land between Profundidad and Cerro Corá (Ensanche Cerro Corá SW) from individuals who possessed invalidated titles.[41] Once again the official instructions were to lay out a damero settlement to match that of Cerro Corá, but Fouilland requested and received approval to alter the plan. The boundaries of this area, and hence its narrow shape, were similar to those of Profundidad, and had been dictated again by legal circumstances. However, in the Ensanche Cerro Corá SW some streams paralleled the principle axis of the colony. As a consequence, only 20 per cent of the holdings are without permanent surface water. Colonia San José was added in a similar fashion at the southern end of Profundidad in 1905. Both were rapidly settled.

In 1905 there was a Russian revolution which resulted in large numbers of displaced persons in Europe, particularly Cossacks and Finns. At that time a Finnish commission journeyed to Misiones to look for land for settling refugees and decided on an area of federal holdings east of Bonpland.[42] The Argentine government was anxious to establish colonization in the Selva of Misiones but had had no experience there. A very real fear of the dense forest existed and in order to assure the Finns of contact between civilization and a zone of wild yerba mate which could be exploited for sale, the government promised to open a picada from Bonpland to Yerbal Viejo, and to survey lots on either side of this crude roadway. Fouilland was employed to carry out the task, and was instructed to lay out reserve areas at 15 to 20 km intervals along the picada for future urban facilities, just as he had done in other government colonies. This resulted in centers at Caá Yarí and Salta, although only the former has developed into a hamlet. Again Fouilland was able to alter the settlement form and created one more Type A project in Misiones: the Colonia Picada Bonpland a Yerbal Viejo.[43]

Half the rural lots in the new colony were reserved for Finnish settlers. One hundred and twelve people arrived from Finland in 1906, two or three of whom went north into the forest beyond the Yabebiry River, while the rest settled in lots along the new picada and formed the Colonia Finlandesa.[44] Although a little over 15 per cent of the 189 lots in the Colonia Picada Bonpland a Yerbal Viejo lacked water, particularly along the south side of the settlement which paralleled no major streams, and many possessed excessively rocky or steep surfaces, the settlers were enthusiastic and began at once to make neat clearings in the Selva. Unhappily, during the first year a severe drought occurred and caused irreparable crop damage.[45] A rare invasion of locusts attacked plants, and fires created widespread damage and fear. Soon afterward the price of tobacco on which pioneers had pinned their hopes began to drop rapidly. Careless harvesting and drying had much to do with this failure, as such a poor quality was achieved that tobacco buyers objected. Even later, with improved tobacco production and when yerba mate commanded good market prices, previous discouragement, continued lack of water, poor transportation facilities, and long-lasting language problems kept the colony from progressing. A total of sixty families had arrived, but they did not band together to survive, and moved independently to other parts of the Territory and nation. Those who remained neglected their tobacco plantings, stayed in palm board and bamboo huts, often without making improvements, and soon were raising only subsistence crops. By 1932 only half the colony's 300 settlers remained; the rest were divided between Bonpland Norte (40) and Yerbal Viejo (80).[46] Today there are only a few original families of older people in the former Colonia Finlandesa. The children have all departed for Yerbal Viejo, Aristóbulo del Valle, and San Pedro in northeastern Misiones. Thus, one of the first sizeable groups of European settlers did not create a favorable image for colonization in the Misiones Selva and might have confirmed the widespread fears of other colonists as well as of the federal government regarding forest settlement had it not been for the success of small groups of German pioneers in the same region.

WALDHUFEN-LIKE SETTLEMENTS: TYPE B

One of the factors which motivated German colonization in the Selva was the introduction in 1903 of a technique for the successful planting of yerba mate seeds. The exploitation of wild yerba mate had been excessive since the end of the War of the Triple Alliance, although by the 1880s the product had so stimulated traffic on the Alto Paraná that steamboats made the coast of Misiones accessible with fair regularity.[47] The new boats brought rugged forest men to the Territory who explored the interior and helped in the establishment of large yerba mate processing plants, particularly on the private estates. Even on government land the exploitation was rapid enough so that by 1904 it was reported that only a small number of trees were left out of the "hundreds of thousands" formerly in Yerbal Viejo, Campo Grande, and San Pedro.[48] The disappearance of the limited wild resources of Misiones made it imperative to experiment with the planting of yerba mate. Up to this time the greatest success had been achieved by bending a branch and burying part of it until roots formed. A few plantings had been made in San Javier, Bonpland, San Ignacio, Corpus, and Santa Ana by this method or by patiently waiting for seeds to germinate naturally — a process which was uncertain and took up to a year or more. Luckily, prior to the turn of the century F. Neumann successfully brought about rapid germination of yerba mate seeds in the colony of Nueva Germania, Paraguay.[49] In 1903 an agronomist in San Ignacio imported the treated seeds from Nueva Germania and began a new era of prosperity in Misiones just as the wild product was giving out.[50] Yerba mate was a native plant already adapted to soil, climatic, and disease conditions. It was also a perennial, or tree crop, which prevented erosion better than annual types, so it proved ideal for everyone as long as the market was good.

The simultaneous combination of simplified yerba mate cultivation, a good market, and plentiful land in Misiones attracted more and more foreign families to the region, the largest numbers of whom were German. German pioneers came either from southern Brazil, where they had begun to settle in 1824, or directly from Germany. All were attracted by the liberal attitude of the Argentine government with regard to land grants, and by propaganda of various kinds. In 1883, just after territorialization of Misiones, an official Argentine commission had traveled as far as the Iguazú Falls in search of appropriate colonization land. The voyage was made on an Argentine naval vessel, the *Vigilante*, and received much publicity. A German naturalist, G. Niederlein, was one of the commission members, and his publications about the Misiones region became well known in Europe.[51] The same year some twenty German families travelled to Misiones and settled in the forested land east of Cerro Corá.[52] Eleven years later the Argentine government created the colony of Bonpland in recognition of German settlement efforts there. These colonists helped to stimulate interest in yerba mate over the years and attracted immigrants by their own letters to Germany and Brazil.

A new group of thirty German families who arrived in 1905 set off into the forest south of Bonpland and, recognizing the value of the grown-over picada from Cerro Corá to San Javier, surveyed their own 25-ha lots by reopening the roadway. They followed the 500-meter markers Fouilland had been ordered to build.[53] As a result, many of the holdings are square or nearly square as in the damero, but all are strung out in a line just as they are in a Waldhufen settlement. Whenever the settlers observed that their own lots were going to be deprived of water by following the government markers, they took matters into their own experienced hands and altered the settlement form; hence certain sections of this colony have a truly Waldhufen appearance (Fig. 10). Lot 85, for example, is 281 meters wide and 1079 meters long.[54] Other settlers discovered that bedrock prevented the construction of wells, and since they had no running water available, deserted their land. Colonists also searched for better routing for the old picada and organized informally into groups just as had been done earlier in Europe in order to construct new sections through the dense forest.[55] Some of the holdings were on land so steep that transverse roads had to be left out entirely (lots 71–100), and, unlike the Waldhufendörfer of Europe, most of the feeder paths or roads had to be devious and could not be built straight into the forest because of the rough terrain.

After several years of rapid adjustment in the Selva, successful planting of yerba mate, good market conditions, and Argentine advertising in Europe attracted still other Germans from the Old World and southern Brazil. By 1910 the picada was so nearly filled that colonists spilled over into private lands owned by the Sociedad Errecaborde. Normally this would have constituted serious trespassing. However, exploitative practices on private estates had created a situation in which the average laborer, called a *mensú* in Misiones, was kept imprisoned on the land by means of constant indebtedness, or even by armed force. Thus the federal government took a firm attitude against the latifundistas when it could. In this instance, the Sociedad was forced to sell 6,000 ha to the government in 1911 on the grounds that the owners had not complied with the legal requirements of their concession.[56] By 1912 only 15 lots along the picada were not occupied. Almost 70 per cent of the pioneers were German; slightly over 25 per cent were Argentine. The rest were Polish, Scandinavian, Italian, and French.

Russian settlers arrived in 1912 and adopted the surveying techniques used by the Germans to cut a transverse picada northward from lot 41 to the picada from Bonpland to Yerbal Viejo. They settled along both sides of the new route which soon became known as the *Picada Rusa* (Fig. 10). By 1914 Swedish settlers had employed the same methods along the *Picada Sueca* from lots 44 and 45 northward to Villa Svea just outside Oberá.[57]

The rush of settlers to this area was so impressive that in 1915 the government established the Picada de Cerro Corá a San Javier as an official colony. The Argentine surveyor had to do the best he could with orders to mark off square 25-ha lots on land already thickly inhabited. Although some effort was made to follow the private long-lot surveys, many boundary alterations were carried out by this official and not a few colonists lost valuable land to others, and much hardship and enmity resulted.[58] On the southeast border of Colonia Bonpland, for example, survey lines were drawn in 1916 which passed through the houses of some Swedish settlers.[59] In other places, where the land was flooded or rose too steeply, it was impossible to place markers for lot boundaries and the uncertainty of affairs discouraged colonists. The whole experience stands as a good example of what happens when a wave of settlers precedes government surveyors; but this lesson was soon forgotten and the mistake was repeated in other parts of the Selva.

Although the Colonia Picada de Cerro Corá a San Javier has an intermediate settlement form it may be seen that the causes and results are somewhat different from those where Fouilland had a more direct hand in planning. The Argentine official who surveyed the Colonia Picada de Cerro Corá a San Javier created a line settlement with both square and long lots — quite a different situation from that of Profundidad or Colonia Bonpland a Yerbal Viejo. This Waldhufen-like form with square and long lots will be referred to as intermediate Type B.

The surveyor of Type B also observed that the Germans had established a number of urban functions along their picada between lots 41 and 64 (between the Picada Rusa and the Picada Sueca) where there were several stores, a Protestant church, and a cemetery. Because of the more concentrated activities in this area, an official urban zone was demarcated there. The first solares, or urban lots, were made by subdividing the holdings of A. Ullrich, A. Schurich, W. Alwardt, and E. Mecking. The latter was a community leader who had established one of the colony's general stores, and the pueblo was named Mecking (now Leandro N. Alem) in his honor (Fig. 10).[60] It is to be noted that the government once again maintained its attitude favoring the creation of urban areas in its colonies, whatever the shape.

During this period one other Waldhufen-like settlement resulted from the work of F. Fouilland. The Colonia Itacaruaré, which he was asked to survey on private land east of the Itacaruaré River in 1914 (Fig. 3), was the last colony demarcated by this perceptive individual. True to his earlier conviction that settlers were much better off if their lots all faced a central road, he planned a Type A settlement. This was the first private settlement scheme in Misiones not of the damero type. In fact, during Fouilland's employment as a government surveyor, only one damero settlement appeared even on state lands. This was a forty-eight-lot extension in 1904 of Cerro Corá, called Ensanche NE de Cerro Corá, and was surveyed by another individual.

The Waldhufen-like settlement forms developed by Fouilland and by groups of other settlers in the Colonia Picada de Cerro Corá a San Javier represent a marked deviation from the damero system and were the direct result of the recognition of the inadequacy of the latter form in the hilly, forested landscape of Misiones. Regrettably, the first Waldhufen-like settlement forms were the work of only a few people who never convinced the authorities in Buenos Aires that a permanent change was badly needed. Granted that Fouilland and the others left their mark on the landscape in several places, the new forms were never officially adopted. When the next phase of colonization occurred on government lands, Fouilland had retired, and without his prestige and influence his successors reestablished the damero in the interior of the Territory. Analysis reveals that, on the average, 30 to 35 per cent of the holdings surveyed in this settlement form were unusable compared to between 15 and 20 per cent for the Waldhufen-like types developed by Fouilland and the European settlers of Colonia Picada de Cerro Corá a San Javier.

EXPANSION OF WALDHUFEN-LIKE AND DAMERO SETTLEMENTS

Colonia Picada de Cerro Corá a San Javier. The small urban center of Mecking in the Colonia Picada de Cerro Corá a San Javier had an exceptionally favorable location since it was the dispersal point from which colonists had spread into the most accessible of the large government forests in the Selva. In 1912 a railroad from Buenos Aires to Posadas was completed and this increased the amount of traffic to the interior by way of Mecking. By 1915 the movement of pioneers from Posadas was heavy enough to warrant construction of a bridge over the Río Mártires. This was accomplished with great ingenuity by the settlers themselves, who organized labor and capital. A German engineer built the bridge with funds acquired from the colonists of Bonpland and Mecking (6,500 pesos), the Territorial government (1,000 pesos), the National Tobacco Company (500 pesos), and the Piccardo (tobacco)

Company (500 pesos). Thereafter the large, four-wheeled freight wagons did not have to be dismantled to cross the swampy area.[61] The value of having attracted colonists from Germany and other parts of Europe where road maintenance was expected of individual farmers is illustrated by this cooperative innovation. The system of voluntary cooperation is especially typical of colonies where German settlers predominated, and soon spread to other groups. It is a tribute to the organizational ability of these pioneers that L. de la Torre commented in 1924 that every road in this part of Misiones had been privately constructed.[62]

Since Mecking had been given a rectangular town plan, the settlement began to lose the incipient Waldhufendorf form as it expanded. The community was renamed Leandro N. Alem in 1926. Growth was steady and pioneers of many nationalities eventually absorbed the original group. Both Protestant and Catholic churches appeared, although as late as 1928 Suaiter complained that not a single priest in the entire region was Argentine.[63]

One of the first formally organized agricultural cooperatives in Misiones was begun by European farmers in Leandro N. Alem in 1930 (Cooperativa Agrícola Ltda. de Picada Libertad). By 1934 the colony had 5,000 settlers, 4,750 of whom were foreigners, mainly so-called *Volks-* and *Reichsdeutschen*, from Brazil and Germany, respectively, and 250 of whom were Argentineans.[64] The next year the urban area had to be enlarged — an action that caused much litigation but which was successfully carried out by the Territory which took land from colonists who had not complied with legal requirements.[65] Five years later there were millers, shoemakers, tailors, mechanics, doctors, three hotels, and religious services from two Lutheran synods as well as one Catholic and one Orthodox church.[66] The city of Leandro N. Alem alone had 5,000 residents according to a 1965 estimate and was one of the most important settlements in Misiones (Pl. 2).

Ensanche San Javier N. The federal government did not make any other substantial surveys on public land in Misiones until after the end of World War I. At that time the movement of homeless people who wanted a new life outside Europe began on a large scale. The first sizeable project was the enlargement of San Javier, known as Ensanche San Javier N, which consisted of 5,657 ha. The Argentine government had no funds to spare and apparently no desire to experiment after the fashion of Fouilland, so the new surveyor was instructed to complete another damero plan and told not to exceed the amount of money granted for the task.[67] Surveys were approved in 1923, but the usual difficulties of lack of roads and water and rocky land made settlement so precarious that by the late 1960s less than 15 titles had been granted in the 206-lot area (Fig. 11). Over 100 lots were still classified as federal land and were either not occupiable or were used only in part by squatters with small plantings of manioc, maize, tobacco, and yerba mate.

Picadas Libertad and Sueca.   Although settlement was unsuccessful in the remote area of San Javier, another attempted land boom succeeded northeast of Leandro N. Alem. The national demand for yerba mate was increasing rapidly with the growth of the Argentine population and seemed assured of a good market for some time to come. The Picada Rusa, which was established just prior to the war, continued to fill up primarily with German settlers and later became known as the *Picada Libertad.* Large numbers of colonists also took land along the Picada Sueca which proved a better route to the interior and subsequently was chosen for the path of the main road to Oberá (Fig. 10).

Yabebiry.   In 1925 Atilio Fernández de la Puente, then chief of the Oficina de Tierras in Misiones, proposed formation of a strictly "Argentine" colony for raising yerba mate.[68] This colony was authorized in October, 1925, and was named Yabebiry. It was not opened exclusively by Argentine citizens and was slow to develop because of its distance from the main stream of settlement and the less favorable survey conditions compared with those found along the Picada Sueca. Yabebiry was an official colony and lots were not only surveyed by the damero method, but the task was not completed until 1937 — a delay which discouraged settlers. (See zone 12 in Fig. 19, p. 188.)

Picada San Martín.   Yabebiry was linked with the north end of the Picada San Martín to the vicinity of the Swedish settlement of Villa Svea. The small village of San Martín was laid out along the picada bearing its name but never grew beyond the 12 houses strung out, 6 on each side of the thoroughfare, over a distance of about one-half km. This line village has proven to be the most practical form of group settlement in spite of the government damero survey which has forced extraordinarily wide spacing between the village lots.

As a result of rapid settlement another urban center was created on government land where tierra colorada soils were found to be deep and fertile only 25 km northeast of Leandro N. Alem. The new center was chosen beyond the end of Picada Sueca when the latter became filled in 1913–14. Since it showed signs of possessing an important hinterland it was officially established as the pueblo of Oberá in 1928.[69] By that time Oberá had several links with Posadas: one via the San Martín picada, and two others, via the Picada Rusa and the Picada Sueca, through Leandro S. Alem. The hard-working, thrifty colonists created neat rectangular farmsteads on which tobacco, yerba mate, citrus fruit, and tung trees were produced within a radius of several km of the pueblo. Later, tea and lumber were added to the diversified list of cash crops. By 1929 a yerba mate cooperative was founded, and within six years of the official establishment of the urban center, some 75 per cent of all land in the colony was officially surveyed.[70] Titles have been granted fairly rapidly and the combination of advantageous cultural (especially roads) and physical (especially good soils) geofactors in the area has somewhat mitigated the usual problems associated with the damero settlement form. Oberá itself received electricity and had telephone services as early as 1937. In 1945 financial aid from the government was obtained and a municipio was organized with Oberá as its center. Ten years later the population had risen to about 10,000 and there were a number of large businesses, including transportation and banking. There were also a 150-bed hospital, several churches, two drug stores, and a hotel. A few streets were paved and the community was served by an airport. In fact, one could even buy light plane repair parts at one of the general stores.

Between visits in 1955 and 1960 the author noted that Oberá had lost much of its pioneer atmosphere and had become a stabilized community (Pls. 3 and 4). Wide, paved streets and many new buildings had appeared. The four-wheeled, horse-drawn wagon had practically vanished, at least on the paved streets, as had the mud that formerly gave the city its frontier appearance. Five years later relatively little downtown change had occurred, but it was apparent that the effects of modernization were then spreading outward from the city center. By then the population around Oberá had grown to almost 20,000 and had become second only to that of the provincial Capital District of Posadas (population 75,000). Since then Oberá has been recognized as the undisputed capital of the Selva of Misiones.

Campo Grande. In contrast with Oberá is the settlement of Campo Grande, begun even earlier. Although located in a good yerbal at an important crossroads, Campo Grande settlers were poorer, and became disheartened when land titles were not granted to the majority of the oldest settlers until 1943. Soils were less fertile in this forest opening, or campiña, and the colonists, who were descendents of the original Campo settlers, arrived just as yerba mate prices began falling. Consequently, they were forced to raise tobacco and to deal in lumber. The Cooperativa de Productores Forestales de Campo Grande was founded after the style of the yerba mate cooperatives in an attempt to promote the lumber industry. But the colony has progressed slowly, and only since 1959 has its center been officially designated as a "town." In reality Campo Grande is a line village extending over 5 km in length. A tung oil factory is at one end (km 1), followed by a yerba mate drier (km 2), an inn and repair shop (km 2.5), several houses and another repair shop (km 3.5), the police station (km 4) and store, gasoline station, movie house and church (km 5). Since 1959, a rectangular grid has been laid out at the end of km 5. Several houses and a sawmill have been erected at the new "center."

Cerro Corá, Secciones. The wave of settlers in the Oberá area during the 1920s and 1930s caused the government to enlarge some old colonies as well as to found new settlements. Expansion of Cerro Corá, Sección A, by damero survey was approved in 1926. The new section was located between the old settlements of Cerro Corá and Leandro N. Alem. The village O.V. Andrade which had been founded by German colonists served as a center for the addition. Still other sections of Cerro Corá (B, C, D, E, and F) were settled about the same time, but their quadrate surveys were not completed until 1941. The village of Cerro Azul was founded in Section B and as of 1970 was the only other central place in Cerro Corá.

Bonpland, Secciones. Southward expansion of the colony of

Bonpland was carried out in a similar fashion between 1932 and 1935. Section 1, mapped in 1932, is served by the small village of Almafuerte. Survey of the southernmost section (III) was not approved until 1933, more than fifteen years after the formation of the Picada Rusa (Libertad) which lies within its boundaries. This section is also a damero type but shows considerable variation in lot sizes because of the surveys of the original settlers which long preceded those of the government. Discrepancies between the two systems caused by overlapping holdings, water sources, and communication lines brought about much hardship and bitterness just as has always occurred wherever the state system was superimposed on the private, and accounts in part for the long delayed titling program in the area.[71]

Caá-Guazú, Guaraní and Yerbal Viejo.   Other colonies formed during the 1920s and 1930s were Caá-Guazú, Guaraní, and Yerbal Viejo. All of them, with the exception of the areas along the Picadas Libertad and Sueca, and the *Picada Africana* which was cut and settled by German refugees from Africa in 1930, were surveyed by the damero method. Several small hamlets with incipient linear forms have been established in these sections, including Villa Rural in Colonia Caá-Guazú; Dos Arroyos, Gobernador López, and Guaraní in Colonia Guaraní; and Los Helechos, C. Ramón, and General Alvear in Yerbal Viejo. None consists of more than six or seven houses and buildings and all but General Alvear and Guaraní are located near the Río Uruguay in areas of relatively poor accessibility.

Land for the colony of Yerbal Viejo was set aside in a 10,000-ha tract in 1916 for the specific purpose of raising yerba mate.[72] Before surveys were made, hundreds of pioneers, mainly White Russians, entered this area and became squatters, frequently along piques and picadas which they cut into the forest. Such was the degree of "illegal" land opening that in 1927 the colony had to be expanded to 58,000 ha. The Dirección General de Tierras belatedly ordered a surveyor, J. F. Artigas, into the area. He was instructed to measure lots on either side of existing picadas in the zone because of colonists' complaints about the damero settlement form. This (Type B) would have been a more practical solution to land opening than that offered by the quadrate system, but Artigas found that there were already so many people in the area that any such survey would create serious disputes among settlers. He demarcated only a few irregular lots of German and Scandinavian colonists who had settled along streams before he applied the damero system irrespective of the location of people or the buildings or crop areas they had established.[73] Evidently the legal adjustments and expenses required to establish a Waldhufen-like settlement system were considered too great, so the damero form was extended once again. That this decision only postponed problems is apparent from a closer investigation of Sección 13, which is a typical part of Yerbal Viejo and is representative of most of the government colonies established in the 1930s.

Sección 13 of Yerbal Viejo consists of 7,395 ha of land surveyed 1937–39 (Fig. 12). The area is hilly to rugged and was completely settled between 1928 and 1930. The colonists were primarily White Russian (70 per cent) and Poles from Galicia (20 per cent) or their descendants, and had come via Azara and Apóstoles from farms that had quickly become uneconomical in the so-called Poor Zone of Misiones. Germans, Japanese, Lithuanians, Swedes, Spaniards, Czechs, English, and Russians completed the list (10 per cent). Colonists felled the most valuable trees such as *lapacho*, *incienso*, and *timbó* and built the wooden frame houses with board sides typical of the area. Many fortunate enough to settle near streams dammed them and created ponds in order to raise carp, and a few harnessed falling water to make electricity. Nearly everyone planted yerba mate in forest clearings and accumulated cash. Within a few years they built better homes, often of stucco, and purchased mechanical farm equipment. More land was cleared for yerba mate and some years later tung trees were added as a second cash crop.

When Artigas arrived in September, 1937, to superimpose the damero survey on this squatter landscape the yerba mate market had gone bad because of overproduction and other crop prices were not good. Unfortunately communications were still difficult and settlers complained they could not get their products to market before prices dropped, or spoilage occurred. To these problems were added the litigation that began when farmers learned that new survey lines frequently cut across plantations, left some without a trace of water, and placed roads through swamps

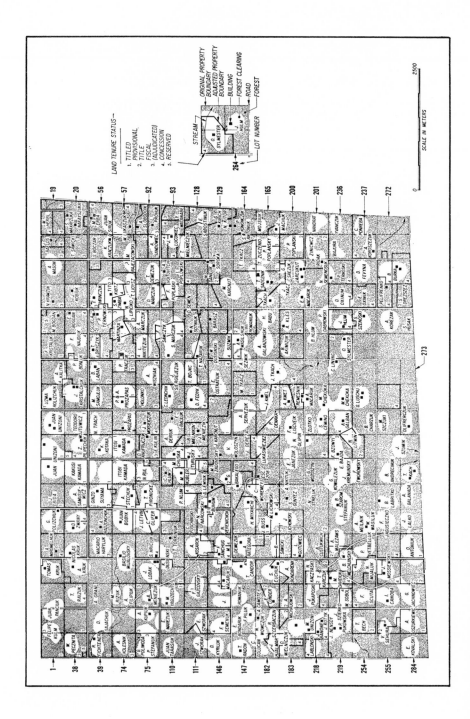

and houses. The survey was bound to create strife between neighbors so that formerly peaceful settlers took to arms and have quarreled through the years over the difficult situation.[74]

The example of Yerbal Viejo raises some obvious points of contention, as to both the official land policy in Misiones and the damero system. The government previously had made no effort to guide settlers to certain areas and people of many nationalities and differing religions settled anywhere land suited them. To all outward appearances these social differences did not matter during the initial phases of settlement when pioneers were extremely busy clearing and planting. However, they were later realized to be significant as is demonstrated by the fact that neighboring government colonies formed with pioneers from the same home communities and religious faith progressed more rapidly — an understandable phenomenon because old neighbors trusted one another and worked together more easily from the start. Informally organized cooperatives among these people sped the building of roads, schools, clinics, purchase of equipment, and sale of crops in their more homogeneous colonies. Later the cooperatives were formally organized and became thriving enterprises in such areas.

Cultural differences are deeply ingrained among farm peoples the world over, and this has been quite evident in the lack of mutual trust during times of stress in the randomly mixed colonies on this difficult landscape. If Yerbal Viejo, Sección 13, can serve as a representative cross section of life on the Latin American frontier, then the conclusion to be drawn is that the percentage of cultural mixing in the colony (30 per cent) was too high for efficient growth and that it would have been wiser to form separate adjacent settlements with people of similar background in this heavily forested area so demanding of specialized solutions to its problems.

Other problems have been created by the damero surveys in vogue at the time. The roads which have finally been built have had to deviate from the original plans because of terrain difficulties. In addition, bridges often have had to span the worst sections of rivers and streams. Finally, many more roads and bridges

Fig. 12 (facing page). Yerbal Viejo colony, Misiones, section 13 (compare with Pl. 7).

have been needed to serve the same number of colonists than are required in line settlements, and internal urban subdivisions have had to be inefficiently widespread.

The surveyor at Sección 13 was given full discretion as to whether an urban center should be created, but since there were paths leading to Oberá he reported no need to reserve land for this purpose. However, the colonists have felt differently and have gradually established stores along *Ruta* 5 on lots 9 and 30, as well as a school and a "plaza." A police station has also been located in the "village" near the school. All these units extend over several km along the east side of the road and make a loose, one-sided, linear village, known as Los Helechos. The lack of land reserved for a village is somewhat unusual for a damero colony, where government planning has always stressed this need, but such seems to be the trend in recent years. The need for village planning in areas which may be adjacent to large urban centers, but cannot communicate easily with them, is borne out by the formation of this and other centers in Misiones such as Aristóbulo de Valle, Campo Viera, Tobuna, and Dos de Mayo. Even if every urban center planned does not prove highly successful, it is far better to reserve space for many such settlements, particularly in sizeable but isolated forest colonies — a fact that the government itself had already proved when it assisted with town formations at Leandro N. Alem and Oberá which were only 25 km apart.[75]

WALDHUFEN-LIKE SETTLEMENTS: TYPE C

One of the largest of all the government colonies was formed on July 11, 1921. A 150,000-ha region named Aristóbulo del Valle was designated that year as a yerba mate colony. The first three sections surveyed (1, 2, 4) were all of the damero type and were approved between 1943 and 1952.[76] Settlers were once again primarily of Germanic stock, Poles with Galician background, some Ukrainians, and a few Swedes, although during the 1960s more and more Argentineans took land in the area. By the time most colonists reached Aristóbulo de Valle enough was known about the problems of the Misiones landscape that individuals sought out water before clearing the forest in order to make certain their lots would support cattle. It should be pointed out that pioneers in this zone had the advantage of experience and could easily compare the private Waldhufen settlements along the north side of the present colony of Aristóbulo del Valle with dameros on the south side. Such were the complaints by then that the government finally conceded to survey the remaining sections of the colony *nach Wasservermessung*, as the Germans put it, i.e., according to the drainage system. Pains were taken to consult each colonist and extra funds were assigned. Roads were built parallel to streams wherever possible and the net result (Fig. 13) is a practical scheme which might well serve as a model for land opening in this type of region except for the obvious lack of an urban center. The lots are variable in size and shape but they resemble the Waldhufen settlement type. Although road requirements are intermediate between those of Waldhufendorf and damero, all lots have water. This topographically adjusted settlement form is classified as Type C and occurs only in the various sections of Aristóbulo de Valle.

For a number of years it appeared that the federal government had developed a settlement form which was more suited to the landscape than the damero. Even when Misiones was made a Province in 1953, the Type C form was continued in surveys designated to expand Aristóbulo del Valle. However, in 1965, when the first official colony under the Provincial government was approved (Sección 1 of the Colonia San Pedro), the damero survey system was employed – a final indication of the hold which this settlement form has on officials who believe it is administratively and traditionally more acceptable. Although official appropriations for survey expenses and map making are initially somewhat lower for the damero form, these are only apparent advantages because expenses are inevitably increased later through alterations made necessary by field conditions. Furthermore, the parts of Misiones where public lands are still available for settlement are mainly in the rugged northern Altiplano de Irigoyen region where the damero form will not be viewed with favor by those who must settle the land. It is indeed unfortunate that the colonist himself has been consulted so little in the planning of settlement forms, especially when his experience has been as broad as it has in Misiones. It would seem that rapid administrative changes and lack of close contact between administrators and surveyors have

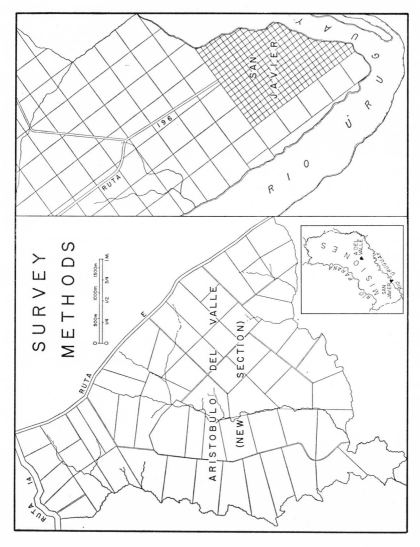

Fig. 13. Aristóbulo del Valle and San Javier, Misiones, a comparison of Type C
and damero settlements.

had strong negative influence on progress in some parts of the federal lands. These are questions which still merit serious attention since over 50 per cent of the public holdings in Misiones remains to be surveyed and subdivided for colonization.

The emergence of damero settlements with awkward linear village forms and of three Waldhufen-like settlement types in the heart of the damero region in Misiones is a measure of the need felt by colonists and by some surveyors for more efficient adjustment between settlement and landscape forms. The continuation of this need and consequently the appearance of still other settlement types was to be expected as more and more colonists arrived, especially from abroad, and became progressively more disenchanted with the damero form. It is not surprising, therefore, to note that subsequent to the initial period of modern settlement discussed above, colonists introduced authentic European Waldhufen settlement types. See Table 8 for a comparison of the major characteristics of all long-lot and damero settlement types which evolved or were introduced in Misiones.

TABLE 8

Major Characteristics of Settlement Types in Misiones

Settlement Types	Settlement Traits					
	Long-lot field form	Parallel fields	Farm-house on farm-land	Access to road along or near one end of lot	Access to stream along or near one end of lot	Central place functions along colony axis
Damero		x	x			Mixed
Waldhufen-like Type A	x	x	x	x		
Waldhufen-like Type B	Mixed	x	x	x		x
Waldhufen-like Type C	Mixed	Mixed	x		x	
Waldhufen-weiler	x	x	x	x	x	—[a]
Waldhufendorf	x	x	x	x	x	x

[a] Few (lower order) or none.

Source: Author's observations.

In spite of the problems encountered by the Argentine government in colonizing this relatively new and difficult part of the national territory, persistent settlement efforts on federal lands have resulted in much progress. One of the outstanding side effects has been that the private estate owners whose lands surround the central strip of public lands have come to realize that more prosperity results from raising crops than renting property, or exploiting only the forests of Misiones. The creation of thousands of farms and the emergence of hamlets, villages, and cities in the Selva proved once and for all that the idea of colonization in the dense forest was not only feasible, but that it could even produce great wealth. In addition, the enticement to form small yerba mate farms on government land was so great that labor shortages were created on the large estates which made it impossible for yerba mate to become a plantation crop. Eventually, therefore, the latifundistas began to experiment with pioneer settlement on their own lands.

CHAPTER 6   FOREIGN COLONIZATION
COMPANIES IN MISIONES

> Success in settlement schemes is, after all, nothing
> but the process of reducing or minimizing the num-
> ber of failures.
>
> A. J. Schwelm, *Some Thoughts on Colonization*

THE GERMAN WALDHUFEN SETTLEMENTS OF PUERTO RICO,
MONTE CARLO, AND ELDORADO

Puerto Rico: Early Settlement. The first modern attempt at
private colonization in Misiones was made in 1910 by the Compañía Introductora, a Buenos Aires firm controlled by the well-
known Tornquist family of Hamburg. A section of land along the
Alto Paraná owned by the Tornquists had already been exploited
for timber, but it was hoped that a further profit might be made
by selling farm plots in a colonization venture.[1] Because it had
earlier been proved on state holdings in Colonia Finlandesa and
Mecking that tobacco could be raised successfully in the Selva,
and since the Argentine tobacco market was growing rapidly and
shipping facilities on the Alto Paraná were excellent, the timing
seemed right for the company to initiate a colonization project.
The Compañía Introductora therefore subdivided its Misiones
property by means of the damero system into 340 farms of 25 ha
each, and 96 town lots. The settlement was named San Alberto
(Fig. 14). A tobacco experimental station was built and some advertising carried on to attract farm settlers. The Company experienced little success, however, and by 1919 only a handful
of German colonists had arrived.

At that time, San Alberto and a considerable amount of land
around it were renamed Puerto Rico and placed under the management of Carl Culmey, a trained surveyor who had emigrated
from Wiesbaden, Germany. Prior to taking over the management

of Puerto Rico, Culmey had pioneered in Rio Grande do Sul, Brazil, where he had helped lay out such linear villages as Santa Rosa.[2] Culmey brought German-Brazilian families to Misiones from Cachoeira, Santa Cruz, São Leopoldo, and Santa Maria in Rio Grande do Sul. All were thoroughly acquainted with German-Brazilian line villages and had helped to build some of them in southern Brazil. These men immediately rejected the damero form used in Misiones and introduced the Waldhufendorf concept.

Their work was made simpler by the forest roadways which had already been cut in the area during the years of lumber exploitation. These picadas, 3–4 meters wide, were slashed through the forest in long lines exactly as the Jesuits had done when they exploited yerba mate and lumber before the Republican period. Main picadas reached inland from crudely built lumber ports to the greatest number of commercially exploitable tree species. Since heavy logs had to be transported along these roadways, they had conveniently been built with a minimum of steep slopes and followed either interfluves or valleys of the main rivers. The lumber firms usually built transverse paths, or piques, at 1 km intervals along both sides of the main picada. Such communication arteries facilitated surveying along Waldhufen lines, but had been largely ignored when the isolated damero lots were established in San Alberto — a factor which contributed heavily to the lack of success of the first colony. Culmey and his associates then established Waldhufen settlements along the lumber roadways adjacent to the old damero area. The new colony of Puerto Rico retains both settlement forms to this day. The Waldhufen section of this colony became so highly successful that the older damero subdivision (San Alberto) was gradually occupied and now makes a substantial contribution to farming in spite of its original disadvantages. Because of the importance of the medieval Waldhufen settlement form introduced after 1919 in Misiones, the next paragraphs are devoted to a brief description of its development in Germany.

Puerto Rico: Waldhufen Origins.   One of the main focal points of early German settlement occurred between the Main and Danube rivers, and was carried out by the Franks and the Bavarians.[3] This region was intensively settled and cultivated between the fifth and sixth centuries and the Carolingian era. Nevertheless, wide expanses of forested lands were bypassed because of rough terrain. An advance toward these places came about as population expanded during the upper Middle Ages when entire forests were cleared for new land. It is not surprising that since many generations were involved in the settlement conquest, systematic colonization methods were developed, especially in the more difficult remnant forest zones. Often similar settlement types appeared on certain parts of the landscape such as the Bayerischer Wald and the Böhmerwald. Since the former area has remained isolated by forests to the present time, it offers an excellent source of field information on the specialized settlement types devised during the Middle Ages but still in use.

Settlers had filled up the Bavarian lowlands and had begun to cut forest breaks at the foot of valley slopes as early as 1,000 A.D. In certain hilly areas pioneers opened their own land and formed *Einzelhöfe,* or isolated individual settlements, but group settlement also occurred along important roads. Semi-fortified royal residences, or *Königshöfe,* were built to watch over these transport lines and to protect boundaries. Typical examples are found at Nabburg and Cham where Kings Henry the First and Otto the Second, respectively, maintained holdings, and near Freyung where bishops assigned from Passau operated the Schloß Wolfstein.

Successful planned settlements imported from other forested parts of Germany or devised by the kings, nobles, and church officials in Bavaria spread out from these conventional strongpoints into the more remote areas. One of the inducements offered pioneers who would settle unknown forested land was the assignment of a single agricultural plot in the new location. This was attractive to most peasants who lived in older, settled areas crowded around the foot of the usual Königshof and who were forced either to cultivate strips of land in several places according to a fixed plan (*Arbeitskalender*), or to work for others because there was no land that could be assigned to them — inconvenient features of the agricultural system then employed. Those who were willing to move were usually carefully selected for past achievement and good health. In order to open the greatest amount of forest and still keep pioneer settlers close together for protection in the new areas, farm plots were frequently surveyed in line form, i.e., in long, narrow strips on one or both sides of a trail or road. Linear settlements were considered the most practical since they could easily be extended along a road or a political boundary, and made road and bridge maintenance and defense easier. Whenever their importance as frontier guards was dominant the armed pioneers in these settlements were called *Wehrbauern*. This type of forest settlement became known as a Waldhufendorf because it was a series of individual forest farms spaced closely enough along a forest trail to have the appearance of a village (Dorf), whether or not village functions actually developed. Waldhufen colony names often had endings like *reut[h]*, e.g., Philippsreut, from the old word *riut*, meaning *Rodung*, or clearing. The endings *schlag*, *grün*, and *schwand* are also typical. These settlements are common on the famous *Goldenen Steig*, or the old *Via Bohemica*, an important salt route between Passau in Germany and Prachatitz in Czechoslovakia. In fact, the last of the Waldhufendörfer in this region were built as late as the nineteenth century.[4]

The Waldhufen idea may have originated in other parts of Germany by evolution from simpler settlement forms which had been developed much earlier. The shorter, narrow strips into which farmland had sometimes been divided around small, loose, primitive settlements called *Drubbel*, may have served as the basic idea on which pioneers drew for expanded Waldhufen settlement.[5] For the sake of greater efficiency, bringing one's village dwelling to a newly assigned strip of land, or consolidating one's land in a strip directly behind the dwelling could, with repetition, have produced either the Waldhufendorf or some similar long-lot settlement type.

When people had an opportunity they may have been stimulated by some prominent physical feature to develop long-lot farm holdings. In small basins around a pond or spring long lots were extended upslope from the water source in radial fashion so that each farmer could have equal access to the water. Various transitional stages in this process are found in the Frankenwald and Fichtelgebirge of southeast Germany. In both areas mentioned, the distribution of basin ponds or springs is common and is directly correlated with the development of the so-called *Radialwaldhufendorf*.[6]

In the Bayerischen Wald, and in the not distant Mühlviertel of

Austria where Waldhufendörfer are also common, narrow ridges frequently had to be occupied in order to avoid the swampy valleys below. In such instances the best lot distribution was the long, downslope strip behind each house since only by this division did every farmer receive fair amounts of dry land, sloping land, and swampland. Such farms were very close to each other, giving settlements with this method of land distribution a more crowded appearance than the usual Waldhufendorf. Exceptionally narrow lots (occasionally less than 50 meters) may also be the result of inheritance practices.

Whether the basis for the formation of Waldhufen settlements is physical, cultural, or a combination of these, it is evident that they developed with particular regard to the shape of the land as well as to the vegetation and drainage types. Consequently, the Waldhufen plan is especially suited to forested areas in more difficult terrain. It has the added advantage of allowing greater contact among the pioneers — a feature of vital necessity in isolated settlement undertakings even today — and at the same time of forming a settlement type which is less exposed than more compact settlements to such dangers as disease and forest fires. Moreover, the changes in microclimate on sloping lands allow for variability of harvest times, an advantage frequently enjoyed in Europe. In the Hinteren Bayerischen Wald, for example, Fehn reports harvests up to 14 days earlier in the lower parts of the long strips than in those of the less sloping upper parts.[7] Thus, the greater distance of fields from houses is compensated for by the advantages of earlier marketing. Advantage of this feature has been taken by Misiones colonists who plant citrus near rivers where frosts are less common than farther inland.

Undoubtedly the colonization agencies active during the Middle Ages observed the fact that the planned Waldhufen settlement form made it easier to send messages to individual farmers, to keep records of all types, and to expand settlements into the densely forested landscapes. This settlement type so favored systematic land management that it has survived to the present time. It is not surprising to note that the Waldhufendörfer in Germany have in certain places remained exactly as they were in medieval times as far as both appearance and function are concerned. Some, however, such as those in the Erzegebirge, have expanded until

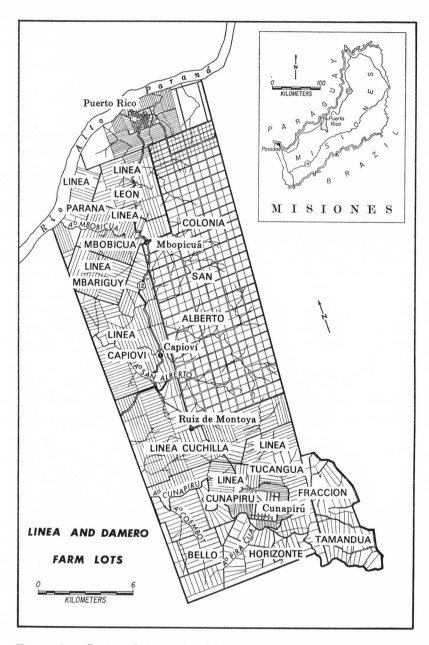

Fig. 14. San Alberto and Puerto Rico, Misiones.

Fig. 15. Monte Carlo colony, Misiones.

the original village form is barely recognizable. This is due partly to mining and industrialization activities as well as to administrative decisions to build centralized urban facilities. The former Waldhufendörfer of Annaberg and Ehrenfriedersdorf are places which have undergone such changes.[8] A few of these Waldhufendörfer also became exceptionally long because upland valleys were lengthier and their gradients gentler than in other parts of Germany.[9]

It was in areas as those just mentioned that *Lokatoren*, or settlement planners and surveyors like Culmey, trained. Some of these men emigrated to southern Brazil and northeastern Argentina where the hilly, forested landscapes are extraordinarily similar to those of Europe and were immediately judged suitable to the Waldhufendorf settlement form.

Culmey was able to attract sufficient colonists — all of whom were experienced Waldhufendorf settlers — to make immediate progress in Puerto Rico. The first pioneer families were offered gratis two times the area they had possessed in Brazil.[10] Some youthful settlers were also enticed to Misiones because they could avoid strict Brazilian draft laws. Still others found economic and political conditions in Argentina relatively better at the time and decided to move. From the very beginning Culmey received requests from both Catholic and Protestant farmers in Brazil but, because of his German cultural background in which the formation of hamlets and villages was limited to members of one religion or the other, he decided to admit only Catholic settlers to Puerto Rico. However, on March 20, 1920, he initiated another colony for Protestant pioneers while continuing to manage Puerto Rico. The new settlement was located 45 km upriver from Puerto Rico and was eventually named Monte Carlo after its manager (originally *Carls Wald*). It was the first settlement modeled entirely after the Waldhufendorf plan.

Monte Carlo: Early Settlement. The original thirty settlers in Monte Carlo were from Brazil. Lots were sold to them at prices varying from 35 to 40 pesos per ha, depending on how much land was bought. Settlers were not charged for the first 7 ha of land purchased — a bonus worth nearly 300 pesos.[11] Holdings varied in size from 8 or 10 ha to 50, although most were approximately 25 ha, which was a size copied from colonization practices on federal lands and believed adequate for one Misiones farm family. After forty German-speaking families from Brazil had arrived, the first pioneers from Germany itself began to join the new colony. The latter came from nearly all parts of Germany, and like the Catholics who went to Puerto Rico, were mostly poor people who used all of their savings to make down payments on land. Not a few wives and children had to remain temporarily in Germany while fathers went to Posadas to seek employment in order to earn money for purchasing lots and transporting families. Many had to borrow food from company stores, *boliches*, and received the dreaded indebtedness book. The practice of supplying tools, seeds, wire, clothes, and even wood to the settler at exorbitant rates had been common in Misiones since the wild yerba mate and lumber period before the turn of the present century. The pioneer was forced to pay at year's end by delivering his harvests. The *bolicheros*, or boliche operators, set prices, weighed all produce, and kept the records. If debt payments were not made, colonists faced a year of restricted credit and in some cases lived like stoics without even salt. Bolicheros earned anywhere between 25 and 40 per cent profit and were described as "insatiable" by one government official.[12] Prices were so high in Monte Carlo that numerous colonists like W. Pohlman, for example, had to pay for twenty years before these debts were cleared. Nevertheless, conditions in Germany and Brazil were so bad that by 1923 most lots in both Puerto Rico and Monte Carlo were sold (Fig. 15).

Eldorado. Another enterprising immigrant by the name of Adolph J. Schwelm organized his own company for colonizing private land along the Alto Paraná River. Although Schwelm was raised in England and had already spent some years in the lumber business in Argentina and Paraguay, he was a perceptive organizer and recognized that the greater the investment in a colonization venture the greater the insurance of success. He therefore took pains to organize international financing and to advertise his project. He also felt that a sizeable number of the pioneers themselves should be well enough off that initial suffering in the new area could be kept to a minimum and land brought into production without delay, thus avoiding conditions that long plagued Puerto Rico, and, to a lesser extent, Monte Carlo. It was his further conviction that company propaganda alone could never maintain the continuous stream of settlers essential to the progress and ultimate success of a colony. He was determined that the first groups of pioneers be successful enough to constitute good advertising in the homeland — a technique which had already proved helpful in Apóstoles and Azara among the Galicians and in Monte Carlo among the Germans, facts well known to Schwelm.

Schwelm's enthusiasm and personal abilities made for an auspicious start for his Eldorado settlement. The first twenty-seven colonists arrived at Easter time in 1921 and were Danish and Argentine-Danes who were attracted by advertising in Buenos Aires newspapers.[13] They settled within 4 km of the Alto Paraná on square holdings fashioned in a damero settlement. The Danes, however, complained of being too isolated from each other and were in desperate need of water and roads. At this time Schwelm invited German-Brazilians to Eldorado because of their renowned ability successfully to open densely forested areas. However, the German-Brazilians refused to settle under the damero system, primarily because of the lack of fresh, running water on Eldorado farm lots.[14] Without water there could be no livestock. Without livestock there could be no plow. And without a plow there could only be hack farming. Furthermore, the children of colonists would have had to go without milk, an especially serious problem in Misiones where neither soils nor water contain adequate supplies of calcium for the needs of plant and man. The German-Brazilians had already established Waldhufen settlements in Puerto Rico and Monte Carlo and were more attracted to these places, so Schwelm changed to their more practical settlement form. By 1922 Eldorado had already begun to look like another *Wurstsiedlung* (sausage settlement) as the Germans jokingly called their Waldhufendörfer. The presence of fresh water and access to a market road were not the only advantages possessed by the Waldhufendorf, as is brought out by one early report from an English official of this colony: "Only experience taught Schwelm that this [the method of 'squares'] was not the best method of working . . . [and that] strips of land have a great advantage over squares and make the possibilities of social life much greater."[15]

The German-Brazilians made other contributions to the initial success of Eldorado as settlers from Germany and Switzerland began to join the colony. The colonists from Brazil preferred to settle close to each other at the very end of the main picada no matter how far it reached into the Selva: the end of the trail meant proximity to future land additions to the colony. Their presence meant to the other settlers that there was always someone else farther on in the forest—a factor which improved settlement morale, especially since most of the Europeans had come from highly urbanized parts of the Continent. The German-Brazilians were also helpful in giving advice to other settlers and not infrequently constituted a labor force eagerly sought after by wealthier pioneers. The technique of forming pioneer settlements with a core of experienced colonists of similar cultural background contributed much to the success of Eldorado and has worked equally well in other private colonies in Misiones, e.g., Garuhapé, discussed in detail elsewhere.

Schwelm advertised his project constantly in newspapers and in special publications; [16] he also established a propaganda agency in Switzerland and contacted various European institutions, including private and semi-official colonization agencies in Germany.[17] However, the main recruitment took place in Buenos Aires, where all immigrants to Argentina received free board and room the first few days they were in the country. There his agents discussed the colony with new arrivals and showed maps and photographs of Eldorado as well as a 16 mm film of life in the new settlement. If a settler decided to go to the Alto Paraná, he was then helped with banking and travel arrangements, and given board and room at his destination where a hostel had been erected. He selected his lot, moved his belongings to it, and began to clear the land, or paid other settlers or native Paraguayans to do so for him. Schwelm, who had been converted from Judaism to Catholicism, built the first Christian church in Eldorado at his own expense, but permitted settlers of all faiths to buy land in the colony as long as they had sufficient funds to assure success. As a result, those with similar backgrounds voluntarily grouped together in different parts of the settlement.

THE GROWTH OF A WALDHUFENDORF: THE EXAMPLE OF MONTE CARLO

European settlement planners such as Schwelm were not unaware of the advantages of building "normal" colonies with outlying farms surrounding well-placed urban centers, but for a combination of reasons, initial attempts at urbanization in private settlements failed. Therefore, the Alto Paraná communities developed along the lines of medieval Waldhufendörfer, as these more detailed illustrations from Monte Carlo demonstrate.

Survey Techniques. By 1923 the colony of Monte Carlo was completely surveyed except for one subdivision, La Horqueta, which was added much later. Culmey and his men accomplished this task in the following manner. First, systematic mapping of 16,000 ha of the concession's 67,500 ha of land (Fig. 15) was carried out so that each farm could be surveyed with one of its borders along a stream or river. This step enabled Waldhufendorf colonists to take full advantage of the natural drainage network for supplying individual farms with water, as may be seen from Fig. 15. Second, there were constructed a main picada along with transverse piques through colony land. This task was accomplished by building the main route along interfluves wherever possible, occasionally following the old lumber trail. Third, demarcation of long farm plots between main picadas, i.e., interfluve survey lines, and streams was carried out. In areas where picadas followed valleys, the demarcation process was reversed.

In order to accommodate the greatest number of lots in the settlement while avoiding isolation of settlers, lot frontage had to be relatively narrow. The farm plots therefore averaged approximately 250 meters wide. With this lot width, families were close enough to call for any kind of help, to socialize, and to exchange ideas about farming during the initial years of colonization when these human factors were most critical. It is also true that, in comparison with the damero where most settlers were isolated, far smaller numbers of colonists in a linear settlement could make much broader and more uniform inroads against the dense forest — an essential feature for rapid and lasting success because of the vigorous ability of the natural vegetation to cover cleared fields, paths, and even roads in a short time. The lot length was 1–2 km, depending on the distance from the river to interfluves. The orientation of lots from valley to interfluve or vice versa assured each farmer of almost identical conditions of microclimatic and slope changes, which meant in turn a fair distribution of soil and lumber types, as well as equal frontage on both streams and communication lines.

In all, nine subdivisions of the colony land were made along major streams, or arroyos, as they are called in Misiones. They were all linked by the central picada which extended inland 20 km from the port. Each subdivision was called a *línea*, after the term *linha* used in southern Brazil for a line settlement. They were:

Línea Paraná	48 lots	Línea Caraguatay	70 lots
Línea Aterrada	32 lots	Línea Piray	71 lots
Línea Bonita	97 lots	Línea Ita-Curuzú	28 lots
Línea Chica	19 lots	Línea Alto Ita-Curuzú	43 lots
Línea Guatambú	48 lots		

TOTAL: 456 lots

In addition to the líneas, forty-four small lots called *quintas* were planned for a suburban area surrounding a large urban zone.[18] Although quintas (100 pesos each) and town lots (50 centavos a square meter) were more expensive, Culmey accepted small down payments for holding land and the sale of these units was brisk. In fact, all of the quintas were sold by 1921, along with one town lot. However, as was pointed out earlier, the urban zone never materialized.

Urban Development.   The main reason for failure of attempted urbanization was a severe attack of malaria just after the colony was opened. The disease was worse in Monte Carlo than elsewhere on the Alto Paraná. Because colony leaders were afraid the government would close the area to future settlement, Argentine health officials were not notified in time. Malaria outbreaks resulted in several deaths and struck Monte Carlo in 1921, 1923, and again in 1930. Under the circumstances settlers were soon convinced of the need to abandon the mosquito-infested port area and moved inland along the main picada. Thus, it was not high prices of urban lots, judging from the active interest in them, that brought on failure of the urban plan.

Between the last two malaria outbreaks in 1923 and 1930, an urban zone might still have developed had it not been for new circumstances. In 1924 Adolph J. Schwelm reorganized his Eldorado company and purchased Puerto Rico and Monte Carlo from

Culmey. He immediately altered the liberal financial policies, which had weakened Culmey's position to the point of bankruptcy, by raising prices and by requiring 50 per cent down payment on all land purchased. Urban lots became so much more costly that people continued to avoid them, and the third malaria outbreak in 1930 more or less underlined the fact that it was better to live on one's own land away from the port. By this time too many farm plots had been sold to provide for a new urban center elsewhere, and none developed in a formal way.

Three other factors were responsible for the failure of an urban center in Monte Carlo: colonists frequently preferred to live on their own farms, which was the main reason for pioneering in the first place; many settlers had lived in Waldhufendörfern in Brazil, or in Germany, Austria, and Poland, and realized that sooner or later a village center would appear along the main road; and for the moment there was much more need to develop the land than there was to establish an urban center.

Eventually schools, churches, and businesses did appear at or beyond the 4-km marker as measured from the port, a distance which was mutually agreed upon as safely beyond the malaria-breeding area. The school, which had been built at km 1 in 1920 and staffed by a teacher from Berlin, was moved to km 4 after the first malaria outbreak. There it was operated by Argentine and German instructors. After the second malaria attack it was moved to km 5. A second school was built in 1924 at km 14 (Línea Guatembú). In 1926 the German-Brazilians established a third school at km 19.2 where most of them had purchased lots (Línea Ita-Curuzú). Each school was built by voluntary cooperative labor of the colonists and was then turned over to the Argentine government. Serious dissatisfaction arose because the government was either unwilling or unable to pay attention to the immediate demand for better educational facilities by these former urban residents. This situation was largely responsible for bringing about a decision to switch to private schools by appealing directly to the German government for assistance. It is evident that greater importance was attached to educational facilities by European pioneers than by the Argentine authorities, and relations between the host country and colonists were severely strained over this point. Judging from this and other similar experiences in Misiones, the provision of adequate educational facilities appears to be a major ingredient in the success of modern pioneer settlements, especially if urban colonists are involved.

A Lutheran church was begun in 1924 at km 5.6, where it is still located. The pastor visited distant areas in the forest by horseback and held services in the homes of colonists. After some degree of wealth had been achieved in the colony, the number of Paraguayan laborers and Argentine settlers increased to the point where the latter were able to build a Catholic church in 1933 at km 5. This church was moved in 1950 to its present site at km 5.3. During the 1930s another Lutheran and a Baptist church were added to the colony.

The first businesses established in Monte Carlo were located at the port. The colony administration office and the store were next to the landing. Postal and police stations were built nearby. After the outbreak of malaria, settlers went farther and farther inland in order to avoid the port and all but the German-Brazilians and those with previous rural experience grew tired of walking many km to carry on business at the river's edge. In 1928 colonist Dürer subdivided his lot at km 5 and sold a small piece of land upon which a butcher shop was built. Another colonist established a general repair shop at km 6. A few months later two other businesses appeared: a small soft drink bottling factory at km 4 and a general store at km 7. The colony administration built a police headquarters at km 4.5 in 1930 and turned it over to the national government. That year a second butcher shop was opened at km 5; in 1936 the postal station was moved inland to the same point on the road.

During the 1930s a bakery, several machine shops, two photographic studios, two barber shops, three general stores, three or four hotels, a brick factory, and other businesses appeared. Pioneers, who by that time had become planters, banded together to build schools and churches and provide linkage roads between piques for the increased activities. Informally organized construction groups planned picnics, games, and dances while roads were built. The custom was practiced by the Germans in Misiones until the Argentine Comisión de Fomento took over such responsibilities in 1933. The same year a government road (Ruta 12) from Posadas reached Monte Carlo and crossed the colony's main road at km 7. New businesses gravitated toward this junction. Their importance grew and resulted in cooperative paving of the central road of Monte Carlo between km 4 and 7. During the 1960s this asphalted section of the old colony picada contrasted sharply with Provincial Ruta 12, which was dirt covered and impassable during heavy rains.

In 1930 market conditions worsened because of the world depression and because of overproduction of the main cash crop, yerba mate. Prices at the private stores were considered so high that colonists decided to form a cooperative society to assist with seed, machinery, and other purchases, and with crop marketing. For these purposes an office building, a large store, and a tobacco drying shed were built at km 6. In 1932 cooperative electric lighting came to the colony — a feat which could not have been carried out so early in the formation of the colony had it not been for the ease with which cables and other equipment could be distributed to colonists in the Waldhufendorf settlement form. The generators were housed at km 6.

By the 1930s it was apparent that a business section was developing in Monte Carlo between km 4 and km 7. Although stores were still up to several hundred meters apart, their density was increasing over this particular stretch of the main road, and a true Waldhufendorf emerged. Even a private village bus line was organized so that wealthier settlers could shop over the 3-km distance without walking. In spite of the service, thrifty European settlers walked or used horse-drawn wagons when making purchases.

Urban Problems. The relatively great distances that settlers have had to cover while on each shopping trip has produced duplication at intervals along the road of basic business establishments such as the general store, bakery, shoe store, pharmacy, etc. As a result of this duplication all businesses have remained small because they are frequented only by the closest residents. As late as 1970 numerous local *Bierstuben* (tap rooms) had *Stammgäste* (regular guests) just as they would in rural community centers of Germany. The heavy rainfall and the desire of colonists to do business close to their farm plots have contributed strongly to this duplication process. In spite of the openly expressed happiness of many of the colonists with their settlement (many came from similar Waldhufendörfern in Brazil, in the

Erzgebirge, in the northern Schwarzwald, and in the Mühlviertel of Austria), there are insufficient financial resources to provide for quality merchandise and services at the surprising number of stores and hostelries in the small community.[19] It is also evident, however, that the average colonist cannot carry heavy loads of groceries and other items long distances from store to store and back home again without great loss of time and energy. Undoubtedly a primary urban area with smaller, well-located outlying villages would have been beneficial to all, but by the time better urban functions became necessary land values had risen so high, and land uses, which emphasized orchard crops, were already so fixed that a compact centralized business district was out of the question. In 1966 a new, shortened road from Posadas was cut 3 km southeast of the old intersection with the main colony road so that the village is bound to continue its slow migration inland from the port and will undoubtedly become at least 6 km long in the next few years. It is rapidly assuming the proportions of the more progressive Waldhufendorf of Eldorado which already has a fairly crowded "central business district" extending 10 km along the main road.

Rural Development: Land Clearing. Clearing the Selva is the hardest task in pioneering and, everywhere except Eldorado, settlers were initially forced to remove the forest with little or no help. The tremendous physical effort required to cut down tropical hardwoods can only be appreciated by first-hand experience with the arduous task: the author was thoroughly convinced by participating in the operation and discussing the problem. Even the highest quality steel axe frequently bounces off metal-hard tree trunks in the Selva and it takes patience and stamina to remain in the forest long enough to finish the cutting task.

Not the least of the hazards is that caused by insects during the initial land clearing period. There are several types of these pests in Misiones which remain especially dangerous until a sizeable amount of the forest is removed. The worst is the so-called *mbarigüí* (*Simulium pertinax*, K.), a tiny fly which appears in swarms and whose bite leaves a small, red blood blister. The bitten area is injected with poison and swells and itches to a degree that makes an honest mosquito bite a welcome relief. If a hand is attacked by a dozen or more of these flies at once, as is usually the case, within several days the swelling incapacitates the limb; fingers remain swollen and stiff for 10 to 15 days longer. Scratching the bites brings on ulceration and infection that may last months. The mbarigüí alone is responsible for many a pioneer defection from the Selva as some 5 per cent of the settlers never seem to become immune. The *ura* (*Dermatobia cyaniventris*), which lays its eggs on the flesh of man and animal and whose larvae burrow into skin, and the *mosca dorada* (*Compsomya macellaria*), whose bite leaves an open wound through which lymphatic fluid drains for weeks, are still other miseries which must be endured. Perhaps the most difficult part is the slow realization that this group of insects works in continuous shifts. The mbarigüí bites from dawn to dusk, after which the common mosquito takes over (malaria is no longer a problem). When it is fully dark, the mosquitos disappear for the most part while the rest of the more dangerous insects become active. Neither is the settler who would make a home in the Selva ever permitted to forget the ant. There are several varieties in Misiones: *Isaú* (*Atta sexdens*), *Akeka* (*Acronyrmex* sp.), *Cuyabana* (*Prenolepis fulva*), and *negra* (*Cryptocerus ater*). Ants have been responsible for the death of at least one child in Monte Carlo who was attacked while sleeping. Inestimable damage to leaves and fruit results from ants, especially among young plantings.

In spite of these difficulties, most pioneers managed to clear and plant a ha or two the first year. If the valuable timber on a farm had not been exploited previously, the owner could be certain that money earned on each ha would suffice to pay others to fell the trees. Paraguayans who crossed the Alto Paraná illegally were hired to do this work, in which case several ha could be cleared the first season. Once the natural vegetation was removed, it was allowed to dry four to six weeks and was then fired in several places on the first clear day. Although it is argued that firing enriches the soil with ashes and removes insects, both advantages offer ephemeral gains. Useful soil bacteria and fungi are destroyed by the intense heat, and crusting occurs which alters percolation characteristics and increases damage from erosion. However, once burning was finished, subsistence crops were planted and other things were done until harvest time. For instance, the majority of colonists, who were too poor to hire laborers, cooperated to pull stumps. The informally organized *Stumpenvereine* (stump-removing societies) were, like all other cooperative efforts, spiced with socializing. Most of these methods are still in use today where new areas are being opened in the forests by descendants of the original pioneers.

Settler's Diet. If the pioneer in Misiones was fortunate, he trapped or shot such animals as deer or armadillos for meat. He may also have encountered wild honey in the trees, made by stingless bees of the region (*Polybia soutellaris* and *Nectarinia lechequana*). Otherwise it was necessary to buy food from neighbors who had already raised manioc and maize, or from the nearest store. In the early days at Monte Carlo some pioneers became ill from malnutrition. Tragedies of this sort were not uncommon, nor were those caused by accidents which had to be treated without proper medical attention. Before the first harvests could be gathered morale plummeted to a new low, waves of despair swept through the colony, and the rapid departures, especially of bachelors, nearly caused a general exodus at one point. Small wonder that surviving pioneers repeat the old German saying: *Der Väter Tod, der Söhne Not, der Enkel Brot* (To the [pioneer] fathers, death; to the sons of pioneers, poverty; to the grandsons, bread).

Shelters. The first shelter was built while clearing the land. This was, and still is, a lean-to made of palm fronds and other large leaves which shed rain easily. As soon as possible the settler replaced his lean-to with a frame house built from the best wood available. Ignorance of tropical tree types, or scarcity of hardwoods, resulted in softwood construction. Pioneers have learned, however, that softwood houses last only about fifteen years in Misiones. Usually, houses built from bricks made at local clay deposits replace the softwood frame types, although the brick variety may be chilly and damp inside. Houses originally built of hardwood are still in excellent condition. Sometimes even these have been replaced by frame houses with hardwood and stucco construction where pioneers have been financially successful. Thus housing materials vary, as do styles in the Monte Carlo community. The typical wood frame structure with a veranda found in the American tropics is commonly used by newcomers in the forest. Roofs are generally made with hardwood shingles and have a simple pitched shape. Even so, the German-Brazilians almost invariably build the German *Krüppelwalmdach*, i.e., the pitched-roof house with a half hip (Pl. 9). Others have copied housing styles from their regions in Europe, and a few have built Spanish-style homes with red tiled roofs. All have adopted the American custom of separating the house from other farm structures. This is done (where land is available) both to insure against simultaneous destruction by fire of all units, and to keep livestock odors away from the house in the case of larger herds with ten or more cattle.

The first house was often located at the low end of the long lot so as to be near the stream, and land was gradually cleared upslope toward the road. After several years had elapsed and the pioneer began to receive money from cash crops, a better home with a well was built near the road. In this way communicating with others was made easier — a factor which is important if medical attention is necessary, if wild animals endanger children on trips to and from school, and if home postal service is desirable. By this time the settler had learned which construction materials were to be preferred, as well as the importance of house orientation. Those who made the mistake originally of building houses that extended E-W did not repeat the error because of the lack of heat on the west side late in the afternoon. If bedrooms were planned on that side they were too cool, especially during the low-sun season. Hence if a house has to be oriented E-W the west side is better used for the kitchen. Also the northern side of roads is much sought after as a building site because prevailing winds are from the north and blow the fine, red dust of tierra colorada soils toward the south. If the house must be built on the south side of the road, it is almost impossible to keep dust out of even well-sealed rooms — a feature not ordinarily associated with such humid regions. In the business district of Monte Carlo there have always been more buildings on the north side for this reason, since store fronts must remain open. However, in recent years land prices in the village have become so high that the trend has almost been halted and buyers are purchasing whatever they can afford. Occasionally, because of the dust problem, incipient villages in Misiones look like the one-sided Waldhufendörfer found in the Bayerischen Wald and in the Mühlviertel of Austria. House and store owners have learned to build back 5 meters or more from either side of the road in order to leave a shelter belt of forest trees and shrubs between buildings and the road edge. This frontal vegetation also serves as protection against gusts of wind which are common during storms and which are sometimes severe enough along roads to destroy exposed house roofs. The combined problems of dust and poor drainage hastened the paving of the main road through Monte Carlo.

Planting: Subsistence Crops. Newly cleared farm lands were planted with crops formerly used by Guaraní Indians and later by the Jesuits. Manioc, which is a staple, has the dual advantage of producing its tubers even in poor soils and of not rotting if left undisturbed in the ground. Thus, manioc may be "stored" for many months and has always been a mainstay for the pioneer who has no other means of food preservation in this climate. Moreover, manioc does not seem to be so disturbed by ants as do other crops; hence the harvest is more certain. Manioc is the easiest food crop to plant — only cuttings are needed — and its uses extend from a baked form (*Mandiokbrägele*, after *schwarzwälder Brägele*) to salad, bread, and cattle fodder. Many a pioneer claims that without manioc it would have been impossible to settle the remote Alto Paraná colonies, and this may well be true. The importance of the plant has given rise to the Misiones saying: *Wer Mandioka hat, hat keine Sorgen* (He who has manioc has no worries).

Maize is another important crop, but it requires better growing conditions than manioc. Vegetables, such as the sweet potato, may be raised in the tierra colorada without much difficulty, provided ants have been eradicated first. The *isaú* (Spanish) or *sauva* (Portuguese), sometimes called the parasol ant (*Atta sexdens*) is especially dangerous to non-native plants. The indigenous peoples did not combat ants and when these insects became oppressive probably moved their plantings to another part of the forest. This ant has done its share to make modern settlers move on occasion or give up entirely. It is significant that the main concentrations of *Atta sexdens* are in the Campo. However, since the fertilization of females takes place in the air, especially when south winds are blowing, the plague is slowly spreading to new agricultural clearings. Successful eradication has been achieved by prolonged use of ant poisons like arsenic, cyanide, DDT, Clordane, and Dieldrin, but thousands of pesos must be spent annually in order to combat ants chemically on 50 ha of commercial cropland.

Cash Crops: Tobacco. The first cash crop to be planted in Monte Carlo was tobacco, which provided a fairly rapid source of income. Several tobacco companies bought harvests in Misiones and paid good prices as long as the tobacco was well cured and sorted. Occasionally one or two careless settlers caused a general depression of tobacco prices, exactly as happened to Finnish colonists, but the cooperative in Monte Carlo was energetic about instructing members and maintaining reasonable enough standards to save the situation. Kentucky, Maryland, and *Criollo Misionero* were some of the principal types raised. Tobacco has continued to be an important pioneer crop in Misiones and is still grown on freshly cleared land. Criollo Misionero is more popular among new pioneers because the drying sheds are smaller and no fire is used in curing the leaf. However, yields and market prices are both lower for this variety so that other types are raised as soon as means are available. There are now approximately 10,000 ha of small plots cultivated, and Misiones produces nearly one-fourth of the Argentine tobacco crop.[20] As soon as other crops such as yerba mate could be raised, tobacco was often discontinued by European settlers because of the hard work involved. Each plant must be carefully pruned three times during the growing season, a process which has to be done personally and which ruins clothes and discolors hands. Furthermore, several *carpidas*, or weedings, are required during the growing season in order to prevent insect attacks and to control diseases. Nevertheless, by 1965, the long-lasting yerba mate crisis brought on by overproduction finally stimulated some Europeans to raise tobacco again.

Yerba Mate. In the early years of pioneer settlement the successful growing of yerba mate on federal lands pointed the way toward a transfer of this crop to private colonies, just as happened with tobacco. In Monte Carlo a nursery was started by W. E. von Jungenfeld, a colonist who had learned his trade in the settlement of Hohenau in Paraguay.[21] Individual pioneers along the Alto Paraná soon began experimenting with yerba mate and were more or less successful, depending on soil conditions. Not a few pioneers who purchased young plants found that soils were too shallow for yerba mate. This created hard feelings between the

Schwelm company and these pioneers, for neither had investigated land under the dense rainforests before sales contracts were
made, and Schwelm was not disposed to letting settlers change
their lots as Culmey had always done. Schwelm was legally correct in doing this, since precedent had long been established on
its lands by the federal government.[22] The disclosure of rocky
soils after land clearing or of bedrock only 2–3 meters below the
surface precluded successful yerba mate production and could not
have been detected in advance, short of making numerous borings
or doing a complete geological survey. During the initial experimental period, colonists also learned that yerba mate did best on
north-facing slopes. Fortunately the rolling landscape was so subdivided by the Waldhufendorf system as to make it possible for
nearly everyone to raise yerba mate under appropriate exposure
conditions. Within a few years yerba mate turned into the famous
"green gold" of Misiones and had such good market potential in
Argentina that it swept aside consideration of other crops and
was responsible for the establishment of a monocultural economy
in the national territory.

Settlers have been criticized because they did not continue the
development of tobacco, rice, sugar cane, and other crops, but
at least part of the blame may be placed on contrabrand tobacco
from Brazil and on highly organized sugar cane competition from
other farm regions (Tucumán) in Argentina. The government
likewise played an important role by issuing a series of decrees
requiring all colonists on federal land to plant yerba mate. This
legislation came about after it was realized that some colonists
were being lost who went to Misiones with more than adequate
funds and complained that on the usual 25-ha farm lot there was
not enough good land to raise large amounts of the crop. Since
the government wanted the yerba mate region settled by farmers,
H. Barreyro made a proposal as early as 1916 for creating lots of
200 ha if the prospective colonist would plant at least 50 per cent
of his holding in yerba mate.[23] Action was delayed until March 15,
1926, when a decree specified that all colonists on federal lands
"have the obligation of planting and cultivating one-fifth of their
exploitable terrain with yerba mate within two years of the date
of issue of a provisional title."[24] Conditions were liberalized by the
same decree, which allowed purchase of 100 ha of land if 75 per

cent of the exploitable area were planted with yerba mate within four years of the provisional titling. Anyone who planted yerba mate on 50 per cent of this exploitable area within three years was not even required to reside on the land. Each farm had to have a minimum of 840 plants per ha. On January 19, 1927, even greater colonization concessions were approved on federal lands by another *decreto oficial.*[25] These incentives reflected the favorable market conditions in Argentina and it is little wonder that private farmers also strove to plant as much yerba mate as they could. Argentine yerba mate production statistics appear first for 1910, and are illustrated in Table 9 up to 1929, i.e., three years after it became apparent that the market was becoming saturated.[26]

The Argentine government continued to encourage planting

TABLE 9

Production of Yerba Mate in Argentina, 1910–1929

Year	Kilograms Produced	Kilograms Imported
1910	910,000	48,826,000
1911	909,803	50,518,065
1912	896,441	52,807,299
1913	980,212	62,907,993
1914	1,174,136	52,670,333
1915	2,168,601	58,282,918
1916	2,228,388	55,508,237
1917	2,477,799	55,352,664
1918	2,500,000	59,015,921
1919	2,700,000	69,084,038
1920	2,900,000	67,810,912
1921	3,100,000	62,116,343
1922	3,700,000	69,105,750
1923	5,600,000	73,526,347
1924	8,500,000	66,059,951
1925	10,000,000	72,552,209
1926	13,000,000	75,639,511
1927	16,200,000	81,032,092
1928	17,800,000	75,047,133
1929	20,000,000	70,000,000

Source: Republic of Argentina, Comisión Reguladora y Comercio de la Yerba Mate, Unpublished report, Buenos Aires, 1966; Ernesto Daumas, "El problema de la yerba mate," *Revista de la Economía Argentina,* 25 (1930):49.

yerba mate in Misiones, although it never took action to curtail imports of the same product that were increasing just as steadily as home production (Table 9). By 1926 it was apparent that something had to be done as prices began dropping in spite of the fact that Misiones production was still less than 30 per cent of Argentine consumption. Most of the imported yerba mate came from wild collections made in Brazil. The Brazilians realized they were losing the sizeable Argentine market and took dumping action in 1926–27 by ordering a *safrinha*, or an extra cutting, in hopes of discouraging colonists' efforts in Misiones.[27] Making matters easier for Brazil was the fact that the expense of shipping yerba mate from Paranaguá, Brazil, to Buenos Aires was only half that of the Alto Paraná-Buenos Aires route, i.e., 20.45 pesos/ton versus 40.00 pesos/ton.[28] As a result of the price war, 40 percent of Argentina's yerba mate mills (eight of them) closed within a period of five years, since milled yerba mate was the type dumped by Brazil. By 1934, the financial effects on yerba mate growers in the private colonies of Misiones (Puerto Rico, Monte Carlo, and Eldorado) were far greater than those on public lands, the reasons for which may be seen from Table 10.

TABLE 10

Misiones Yerba Mate Production, 1933

Colony Type	Total Farms	Total Acreage	Yerba Plants	Total Production
	%	%	%	%
Federal Colonies	75.5	32.4	46.7	35.6
Private colonies	24.5	67.6	53.3	64.4

Source: "La cercana tragedia de la yerba," *Revista de la Economía Argentina* 32 (1934):41–42.

In 1935, instead of stopping the inflow of Brazilian yerba mate, the Argentine government created the Comisión Reguladora de la Producción y Comercio de la Yerba Mate for controlling the enterprise in Misiones. The first action of the Comisión was a four-peso tax on each new yerba mate plant; three years later harvests were limited to 60 per cent of normal. Controls have existed ever since and have not only effectively stopped Argentine production increases, but have stopped one of the most successful commercial colonization efforts of modern times within such a densely forested area of Latin America. The fact that by 1935 approximately one-half the colonists along the Alto Paraná and a much greater percentage of those on public lands were native Argentineans made no difference to the authorities. Population growth in the colony of Monte Carlo reflects the economic situation during this difficult period. The number of families changed as follows: 100, 1925; 400, 1935; 550, 1945; 552, 1955; 540, 1965.[29]

The increase between 1935 and 1945 was only a little over one-fourth that of the previous decade, and probably would have been eliminated entirely had it not been for the arrival of more than one hundred Polish-German families in 1939. These unfortunate families were personæ non gratæ in both Poland and Germany and had come to Misiones in spite of the bad economic situation.

The principal reason for government interference in Misiones had been the fact that Brazil, long an important market for Argentine wheat from the Pampa, made all trade with Argentina contingent upon Argentine purchases of large quantities of Brazilian yerba mate. The Brazilian request was honored, but as a result established yerba mate colonies in Misiones suffered severely.[30] By its action the Argentine government had put itself in the unenviable position of first encouraging and even requiring colonists to plant yerba mate in small holdings and then, after achieving success, of taking strong steps to undermine their progress by supporting large-scale importation from a competing economy. The yerba mate business has never recovered from this type of interference.

Other yerba mate problems result from the declining yields with age of trees, root exposure from erosion, and harmful over-pruning because of poor quality labor and management. Although after the 1950s yerba mate trees were harvested less intensively and a crown of leaves left to help the plant through the frost period, this was done primarily because the pruning time was interrupted by the increased demand for labor during the tea harvest.

Unfortunately yerba mate leaves must be transported to driers not more than 60 km from the harvest place because of instability of the leaf chemistry. Transportation is another difficulty. The carro polaco, or horse-drawn wagon, is used to carry the leaves, although trucks have become more and more common since the 1950s. Both types of vehicle, however, are subjected to precarious delays whenever rainfall is intensive. If delays last more than twenty-four hours, yerba mate leaves begin to deteriorate. Fortunately the muddy roads in tierra colorada soils tend to dry within a few hours after full sunshine, but quite possibly this "convenient" trait has precluded more rapid paving in the Province.

Once the yerba mate leaves have been taken to a drier they are heated over open flames to fix the chlorophyl (called the *sapecado* stage locally). They are then subjected to a longer drying process or *secanza*, after which they are finally milled to produce *yerba canchada*. Only about 10 per cent of the yerba mate is milled in Misiones; over 80 per cent is processed in Buenos Aires and Santa Fe. About 75 per cent of the bulky dried product is shipped by river to Santa Fe and Buenos Aires. Rail transport is used for approximately 25 per cent, especially when river freight rates are unfavorable because of high labor costs or when water levels on the Paraná are exceptionally low. Rising prices and competition from tea and imported coffee have brought about a declining national consumption of the product.

Tung Trees. Colonists have taken several forms of action to combat the deteriorating yerba mate economy in Misiones. As early as 1928 those who had foreseen the difficulties with yerba mate had begun to experiment with the tung tree (*Aleurites Fordii*) for a cushion crop. Oil pressed from the fruit of this tree had a relatively good world market price. The pale yellow tung oil is used in varnishes and paints as well as in certain inks because of its rapid drying quality, and as an isolating agent in various chemical processes. In Eldorado seeds were imported from China; in Santo Pipó, a private Swiss colony on the Alto Paraná founded in 1924, seeds were imported from Florida. It became immediately evident that the tree was ecologically at home in Misiones, but adoption was slow because the best planting and harvesting techniques had to be worked out, and because most colonists made the mistake of resisting diversification with unknown plants until long after the yerba mate market had collapsed. The fruit of the tung tree had to be gathered from the ground several times during the ripening period, and factories for extracting the oil had to be built.

More problems arose because of lack of transport tanks. Tung oil is toxic and flammable and must be shipped in special trucks to ports where boats carry the heavy product to Buenos Aires.

It was not until the late 1940s that tung production began to increase rapidly. Since then it has replaced yerba mate as the principal cash crop in new colonies. Settlers have cultivated tung trees after the fashion of yerba mate on plots averaging only 5 ha. Since tung yields of 2,000–3,000 kilograms/ha of fruit may be obtained for many years and there are few pathological problems, the tree is now quite common. On many farms tung earnings have paid labor costs for the yerba mate harvests and have proved the advantages of diversification. It is significant, however, that thin soils in the Campo have been found generally inadequate for tung production, and there are lower yields in this part of Misiones.

In spite of many favorable features, the overproduction history of yerba mate was repeated with tung trees. But direct government competition was not a factor, since 95 per cent of Misiones's production was exported, mainly to the United States and to Europe, and settlers quickly adjusted to obvious world market conditions. Recently, production in the United States and in China, as well as adverse agricultural policies during the Perón administration, have made continuous expansion of tung acreage difficult. Protection of domestic tung in the United States, and chemical substitutes manufactured there have also curtailed prospects. One of the inevitable results of world marketing problems has been the rapid development of tung cooperatives after the style of their yerba mate counterparts.

Agricultural Cooperatives.   The unusually large number of cooperatives developed in Misiones indicates that Alto Paraná colonists felt there was only one effective way to remedy agricultural problems without government help. Agricultural cooperatives were introduced by the Germans in a private settlement in the Campo of Misiones as early as 1924. They were begun in 1931 by the colonies along the Alto Paraná but developed later in many federal colonies. One of the primary reasons for this difference may be that greater dispersal of farmers in the damero system has militated against cooperation. The Waldhufen settlements, on the other hand, not only had transportation features which facilitated close coordination, but were made up largely of settlers who spoke the same language and who knew each other well. In addition, they were settled by people whose original background provided a long history of organizational training. A brief summary of the growth of cooperatives in the colonies of Eldorado and Monte Carlo is illustrative of their rapid success.

The Cooperativa Agrícola Eldorado was founded in 1931 with only 26 members and a capital of 2,600 pesos. Thirty-eight years later, this cooperative had almost 2,000 members and a subscribed capital of over 100,000,000 pesos. The total capital value had reached approximately 375,000,000 pesos.[31] A similar advance has been made by the smaller Cooperativa Agrícola Mixta de Monte Carlo. It too was begun in 1931 when 94 colonists pooled resources which totaled only 4,800 pesos. By 1969 membership had grown to 762, and subscribed capital had reached 107,669,000 pesos. The total value of land, buildings, equipment, and expenses was recorded as 138,974,881 pesos for that year.[32]

Both of these are representative of the type of cooperative founded in the colonies of Misiones. They were credit cooperatives which were modeled after those established in Germany in 1854 by F. G. Raiffeisen. The so-called Raiffeisen cooperative was designed with the small farmer in mind, and probably originated as a more formal expression of the well-known German *Landschaften*. These rural societies were begun by Frederick II, King of Prussia, in order to drive down interest rates and to eliminate the medieval practice of usury. The cooperatives formed in Germany usually had less than 100 members. The smaller organizations joined to form central cooperative societies, which in turn united to form provincial entities. The latter still make up a national federation of cooperatives. In 1913, four years after federation began, there were already 27,192 agricultural cooperatives in Germany. Over half of them were of the rural credit variety.[33]

The popularity of the German Raiffeisen cooperative was so great that in 1866 it was transferred to Italy, and subsequently to many other countries in the world. Since many Italians emigrated to Argentina, there is much sympathy for this kind of cooperative in the pertinent general laws of the nation which date from 1926.[34] Rural cooperatives of the Raiffeisen type were begun in Misiones by the president of the Liebig colony of La Merced in 1924. This Waldhufen colony was established by settlers from Württemberg, where the first formally organized agricultural cooperative in Germany was begun in 1873. The president of the Colonia Liebig was also responsible for initiating federation of Misiones cooperatives after the German style in 1930, and is much honored today for his achievement.

The growth of the cooperative movement in Misiones is an indication that settlers have passed the primitive stage of self-sufficiency and need to purchase sophisticated goods made in other parts of the country. Consumer cooperatives have the advantage that bulk goods of many types can be purchased at wholesale prices and sold at little or no profit to members — essential features of economy in a place where individual investment is low and transportation costs are exceptionally high. The degree of success of the cooperatives in Misiones also illustrates the contribution of this region to other parts of Argentina where markets have been found for provincial goods. Nor have voluntary cooperatives prevented competition from normal retail outlets, since not everyone joins cooperatives; this is demonstrated by the presence of both types of businesses in each of the colonies.

The fact that cooperatives in Misiones are multifaceted, i.e., have been developed to handle consumer needs, agricultural product sales, and rural credit arrangements, has undoubtedly stimulated growth rates of pioneer settlements. Recognition of the importance of cooperatives was made in 1953 when the study of these multifaceted entities was placed on the curriculum in the primary schools of Misiones.[35] Although new colonies being established in other parts of Latin America generally recognize the importance of the cooperative principle, Misiones techniques of operation and of preparation of future generations are not widely known and should afford an ample supply of workable ideas to those interested in land opening.

Recent Agricultural Developments. At the time yerba mate prices declined in the late 1920s there was an increase in citrus production because of the hope that oranges, mandarins, grapefruit, and lemons might help the diversification process. Citrus plants had been introduced by the Jesuits and were already raised in nearly every colony in Misiones. In fact, during the lean years wild stands of oranges provided many a pioneer with food until harvest season. Commercialization of these crops has occurred most rapidly in the Alto Paraná colonies, but production has also increased on government lands. Today oranges make up 85 per cent of the citrus crop.

Monte Carlo has become one of the most important orange centers, especially of the late Valencia variety, although Calderón and Lue Ging Gong are also to be found. Production and marketing have been handled by a cooperative after the fashion of yerba mate, but the crop is so expensive to produce properly for commercial fruit sales that most farmers cannot afford to maintain the required standards. Spray is needed four to six times a year for fungus and insects, and after the fourth or fifth year substantial fertilizer applications must be made for quality yields. Harvests vary even within a single colony from 0.5 to 25 tons per ha, depending on the care given the trees.

When good oranges are produced, the problems of shipment to large markets are great and have never been solved. River transportation is too expensive for most growers since the trade organizations have monopolistic control of this form of shipping and charge the highest surface transportation prices in Argentina. This reversal of the usual role of water transportation is aggravated by railroad service, which is available but unreliable. Trains, for example, went out of action for two-and-one-half months in 1961 just as orange harvests reached Posadas. It is estimated that 75 per cent of the Misiones harvest spoiled. Only since 1965 have roads been improved enough for truck shipments to reach the large cities along the Paraná River, but during heavy rains all trade traffic must halt and wait for dry ground. Occasionally this requires several weeks. Meanwhile the oranges are usually given away. When transportation problems have been solved, production of quality oranges for the consumer's market may become feasible.

Because of the marketing problem, juice factories have recently been given more attention. In Eldorado and Puerto Rico concentrated orange juice is now made and the product is exported to West Germany, Holland, and Belgium. Since the Puerto Rico factory was built in 1963 it has been expanded 60 per cent and can handle 10,000 tons of fruit per year. Oranges are harvested from March through December in the Alto Paraná area so there is a certain amount of optimism about the future of orange juice manufacture, providing prices remain good.

Another of the most recent agricultural developments in Misiones is that of tea cultivation. Although this plant was introduced by A. J. Schwelm as a possible cash crop for Misiones, settlers did nothing with it until the yerba mate crisis brought on a search for new products. In 1939, F. Kühnlein, a colonist from Oberá, began experiments with tea. Within a few years he was producing such a high quality product that export was assured. Tea culture has spread to numerous Misiones settlements, both private and public.[36] Since 1958 growers have successfully competed on the European market. Following yerba mate, tung, and orange planting practices, tea is raised on small holdings of only 2–3 ha, and is already a cooperative industry. It has been discovered that tea grows well in old yerba mate orchards so there is added incentive to diversify further in this respect. However, the leaves must be picked with expert care, and the first harvests of new growers in Monte Carlo, where it became an important crop by 1965, were rejected by the local tea factory.

The Monte Carlo tea factory was built in 1958 by the H. G. Th. Crone Company, formerly of Java. Other factories existed in the Province by then (Campo Viera), but poor road conditions require locating drying establishments within 30 km of growing areas so that leaves will not lose quality in shipping. Eventually the Company sponsored a Dutch-Indonesian pioneer colony to raise tea just south of Monte Carlo. The Colonia Alo was begun in 1965 on 300 ha of land subdivided into 10 long lots by the surveyor from Monte Carlo. Most of the forest has been removed by hand methods, but the Indonesians introduced portable chain saws for more rapid clearing of vegetation — a technique which works well and makes simpler the piling of debris for burning at edges of clearings rather than where planting must occur.

Since tea is processed in Misiones factories there is no transport-spoilage problem as occurs with citrus fruit. Other drawbacks have appeared because the domestic market has experienced extraordinary price oscillations. Poor quality tea and over speculation characterized the operation in early years. Moreover, the presence of numerous small driers makes it difficult to control quality even when demand is stable — a problem which has also plagued yerba mate production in Misiones.

Lumbering was important long before the modern colonization period in Misiones, but difficulties with yerba mate have hastened development of this industry too. Tree production became noticeable between 1960 and 1965 when even the formerly open appearance of the Campo was altered by the planting of extensive eucalyptus groves. *Eucalyptus saligna* was found to mature in eight or nine years in Misiones, after which colonists realized approximately 700 pesos a ton. A good yield is 200 tons per ha, which farmers readily obtained. After about the same growing time, Paraná pine (*Araucaria angustofolia*) can be harvested for pulp. The Alto Paraná colonies find a ready pulp market at one of Argentina's two paper mills which is located just north of Monte Carlo. A plywood factory in Puerto Rico whose output was expanded during the 1960s is another boon to the wood industry. Since the yerba mate crisis, pioneers have begun to clear land for reforestation with these tree types, and, to a lesser extent, with *Pinus Elliottii* (slash pine) and *Melia azedarach* (*paraíso*), both of which are used in furniture making.

During the early 1960s Misiones began to produce 50 per cent of the plywood consumed in Argentina, and 25 per cent of the logs, posts, and fuel wood needed by the country. Because of good market conditions, approximately 20,000 ha were reforested, mostly on private land, and large areas of the Alto Paraná began to look exactly like sections of the Schwarzwald and of the Bayerischen Wald. Fortunately lumbering — one of the original and continuing occupations of people from the Waldhufendörfern of Brazil, Germany, Austria, and other places — is an economic activity with which Misiones pioneers are well prepared to cope.

Since 1959 colonists from Monte Carlo and other parts of Misiones have been able to obtain tree seeds without charge from the government. Public land designated specifically for forest exploitation can be colonized.[37] Settlers pay nothing down, have ten years to make payments, and must reforest 80 per cent of the land in that time, mainly with pines. Even with these inducements, attracting colonists to federal lands is hampered by remoteness and poor accessibility, especially in higher places like the Altiplano de Irigoyen where good pine growth is possible.

There are approximately 100 large *obrajes,* or lumber operations in Misiones, most of which have established sizeable permanent settlements. *Celulosa Argentina,* for example, employs and
houses more than 500 workers, has built many km of roads to its
forest plantings, and operates its own port near Monte Carlo
(*Puerto Piray*). There are also over 500 smaller processing centers
in the Province.

Logs are transported mainly by truck to the sawmills. Actually,
half the trucks in Misiones are used in the lumber business, but
a general lack of adequate transportation facilities still makes it
necessary to ship forest products via the expensive Alto Paraná
and Uruguay rivers. Because of the high cost of labor on the river
boats, fluvial traffic is used mainly for shipments over 200 km.
River prices are often above railway costs and, when this occurs,
wood products are shipped from Posadas to Buenos Aires by
train. Because of this peculiar situation Paraguayan lumber com-
petes easily with that from Misiones, and Argentina continues to
import wood. Since Argentina spends over $200,000,000 annually
to import wood products, there is strong hope that Misiones may
yet provide more of these vital materials to the nation through
the reforestation phase of the colonization program.

Cultural Problems and Decline of the Colony. Although crop
diversification and cooperatives have been successfully adopted
by colonists to combat economic difficulties, lack of educational
assistance from the host country caused much early resentment
among the colonists. This attitude was exploited, although generally unsuccessfully, during the rise of Hitler in Germany. For
instance, whereas the Argentine government refused to provide
acceptable school facilities, the German government understood
the plight of these sophisticated, formerly urban residents, and
offered aid, not, of course, without ulterior motives. In 1937 private
schools were built in Eldorado and Monte Carlo with money from
Germany. Not only were good educational facilities provided but
the schools were supplied with propaganda as well. The latter
helped deepen the rift already formed between colonist and host
country.[38] Later, with World War II under way, the Argentine
government prohibited classroom use of the German language
and finally confiscated all private schools. It even became difficult
for anyone to use German in public. Although the Argentine gov-

ernment paid for new private schools in 1965, and permitted half the teaching to be carried on in German, it appeared that the private educational system would not again hold the position of prestige it formerly enjoyed in the colony in spite of the undesirable propaganda associated with the old program. Thus, the school situation has never been entirely solved and the original educational rift has persisted through the post-war years.

Several other reasons for colonist resentment have occurred in Misiones. One is the fact that the German, Austrian, and Swiss pioneers have always been more interested in agricultural success than in the political control and management of colonies. In Monte Carlo, for example, political control passed into Argentine hands as soon as the colony had organized its local government. This has since been the case with but one brief exception. Although there is deep feeling about the political situation, the fault lies with the colonists rather than with the host country, which has provided the means for a democratic form of government. The greater interest and leadership of the Europeans for management of farm cooperatives rather than political affairs is made clear by comparing activities of Argentine colonists in these fields. For example, of four mayors between 1932 and 1966, three were Argentineans and one a German, whereas of eight presidents of the cooperative during the same period, seven were Germans and one a Swiss.[39]

Still another reason for deepening discontent among the colonists is based on economic discouragement in the Province. Although the German Federal Republic provides some assistance to the colonists, there is not sufficient aid to combat Argentine inflation, which has been serious since 1956. Because of the declining economy, numerous young people have been encouraged to depart from Monte Carlo and Eldorado, and will undoubtedly never return. The pastor of the Lutheran church in Monte Carlo and the head of the accounting section of the cooperative estimated that one hundred and twenty-five of the best young people left in the period 1964–66. Older colony leaders have become fearful that this exodus may not be halted. European and North American economic conditions have become too attractive, and some of the colony members have even begun to settle in Australia since that country pays transportation for qualified immigrants.

Educational and economic hardship notwithstanding, there are other motives which have added impetus to the general departure of people from Monte Carlo. One of the most serious is the scarcity of land for farming. The normal holding size is still only 25 ha, although much more than that is needed to earn a comfortable living. Thus, it is not economically feasible to subdivide property among the children of settlers. A few of the younger sons were fortunate enough to take over forested land which parents bought adjacent to their original farm plots. However, most parents were unable to save enough money to think of the future until many years had passed. By then all the lots in the colony had been sold and nearby land was no longer available. Fortunately, in 1935, when the second wave of land hunting began, a new private colony was opened along the north side of Monte Carlo; over three hundred farm lots were sold in this area, now called Colonia Laharrague. Although from the center of Monte Carlo to the most remote part of the new colony is only 15 km, families have been split and the inadequate 25-ha family size holding has been maintained. These circumstances have meant the creation of another set of problems identical to those faced by the mother colony: not only has it been extremely difficult for Laharrague pioneers to clear enough land out of the hilly 25-ha farm plots in order to mechanize, but there has been little opportunity to save sufficient money for improvements. Moreover, each farm, i.e., the parent's farm in Monte Carlo and the children's farm in Laharrague, must now function through the efforts of only part of the former family — a difficult task at best in tropical and semitropical rainforest areas where specialized agricultural techniques require that year around labor be employed for efficient farming. South of Monte Carlo 25-ha holdings have also been opened for sale since 1946 when the third wave of land buying began — this time in part for grandchildren of original pioneers. These lots are even farther away from Monte Carlo than is Laharrague, in the Tarumá section of the neighboring Colonia Caraguatay (Fig. 16). The same difficulties are present there: settlers cannot afford more than approximately 25 ha of land at prices of 10,000 pesos or more per ha; there is on the average only 60–70 per cent of cultivable land; labor and machinery costs are both so high and market prices so low that little effort can be made toward mechanization.[40]

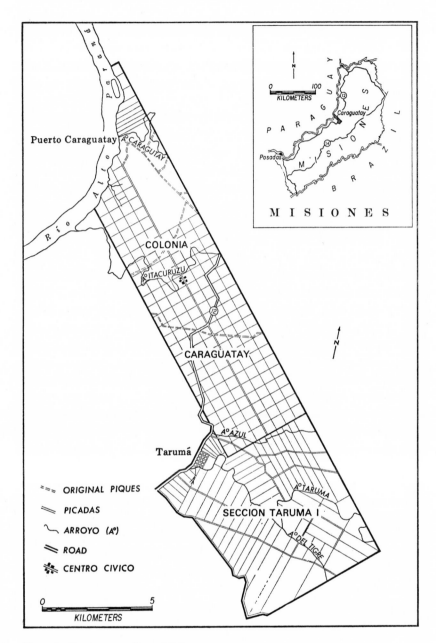

Fig. 16. Caraguatay colony, Misiones.

One other factor compounding the Monte Carlo exodus is the general lack of understanding of the inheritance laws in Argentina. Argentine civil law requires that after the death of a land owner property be divided equally between the remaining family head and the children. Since the officially recognized minimum economical farm size in Misiones is 25 ha, and the average holding size is the same, subdivision of farm property should be avoided at all costs. Although some widowed settlers have managed by paying the children for their share of the land, this has not always been possible. Unfortunately, when land has to be subdivided, the combined lawyer's fee and inheritance tax cost almost half the assessed value of the holding. Often land must be sold to meet these expenses, and a risky subdivision of 25-ha lots has already begun in the Province.

In order to prevent the uneconomical breakup of holdings that financial need can precipitate, colonists have often "sold" their land before death to a trusted friend who later "sells" the same land back to one child of the original owner. Such action has permitted many 25-ha holdings to remain intact in practice, although hardship has been created where personality conflicts develop. There have even been instances of physical violence in the colony of Monte Carlo over these inheritance practices. It is perhaps characteristic of colonization in Latin America, whether private or governmental, that foreign settlers have not been informed about inheritance laws until too late. Settlers in Monte Carlo did not know enough about Argentine laws until after 1960 when the first *escribano*, or notary public, joined the colony to find out that the civil code in Argentina permits *intervivos* trust deeds by which land holders may give their property to another family member before death to avoid lawyer's fees and forced subdivision (Law 11,357, Articles 1,789–1,868). Even today, the vast majority of colonists are still unaware of this equitable solution to a vexing problem. It is to be hoped that knowledge will spread, but as long as such a solution is not made clear, or perhaps because it is already too late, colonists will continue to leave the area.

WALDHUFEN SETTLEMENT VARIATIONS

Field inspections among the previously discussed colonies of Puerto Rico, Eldorado, and Monte Carlo reveal some fundamental differences among the original Waldhufen settlements of Misiones. There are also some subtle differences between these colonies and their medieval counterparts in Germany which have resulted from adaptations made to suit the Misiones landscape. Since all of the changes are interrelated and affect economic growth, it seems best to analyze the processes of their formation at this point. In Misiones the small-scale differences in landforms, the difficulties of accessibility, and the limiting nature of colony boundaries have all produced changes in the settlement form. Thus the Waldhufen settlements of this region are smaller and more crowded than many of those in the Old World. The landscape consists of various adjacent but individual Waldhufen colonies whose shorter lots are easy to recognize on detailed maps (Fig. 17). Usually one of these — the central one for a particular area and often situated on an interfluve — becomes the location for the main Waldhufen*dorf*, or settlement village, whereas the rest are tributary and have only a few lower order or no central-place functions; hence the term Waldhufenweiler, or Waldhufen hamlet for these smaller units. As each tributary Waldhufenweiler is surveyed and land is cleared, the forest recedes from its valley to the adjacent interfluve where it meets the same phenomenon from the next valley. In Monte Carlo, where nearly all the land has been cleared, several merging Waldhufenweiler surround a long central Waldhufendorf. Eldorado developed in the same way, but the main village has already expanded laterally because settlers have become wealthy enough to buy land to form what may ultimately become a rectangular "town." Because such a process of urbanization is only beginning in Monte Carlo (Pl. 8) it is suggested that its more primitive central place be classified as Stage 2 in the development process. Eldorado would be at Stage 3, and any incipient Waldhufendorf, i.e., Waldhufenweiler, such as that more recently begun by the Japanese between Puerto Rico and Monte Carlo, where few central-place functions exist and where homes are still located near a stream rather than along the road, would be clearly recognized as a Stage 1 colony. (See p. 172, Pl. 6, and Fig. 17).

Since in Misiones the main Dorf is often located on an interfluve and individual satellite colonies occasionally exist in adjacent valleys, these Waldhufen settlements resemble both the Black

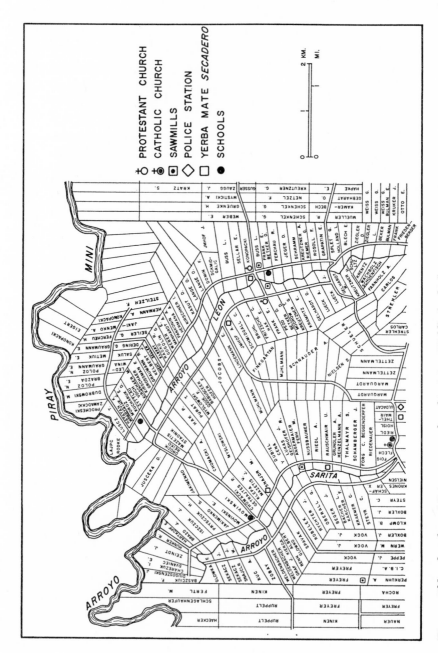

Fig. 17. Eldorado colony, Misiones, examples of incipient Waldhufendörfer.

Forest and Mühlviertel types, as well as the Erzgebirge variety. Although the relationships between landforms and settlement forms are similar to those in the Old World, there are important distinctions. First, in Misiones the density of hilltops is greater and valleys are shorter than in Germany. This accounts for numerous tributary Waldhufenweiler which have need of ony one main village, or later, urban center. The smaller number of settlements with central places compared with European counterparts makes for more efficient regional development, provided land clearing and road building occur rapidly and uniformly throughout the early pioneering phase. Second, the precise surveying of colony long-lot boundaries prior to settlement makes the Argentine Waldhufen settlements much more regular in appearance. Thus microrelief features have less influence on settlement form, but the practical aspects of surveying with straight lines have overridden to some extent consideration of this factor. The custom of surveying lots prior to land sales has also resulted in more uniform lot lengths than are generally found in Europe, where rear lot boundaries varied with the land-opening activity of individual settlers over longer periods of time. Third, cottage industries, developed in the Waldhufendörfern of Germany, have not come to characterize the linear villages of Misiones. The reason for this major difference is that in Europe the long winter months make for less farm productivity and prevent most outside activities, hence the time is used to make wood carvings, clocks, Christmas ornaments, etc. These are later sold to tourists and in the cities. The climate in Misiones, by contrast, permits agricultural activities the year around and is not conducive to development of industry of this type. Nevertheless a few cuckoo clocks and furniture items have been made and sold far and wide in Misiones for good prices. The unusual number of artisans in these colonies could still form the basis for a hand industry to act as an economic cushion when crop prices fail.

It is commonly believed in Argentina that the German pioneers who came to the colonies of the Alto Paraná were farmers well prepared to develop a rural economy. However this is not true, since approximately 60 per cent of the settlers in Eldorado and 80 per cent of those in Monte Carlo came from the highly urbanized areas of Berlin, Hamburg, Leipzig, and Stuttgart. Even in Puerto

Rico, where mainly German-Brazilian farmers settled, nearly 20 per cent of the pioneers had an urban background. The farming success of these "city" residents is explained by cultural factors. First, the average city resident in Germany is close to the rural landscape. The German practice whereby even city apartment dwellers rent garden lands (*Schrebergärten*) speaks for this closeness. In fact, nearly one-half the non-rural dwellers in Germany own small amounts of farm land (0.5–2.5 ha). There is even a special term applied to these people in Germany, *Arbeiterbauern*.[41] The fact that the interior of practically any German city home contains dozens of plants indicates a continued closeness to the planting idea. Second, the German people have a long history of organizational experience. Time and again the combined voluntary efforts of colonists made it possible to build schools, churches, roads, and agricultural cooperatives during the critical early years. Third, nearly everyone desired to escape permanently the persecution of wars and inflation which beset the Old World, and they were determined to succeed. Finally, settlers with common backgrounds were in physical proximity in the three colonies. Close cultural links with neighbors made it far easier for pioneers to cooperate when mutual effort was required. Even in the largest colony of Eldorado (110,000 ha) which harbored wealthy settlers of different religions, Catholics and Protestants formed voluntary areal subdivisions (Fig. 17). These cultural factors in combination meant that the colonies of the Alto Paraná, which were more remote than others in Misiones, made rapid progress.

Monte Carlo provides the classic example of the advantages accruing from voluntary subdivision of settlers within a colony — a technique that promotes especially amiable and rapid growth conditions. The German-Brazilians, who were considered old-fashioned and were sometimes harassed by the more cosmopolitan immigrants, all chose to settle in Línea Ita-Curuzú at the far end of the main picada. Others went with close friends to the numerous separate valleys such as the *Schwabental*, i.e., Línea Bonita. During the late 1930s, when a wave of Wolhynian colonists from Poland arrived, a new section was created for them. Although its official name was La Horqueta, it has long been called *Neu Warschau*. Eldorado, because of its greater size, has even more numerous community subdivisions, the most important of which are:

Bayerntal, Biberacher Tal, Dänin Ecke, Schweizer Tal, Württem-
berger Tal, Apostelschneise, Schwabental, and Schöntal (Polish).

ON THE ORIGINS OF MISIONES WALDHUFEN SETTLEMENTS

The question of the origins of Waldhufen settlements in Misiones does not have a clear answer. Although Waldhufen lots were
first established by mixed groups of settlers on public lands, it
seems likely that this was done mainly by people of German background who had already lived in Waldhufendörfern in southern
Brazil. This was also the case on private lands in Misiones where
Culmey and his German-Brazilians pioneered at a later date.
There exists the possibility that the Waldhufen idea was introduced in some places by colonists directly from Germany (Mecking, Colonia Liebig). Even though the total number of people
acquainted with Waldhufendörfern in any given colony may not
have been large, experience in Puerto Rico, Eldorado, and Colonia
Liebig (described below) indicates that when only a few settlers
objected to the damero form, the Waldhufen plan was quickly sub-
stituted. Certainly the ease with which the Wurstsiedlungen, the
sausage settlements, were accepted was due to the strong cultural
influence of long-lot field and/or settlement forms in nearly every
part of Germany, whether rural or urban. We know that Misiones
colonists came from practically every part of Germany that has
a record of either long-lot or -hufen settlement, i.e., Wald-, Moor-,
Marschhufen, land history. In this regard, the author has verified
colonist origins from the lower Rhine, Weser-Bergland, Erzgebirge,
northern Schwarzwald, Vogtland, northern Austria, and other regions where Waldhufendörfer are found, as well as from rural and
urban areas characterized by other types of long-lot field or
garden forms (central Schwarzwald, Vierlande).[42]

A more difficult but related question still to be answered by land
investigators is that posed by the presence of Waldhufen settlements in southern Brazil. Here the record is much older and even
harder to trace. German settlers were officially invited to southern
Brazil in 1824 when they established the colony of São Leopoldo
25 km north of Pôrto Alegre. Only from that time on did numerous
Waldhufen settlements appear in the forested land of Rio Grande
do Sul, Santa Catarina, and Paraná states. Despite this, one authority, Leo Waibel, is sometimes quoted for his suggestion that

the Waldhufen colonies of southern Brazil were not introduced by German settlers.[43] Waibel's reasoning was that the settlers came from west and south Germany where, according to him, there were no Waldhufendörfer. It should be pointed out that this work was published posthumously in German and that Waibel had been more careful about his assessment of the problem in an earlier study which appeared in Portuguese as "Principios da Colonização Euro-péia no sul do Brasil."[44] Here he stated that there were settlers from northern, western, and southern Germany where Waldhu-fendörfer are almost unknown. (He does not mention probable acquaintance with other long-lot forms.) On the other hand, Al-fred Hettner, who visited the German-Brazilian colonies before the turn of the century, stated on the basis of existing records of colonist origins, that settlers came from "every German landscape" and were organized into colonies by government and private groups.[45] He went on to say that the organization of German set-tlements was carried out in the same fashion nearly everywhere "after the style of Waldhufen colonies which are found in many parts of the central German mountain region."[46] It may also be pointed out that sizeable numbers of the earliest settlers originated in the Hunsrück, Schlesien, and Hinteren Pommern districts where linear settlements, if not actual Waldhufendörfer, and their closely related forms such as *Hagenhufendörfer*, are well known.[47]

Since the appearance of H. Zschocke's book in 1963 dealing with Waldhufen remnants found along the lower Rhine, it is evi-dent that the distribution of nineteenth-century linear settlements (especially Waldhufen types) in Germany was broader than it has been during the present century and that much more is known about these forms than even in Waibel's time.[48] All things con-sidered, it is probable that some nineteenth-century settlers even from western Germany were well acquainted with linear settle-ment forms and could have introduced them to southern Brazil. As the historical record makes it quite clear that the earliest of-ficial and private colony surveying in southern Brazil was carried out by Germans, it is also possible that surveyors were responsible for the introduction of Waldhufen settlements.[49] In any case, judging from examples in Misiones, a relatively small number of colonists with Waldhufen experience could have organized their

own settlements or may even have convinced Brazilian land planners of the merits of their long-lot form.

It is sometimes suggested that the Brazilian government imposed the Waldhufen form on all ethnic colonial groups in south
Brazil. However, in the earliest years of colonization in southern
Brazil the government specified only that lot boundaries run according to the eight-part wind rose, i.e., as simply as possible.
The rest was left to the surveyor. Later, long-lot fields were officially established on some individual farms surrounding agglomerated settlements.[50] It may be that in southern Brazil even this
official field pattern came about because of the influence of German settlers, many of whom established Waldhufen holdings
along picadas prior to the arrival of government surveyors just as
has been done on state lands in Misiones. On the other hand, it
is certain that the line village typical of Waldhufendörfer was not
imposed as a central-place form to serve these long-lot fields.
Italians, Germans, and probably others were settled in damero
villages.[51] In some places the record indicates that colonists originally formed cluster villages (*Haufendörfer*) in which people
lived in a compact settlement but farmed long lots strung along
the road. However, Indian attacks on women and children while
men were away in the fields forced pioneer families to move out
onto their long lots and hence to create the Waldhufen form of
settlement.[52] Evidently Waldhufen settlements were also created
voluntarily, as at Dois Irmãos, Ana Rech, Farroupilha, and Em-
boaba, some km north of São Leopoldo.[53]

So far as I am aware, the observation that Waldhufen colonies
in southern Brazil first emerged after the appearance of German
settlers is also true of Misiones where ethnic Europeans (German-
Brazilians) and possibly new European immigrants established
Waldhufenweiler and Waldhufendörfer in the areas already partly
settled under damero surveys.[54]

CARAGUATAY: A GERMAN DAMERO SETTLEMENT

The colony of Caraguatay (pronounced "Caraguatahee") was
founded in 1925 by the La Misionera lumber company of Buenos
Aires. Approximately 5,000 ha were surveyed and administered
by Charles H. Benson, a retired railroad engineer who had spent

many years in the Argentine. Although Benson was familiar with the Monte Carlo project which his colony bordered, he surveyed Caraguatay along damero lines. The result was predictable: 35 per cent of the colony's 195 lots had no running water, and 65 per cent had no access to roads (Fig. 16). The first settlers were Germans from Europe who were warned by the colonists in Monte Carlo to buy only where water was available. Only a few lots were sold by La Misionera and a kind of checkerboard settlement occurred. This form, therefore, was not caused by Company refusal to sell certain lots while withholding others in order to bring about land speculation.

Later, as the few scattered colonists in Caraguatay made good, they spent savings to purchase adjacent lots for their children. Some wealthy owners bought up to 6 or more adjacent farm plots of 25 ha each. Other pioneers who could afford to buy and develop several lots simultaneously have been strongly attracted to Caraguatay in recent years because of more favorable land prices. Gradually large-sized holdings have evolved which now represent this colony's major farm type and which make the landscape vastly different from the neighboring one at Monte Carlo. Approximately 50 per cent of the colony's present property holders are absentee owners and live elsewhere in Argentina, or in Europe.

In spite of this development, growth remained exceptionally slow in Caraguatay because of the expense of building wells and roads on private property. Because of the isolation of settlers and because they were wealthier to begin with, there was no cooperative established in Caraguatay until long after those in Monte Carlo and Eldorado had been founded. When this finally happened in 1933 there were already 10 German-Polish families and several other farm families with small holdings who were responsible for attracting a branch office of the Monte Carlo cooperative.

Although Benson left the colony in 1933, the Company continued to offer lots until the mid-1940s, when nearly all land was gone even though much of it was still inaccessible and too rough to be developed. The arrival of a government road in 1933 from Posadas helped stimulate progress in the colony. Caraguatay was crossed diagonally and linked with Monte Carlo for the first time. It was only after this that building the branch cooperative became possible. Gradually the Company and the colonists built more roads and made more of the isolated areas accessible.

Benson originally planned an urban center for Caraguatay which was located over 4 km from the Alto Paraná River. However, its great distance and isolation from many of the lots that were actually settled, the rugged terrain chosen for the townsite, and the slow growth of the colony have prevented its development. Although the urban site was on the main road through Caraguatay, colonists elected to open various places of business at far-flung intervals along this route. The first store appeared at km 4.5 from the river in late 1927. A school was erected at km 4 in 1928, the cooperative building at km 6.5 in 1933. The police station was established in 1936 near km 4.5, and a postal office at km 6 in 1940, where the original town was planned. An Evangelical Lutheran church was built in 1944 at km 2 after holding services for seventeen years in the nearby schoolhouse. Later, another school was built at km 11. This natural development of a Waldhufen village in a damero colony might have been prevented had the Company or the colonists understood the whole settlement process better. Because the form of the settlement was given little attention, the wide spacing between farm holdings (500 meters) separated the randomly placed schools, church, businesses, and normal urban functions that were built as colonists became linked with the road, even farther apart than they would be in a normal Waldhufendorf. In 1960, Sr. Fausch, one of the leaders of the colony, attempted to solve this problem by donating land on one of his lots near where the cooperative had been built, so that at least the primary urban needs could be met at one place. His offer was accepted and the "Centro Cívico" was built. Unhappily, the land along this section of the road is steep and there is little room for future expansion (Pl. 5), with the result that some colonists feel frustrated and complain bitterly about the entire situation.

After Monte Carlo residents had purchased lots in Laharrague and had turned southward in the third buying wave during the 1940s, the La Misionera Company was convinced that its original damero survey had been a mistake and decided to open new land south and east of Caraguatay by using the Waldhufendorf method. In 1946, a surveyor from Monte Carlo was employed to demarcate ninety-six long lots, all of which were sold within a few years in a subdivision called Tarumá I (Fig. 16). In 1958 Tarumá II was surveyed and was so successful that two years later Tarumá III was prepared. Many of the farm plots have been sold to Argentine citizens, as very few foreigners have arrived in Misiones since the beginning of World War II. It appears evident that the ordinary colonist of Argentine extraction appreciates the advantages of the Waldhufendorf as much as the European colonist, provided he has some opportunity to learn how the new settlement type functions either from neighboring settlements or experienced colonists.

OTHER FOREIGN COLONIZATION ATTEMPTS

Of the numerous private colonization attempts in Misiones that have followed Puerto Rico, Monte Carlo, Eldorado, and Caragua-tay, the Neu-Karlsruhe and Victoria settlements merit special attention. Each of these smaller colonies has contributed in its own way to knowledge about successful settlement techniques. The first, Neu-Karlsruhe, was established in 1923 by one of the numerous colonization organizations founded in Germany during the 1920s. The Siedlungs- und Handelsgesellschaft Neu-Karlsruhe (Eingetragener Verein) began as an agricultural society which had as its main object the formation of a farm settlement in Latin America.[55] Little was known about the hard facts of life in the interior of Latin America, and settlers, mainly idealists with almost no practical experience in farming, planned a damero settlement to be located in Paraguay, where they mistakenly thought they could harness electric power from the Iguazú Falls.[56] Most of the colonists were from the northern Schwarzwald region; only 5 of the 165 who left Hamburg in 1924 and settled in Misiones were farmers. Half the settlers were unmarried young men. Only after leaving Germany did the group learn that there were insufficient funds for carrying out their plans.

Once in Argentina the fate of these would-be colonists was favored by a government proposal of substantial tax reduction for any private landowner who would subdivide his property for colonization. This prompted the English Liebig's Extract of Meat Company to offer one of their *estancias* (estates) on the border between Misiones and Corrientes to the Neu-Karlsruhe group.[57] The name of the project was changed to Colonia Liebig and the surveys were readied for a damero settlement. Luckily, a few colony members realized that this settlement form resulted in roads and property boundaries that crossed the land without regard to terrain features, so "manche Lotes gar kein Wasser hatten, während andere von einem Bachlauf in zwei Teile zerschnitten wurden" ("many lots had no water whereas others were split in two by a stream").[58] So strong a protest was lodged that the farm plots were all redesigned and surveyed according to the Waldhufen principle.

The Liebig Company originally permitted settlers to rent land for the first five years, with purchase rights thereafter. Ten years were allowed for making property payments. By 1934 none of the one hundred and sixty-five colonists had been able to comply with these requirements and the Liebig Company distinguished itself from most private colonization enterprises by lowering the land price 25 per cent, by cancelling all company store debts, and by allowing 20 years for payment of the remaining land debts.[59] With this kind of aid the colony managed to survive, but without the prosperity evident in other German colonies in Misiones.

Two economic factors involving yerba mate made difficult the success of the colony. First, the yields of this forest plant turned out to be much lower than along the Alto Paraná — a fact which is true of the entire Campo landscape. The reasons for this are: the natural thinness of most of the tierra colorada soils in the Campo; the presence of greater quantities of sandstone derived soils than in the Selva; and previous erosive exploitation of Campo soils during colonial times.

The second factor was that harvests of the Colonia Liebig settlers were initiated after 1926 when yerba mate prices had already begun to drop. In 1931 colonists were forced to diversify by raising rice — a crop they learned about from Polish settlers in the Apóstoles area. By 1934 this crop was raised everywhere in the colony on small plots of 4–6 ha. Water was brought from streams by homemade canals, although electric pumps eventually replaced these less efficient methods. During the late 1930s tung trees were also added, but yields were considerably below those of the Selva. Although tea and reforestation now provide extra cash income, nearly all attempts at diversification have resulted in below-average yields.

As economic conditions worsened in the colony, an agricultural cooperative was founded which was the first formally organized cooperative in Misiones (1926). The Raiffeisen-styled organization was successful from the start, as might have been expected from the Württemberg background of the settlers. The experience of some of them in these matters, along with timely help from the Liebig Company, enabled them to succeed in spite of serious economic misfortune. In fact, many colonists were able to mechanize with small tractors and other farm machinery some years later, as well as to build small but comfortable homes on their farms. Furthermore, some Germans had bought adjacent lots for friends or relatives who never came to the colony because of its initial hardships; these lots were later sold profitably to people of Polish, Ukrainian, and Argentine extraction from Apóstoles and Azara. Many of these late-comers have become modestly successful and now help manage the cooperative.

The first head of the Colonia Liebig cooperative, W. Ostermann, initiated the idea of uniting all cooperatives in Misiones, a project which became reality in 1930 in L.N. Alem at the Hotel zu den Sieben Schwaben. The participating cooperatives were those of Colonia Liebig, Bonpland, Rincón de Bonpland, L.N. Alem, Monte Carlo, and Picada Rusa.[60] Since that time, the Federación de Cooperativas Agrícolas de Misiones, Ltd., has expanded to include over thirty cooperatives and more than 15,000 members, and has been extraordinarily successful. Its first president was C. Lautenschläger, formerly head of the Monte Carlo cooperative.

The Liebig cooperative has also attracted attention by its continuous and intelligent effort to promote agricultural youth cooperatives in order to prepare for better management of farms. The spirit of this youth movement has already spread to various parts of Misiones and is a feature of colonization which other settlements in Latin America should adopt.

The competition from these cooperative ventures in Misiones, and the demands of the colonists' children for more land in the Colonia Liebig prompted the Company to sell the remainder of its farm plots and to cease operations in 1965. Thus the Company

itself did not succeed in the long run in Misiones, but it is evident that its colony would also have joined other Campo members
of the "Poor Zone" had it not been for the combination of Waldhufendorf and Raiffeisen cooperative, and a helpful Liebig policy
through the years.

Victoria. The second private colony of special note, that of
Victoria located just north of Eldorado, was founded by A. J.
Schwelm in 1932. Schwelm's purpose in opening a fourth settlement along the Alto Paraná was to establish a British colony.
Fifty-one families from Great Britain settled in Victoria, but the
colony never prospered and was Schwelm's only failure. Most of
the neighboring settlers in Eldorado and Monte Carlo are agreed
that one of the main difficulties was isolation. Victorians, for example, had to travel overland under great hardship to Eldorado
to reach the only doctor, and at times could not cross the raging
Piray-Guazú River. In 1970 this river still flooded the only low
bridge crossing and halted traffic for lengthy periods. Until about
1946, many a colonist felt forced to leave permanently for medical reasons in spite of the closeness of the Colonia Eldorado.[61] A
second difficulty was that the colonists, unlike those from Eldorado and Monte Carlo, were almost entirely without agricultural
experience (see p. 161). Actually, the Company, which had seen
the success of urban colonists in Eldorado and Monte Carlo, advertised in London in 1935 that "owing to the fertility of the soil and
the technical assistance which newcomers receive, a knowledge
of farming is not essential."[62] They were wrong. A third factor
in the failure of the colony was the desire on the part of romantic
settlers to be "tropical planters," after the fashion of Empire com-
patriots from India. They wanted to pass up the essential pioneering stage, which was not possible in Misiones, and there were
simply insufficient numbers of experienced settlers involved to
convince the large majority to believe otherwise. Neither the fact
that these city people arrived at a time when it was absolutely
necessary to diversify and to grow more complicated crops than
yerba mate, nor the lack of a cooperative in the earliest period
helped matters at all.

Of the initial 51 settlers, 17 had sold out by 1946 and several
others had become absentee land owners.[63] Since 1946 the remaining families have gradually departed, most of them selling their

land to children of colonists from Eldorado and Monte Carlo. To-day Victoria is largely German and looks like a small version of the other Alto Paraná colonies.

The conclusion that must be drawn from the experience of the Victoria colony is that failure was due largely if not entirely to human factors. The physical geography of this colony is in nearly every respect similar to that of Eldorado, Monte Carlo, and Puerto Rico. In fact, physical conditions are superior to those found in Colonia Liebig which has been a more successful settlement than Victoria. Perhaps the explanation lies in the misunderstanding of local conditions by both colonization agency and colonists. Victoria was founded later than any of the other settlements on the Alto Paraná, which meant that pioneers arrived falsely believing that they could live on the profits of "green gold," i.e., yerba mate. In reality this was no longer possible, at least to the degree it had been a few years earlier, and most pioneers did not know enough to attempt crop diversification and so were forced to live at a much lower level than that to which they had been accustomed. The fact that Victoria has been successfully farmed by people better acquainted with rural conditions illustrates with certainty that the original pioneers should not have been brought to Victoria. Had most of the London settlers been selected for possessing agricultural backgrounds they probably not only would have realized the need to diversify crops, but to form road building and farm cooperatives as well. Thus the care and understanding with which a colonization agency selects would-be pioneers from urban areas may become the critical ingredient in opening remote forest regions under difficult circumstances.

GARUHAPE: A JAPANESE WALDHUFEN SETTLEMENT

A more recently founded settlement in Misiones, and one of the most successful in its initial years, is the Japanese colony of Garuhapé. This settlement is illustrative of the fact that modern pioneers can apply many of the favorable ingredients of land opening discussed in the rest of this chapter in order to hasten the pioneering process and insure its viability.

Initial Planning. Preliminary arrangements to send Japanese colonists to Misiones were made in 1957 by the Kaigai Ijyu Jigyodan (KIJ), the official colonization agency of the Japanese government. The KIJ considered Misiones a desirable region because foreign settlers with special ethnic and linguistic problems would be less subject to criticism in such a remote place. Moreover, the cultural landscape of Misiones with its varied pioneer elements was more receptive to the establishment of any new group than older rural areas and therefore offered an atmosphere that would not slow production of sizeable quantities of commercial food and industrial crops. The steady success of the Japanese colony in Misiones during its early years reflects the wisdom of these guidelines. Other factors which contributed to success were the intentional avoidance of mistakes committed by earlier colonists and acceptance of the best features of older pioneer settlements.

Settlement Site and Form. Selection of a settlement site in Misiones was accomplished with the assistance of various long-time Japanese and other residents in the Province. These people convinced the KIJ not to settle on public land, because of inaccessibility, the squatter problem, and official use of the damero settlement form. An examination of private lands was therefore undertaken until a 3,000-ha site was purchased from the La Misionera Company. The land was called Garuhapé, Sección Luján B, and was situated about midway between Puerto Rico and Monte Carlo (Fig. 18). Luján B, as the colony is known locally, had frontage on the Alto Paraná River and along Ruta 12, which links all the river colonies with Posadas. The river transportation outlet afforded security against bad weather conditions along Ruta 12. Although Puerto Rico and Monte Carlo served as important local markets, shipment of agricultural products to Buenos Aires had already begun by the early 1960s.

A major advantage to the Japanese in Luján B was the Waldhufen settlement form possessed by the colony. The Japanese were made quite aware of the fact that even though the Garuhapé area receives an average of 1,700 mm of annual rainfall, wells would be necessary to supply livestock with water during periods of drought. Unfortunately, wells have to be dynamited through bedrock in this area and are so costly that Japanese settlers could not have afforded them.[64] It was equally apparent that a fair distribution of the variable slopes on this land was essential to success of the colony. Access to the main avenue of communication (Ruta 12) and later to electricity, telephone lines, and other

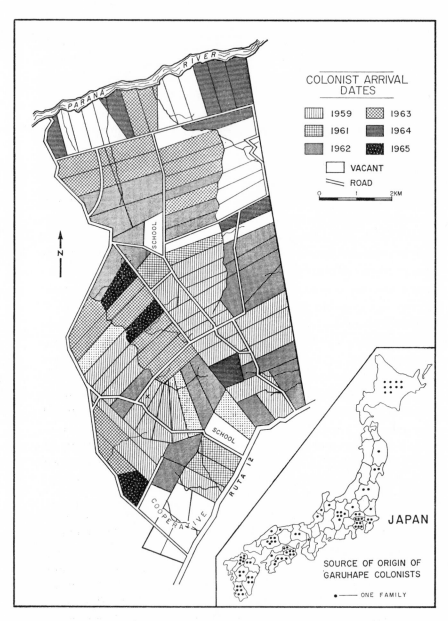

Fig. 18. Garuhapé colony, Misiones, Luján "B," colonist arrival dates.

services which would be provided along this route was considered important. The Japanese were also aware that medical care, shopping, and social intercourse among colonists were all made easier by a linear form of settlement. The fact that government and private lands are in juxtaposition in Misiones, a reflection of the narrowness of the Province and its peculiar land tenure development, was a great advantage to the Japanese who therefore had no difficulty in understanding the differences between the damero and Waldhufen settlement systems. Although they did not themselves survey nach Wasser, or according to the topography of the area, they were attracted to Luján B by the fact that the original owners had a surveyor from Monte Carlo design a long-lot colony.

Selection and Management of Colonists. The Japanese were not only careful about selection of settlement form, but of colonists as well. The choice of people with agricultural experience makes less significant the statistic that some 30 per cent of the settlers in Luján B came from cities in Japan. Colonists were selected from a wide range of Japanese landscapes, just as was true for the German settlers in Monte Carlo and Eldorado; yet the influence of variable homeland conditions does not seem to have had adverse effects on the success of individual settlers in Misiones.

Other Factors. Other reasons for the rapid initial success of Japanese settlers in Argentina included: the practice of crop diversification with Misiones plants as well as with vegetables and rice, crops formerly raised in Japan; the invitation of colonists with previous experience in Latin America to join the project — twelve settlers who spoke some Spanish and who were familiar with American agriculture were dispersed among the others; and the unusual suitability of the Japanese family structure for pioneer settlement, as is explained below.

The close family organization practiced by all Japanese makes for great efficiency in carrying out land opening tasks. For example, the Japanese keep accurate and complete records of most economic progress as a matter of course. The family book, the *nikki*, is therefore a continuous source of valuable data such as profits and losses, weather records, travel, and even character references. Distribution of labor is clear and unquestioned among these people and generally there are few cases of individuals accused of wasting time or of not carrying their share of the work.

In the past such customs have contributed to the rapid advance of the Japanese in Latin America, but have also earned them extreme criticism, sometimes outright clashes with their neighbors, and a tendency to withdraw into isolated groups.

Leaders of the new Misiones settlement tried from the start to eliminate obvious cultural differences between themselves and the local populace. Women stopped carrying children on their backs as they did in Japan, and work kimonos and other Japanese apparel were never worn outside the home. Adoption of Western house styles, children's names, eating utensils, and food habits characterized the settlement. By the mid-1960s, for example, a typical Japanese table setting exhibited Italian dishes common in Argentina (*pasta*) and at the same time imported seaweed (*nori*) and various types of fish. The settlement of Puerto Rico quickly became the supply center for most of these foods, including frozen fish which was regularly ordered from Buenos Aires. In return, the new settlers supplied fresh vegetables to Puerto Rico and Monte Carlo where well-to-do colonists no longer wished to raise them. These contacts improved business conditions in the area and helped the Japanese to overcome important cultural problems to the advantage of the Province.

There were too few settlers in Luján B to initiate a group enterprise for land clearing, house construction, seed purchases, and extra planting and harvesting costs. Therefore the Japanese government organized in 1960 a Raiffeisen-type cooperative with loan facilities. Because of such assistance, the Japanese pioneers progressed more rapidly than the Germans of Monte Carlo who had to clear their own land, build shelters, and undertake agriculture without any help for twelve years before a cooperative was founded. It is apparent that good location of the colony with regard to roads and markets, proper attention to settlement form, careful selection of colonists, and assistance with the early organization of a cooperative enabled the Japanese to produce commercial crops almost from the beginning of their pioneer experience.

Agriculture. Crop production at Luján B was organized by an amalgamation of Japanese and Argentine farm methods. Paddy rice, soya, tea, and vegetables were raised in the Japanese manner. Women and older children worked with men in the fields as they did in Japan. By contrast, orchard crops such as tung, oranges, and other trees were planted, weeded, and harvested with Paraguayan labor. The two systems worked effectively because the hired labor was managed by the cooperative. Otherwise the language barrier would have prevented communications and the Japanese could not easily have continued such a diversified program.

Commercial crop production was enhanced by experimentation with new plants, animals, and farming methods on 40 ha reserved for this purpose near the cooperative headquarters. The success of this approach was attested to by the early adoption, in addition to the new crops, of black and white cows (*Holando argentino*) and of pigs by nearly all colonists. The experimental program provided a constant motivation to mechanize both in order to improve farm efficiency and to eliminate as much outside labor as possible. The role of the cooperative in market experiments was significant and by 1965 resulted in shipment of some six truckloads of vegetables monthly to Puerto Rico and Monte Carlo, 300 tons of tobacco yearly, 2,000 tons of oranges yearly, and increasing amounts of Japanese rice (*mochigame*) and mung beans (*azuki*) to Buenos Aires.

Pioneer farmers in Misiones have usually planted tobacco in new clearings because of the good yields for the first two years and because of favorable market conditions.[65] Although European colonists have given up tobacco as soon as possible because of tedious work requirements, the Japanese have been willing to continue the difficult weeding and pruning tasks. Colonists in Luján B have managed to produce approximately 2 tons per ha, almost twice normal Misiones yields. With appropriate fertilization methods several such colonies could become a major source of tobacco for the Argentine market.[66]

While settlers raised maize, manioc, and vegetables for subsistence, and tobacco for cash, the cooperative provided them with sufficient tung trees for transplanting on cleared land. Tea was planted instead of tung if no Paraguayan laborers were available. Since tea was harvested the third year, it produced a cash crop just as tobacco gave out. Tung, on the other hand, did not mature for four years, but the care and harvesting were simpler than for tea. The wise pioneer planted both crops knowing that a diversified base is good insurance against a selective market decline. In this regard, it is fortunate that the Japanese were not able to count on the traditional cash crop of Misiones, i.e., yerba mate, because of the latter's steady decline in price. Not surprisingly, awareness of the long-lasting yerba mate crisis provided constant motivation to experiment with new crops.

During the third year of land clearing the Japanese frequently planted trees for lumber, furniture, or paper pulp. It is not unusual to find on a typical farm several ha of *Pinus Elliottii* (slash pine) and *Araucaria angustifolia* (Paraná pine) for lumber, *Melia azedarach (paraíso)* for furniture, and *Eucalyptus saligna* for paper pulp.

The fourth year several ha of citrus fruit, usually oranges, several of tobacco, reforestation, and pasture grass were planted. At this time tung could be harvested and some new acreage cleared.

Approximately five years were required before sufficient cash returns from harvests allowed colonists to begin to pay debts. The proceeds from tobacco and other annuals were applied toward land clearing which annually cost some 5,000 pesos per ha. Eradication of ants (*Atta sexdens*) on new clearings required another 1,000 pesos per ha. Because of these expenses, the cooperative did not ask for payments on loans until the fifth year of residence in Luján B. From that time on, income increased steadily each year: by the eighth or ninth year the colonist sold oranges and eucalyptus plantings; by the tenth or eleventh year pine trees were harvested and added another source of income. The pines and eucalyptus were marketed for the manufacture of plywood at the factory in Puerto Rico, and for pulp north of Monte Carlo at one of Argentina's two paper mills.

Land Titles. One of the difficulties of pioneer settlement which the Japanese managed to avoid is poor land titling. Lack of titles and delayed titling have produced so much insecurity in Misiones as to foster squatter settlement, especially as noted on state lands. In the Japanese colony clear titles were assured and no difficulties arose. On the other hand, land inheritance practices can influence seriously the development of any colony. It is not yet clear how Argentine civil law will effect the Japanese, although the results could be similar to those in Monte Carlo. If colony leaders had stopped land sales in order to hold the rest of the farm plots for children of original pioneers there would be some hope for future expansion of Luján B. However, most of the land was sold and prices rose so rapidly in the surrounding area that purchase of extra holdings near Garuhapé appeared doubtful during the late 1960s. Yet if nearby land is not available to the children of colonists, the disintegration of the settlement, abetted by rising Argentine inflation and an exodus of too many original families, could rapidly eliminate the beneficial effects of this much needed agricultural settlement.

Other Difficulties. Japanese colonization efforts have brought about harmony between the new pioneer settlement at Garuhapé and the physical landscape of the Alto Paraná region. But there are certain external difficulties which threaten progress of the colony. These are Argentine inflation, the training and education of children, and the proximity of the colony to an international border.

Pioneers arrived in Misiones at a time when they purchased dollars to repay their cooperative and other loans for 80 pesos per dollar. By 1970 the official exchange rate reached 251 pesos per dollar and the annual rate of inflation was approximately 10 per cent. Serious discontent among settlers resulted which could probably be relieved only if the Japanese authorities decided to permit repayment of loans in pesos instead of dollars. Some additional assistance could be given by increasing loan repayment time. During field research, colony leaders were reluctant to indicate whether the Japanese government would make these changes, but they have been under consideration.

The second problem resulted from insufficient educational facilities in the Luján B area. Colonists built two schools after residing only two months in Misiones because they insisted on a good education for their children. These schools were turned over to the Province without satisfactory results. Classes in Misiones are frequently cancelled on rainy days and children lose several days a week during bad weather. Lack of paved roads precludes adequate bus service, but the rain holiday has become more of a provincial habit than a necessity, according to colonists. These circumstances make it impossible for students who transfer to better schools in the nation to join their peers.

That the education of children is a most important factor in colonization of the wilderness, especially when urban pioneers are involved, has already been made clear in the cases of Monte Carlo and Eldorado. This factor is no less important for other cosmopolitan settlers and leads one to speculate how deep the resentment in Luján B is and how long it will be before private schools are organized. Unfortunately, if the latter are not permitted and if no improvements are forthcoming, the net effect will be to hasten the exodus of talented young people and the decline of the colony. There has been a compromise decision by the Japanese government to build and equip a large school at Luján B which will be staffed by Argentine teachers. It is clear, however, that equipment alone will not suffice, and that if any government seriously expects pioneer settlements to contribute successfully to its economy as well as to become absorbed rapidly by its culture, an extraordinary attempt to supply high educational standards has to be made in the colonization zone.

The third difficulty, like that found in other frontier settlements in Latin America, has been directly related to the proximity of the colony to an international border. The Paraná River is only 600 meters wide at the site of the Japanese settlement and may be crossed illegally day or night. Field laborers do this regularly and settlers claim that there is a substantial contraband movement at the same time. This traffic has become a serious problem which has intensified anti-Paraguayan feelings along the Argentine side of the river. There is simply too much forest completely to patrol the river, but intensification of police activities appears essential to the success of these settlements. Gradually, as forested land is cleared in such places the difficulty will recede, so that the government will not have to provide extra police service in these areas except during the early years of colonization.

These problems and difficulties had already resulted in the departure of some colonists from Luján B by 1970, and it was apparent that discouragement had become serious. However, it must be considered that most settlers were still in debt and could not easily return to Japan or move to other parts of Argentina. Thus indebtedness becomes a stabilizing factor during the initial years of colonization when discontent looms large. Fortunately colony disintegration will not be hastened by less responsible bachelors as happened in Monte Carlo. A few of the Luján B colonists are independently wealthy and have not even joined the cooperative, but all are family heads who came determined to stay. If debts can be paid, better homes built, and the school and international border problems eased or solved fairly rapidly, existing worries may recede into the background as they have in other successful pioneer settlements.

CHAPTER 7

A SUMMING UP:

SETTLEMENT AND POPULATION

GROWTH IN MISIONES

The nation will apply, in keeping with present standards, an agricultural plan designed to populate the
interior of the country, to rationalize rural developments, to subdivide land, establish rural population
on the principle of land ownership, and provide
greater well being for agricultural workers.

Art. 1, National Colonization
Law No. 12,636, 1940

LAND OPENING

Much has been achieved in the Province of Misiones by pioneer settlers during the modern period. There is no question but
that land opening in this remote part of Latin America has already
passed the point of being self-propelled. Indeed, judging from
available evidence it is possible to reach this point when there is
35 percent total effective settlement of land. For example, of the
total 2,980,100 ha in Misiones, 34.8 per cent, or 1,037,477 ha, is
now in use, with 65.2 per cent, or 1,942,623 ha, unused.[1]

Farmsteads and Fields.   In the Province of Misiones four visible
stages of settlement can be recognized among the majority of colonists, i.e., those who have not received substantial amounts of
outside help. These stages are reflected by the type of shelter, the
crop combinations, and the amount of cleared land, all of which
show a parallel progression. The first shelter built by the average
pioneer is a simple lean-to, followed within a few weeks by a crude
shack. The tiny new settlement is called a *rancho*; the second stage
is represented by the appearance in the forest of the typical Latin
American wood frame, board wall house; the third is a stucco or
brick house of greater size and comfort according to the degree
of success achieved by the settlers. The fourth is a small, modern
house constructed on the original property for the eldest son and
his family (Pl. 10). This is usually placed near the parents' home.
The time sequence of these stages may be something like the

following: stage 1, 0–1 year; stage 2, 2–15 years; stage 3, 16–25 years; stage 4, 26 or more years.

The first housing stage is accompanied by the opening of the rainforest by hand methods, the sale of timber, and the planting of subsistence crops such as maize, beans, and manioc. The second is the gradual addition of a cash crop, usually tobacco, after the valuable timber has been removed. In the third stage both tobacco and timber are replaced with yerba mate. The final stage shows a gradual diversification process in which tung, tea, oranges, tree crops, and vegetables play an important role. Only in recent years has the yerba mate stage been bypassed because of poor market conditions.

The extension of field patterns reflects the same progression by showing at first 1–2 ha of cleared land. In the normal progression, the second change is the removal of between 2–15 ha of forest, and in the final stages all the land is cleared except for a few ha of forest kept for wood and fuel.

Field size in Misiones still averages 25 ha — a feature which dates back to early government decisions for this area and which illustrates the persistence of officially sponsored land policies. The 25-ha size was originally developed as a reaction to latifundismo in the Province and has obviously persisted even on privately colonized lands. In fact, over 90 per cent of the holdings registered in the latest census are less than 51 ha in size. Table 11 summarizes the distribution by size ranges in Misiones.

Another feature of the small holding policy inspired by the federal government is that over 75 per cent of the farm lots are owner-operated. Although this percentage includes many people on public lands who do not yet have final property titles, there is little doubt that they will acquire full legal ownership.

AGRICULTURE

Crop production on the farms of Misiones shows a favorable if not a remarkable achievement since the beginning of the modern pioneer movement and is summarized for three different years in Table 12. Although some of the crop types have changed — a few have been abandoned and others have been added — the outstanding growth in Misiones agriculture is made clear by a glance at the acreage increases.

TABLE 11

Holding Sizes and Importance in Misiones

Size Range (ha)	No. of Holdings	% of No.	% of Area
0–5	1,350	7.8	0.4
6–10	1,130	6.6	1.0
11–25	9,801	57.0	19.1
26–50	3,373	19.7	14.7
51–75	739	4.3	5.0
76–100	342	2.0	3.3
101–150	151	0.9	2.0
151–200	91	0.5	1.7
201–250	41	0.2	1.0
251–500	77	0.4	3.1
501–1,000	49	0.3	3.7
1,001–2,000	24	0.1	3.9
2,001–3,000	10	0.1	2.7
3,001–4,000	5	—	1.9
4,001–5,000	1	—	0.5
5,001–10,000	7	—	5.7
10,000–100,000	8[a]	—	31.3
Totals	17,199	99.99[b]	101.0[b]

[a] The two largest size ranges involve extensive areas of commercially developed reforestation.

[b] Sums unequal to 100 are the result of rounding of figures.

Source: Republic of Argentina, *Cuarto censo nacional* (Buenos Aires, 1947).

From Table 12 it is apparent that since the turn of the century yerba mate has become one of the most important commercial plants in Misiones. Indeed, Misiones pioneers made the nation self-sufficient in the national beverage manufactured from this native tree within approximately thirty years of the first planting. By 1928 overproduction was a serious enough problem to prompt a search for other crops with which to bolster the slackening economy. Experiments with tung were then begun and colonists have subsequently planted trees on 4 and 5 ha areas until Argentina has become self-sufficient in tung oil and has initiated exports to the United States and Europe. Whereas yerba mate has never been received favorably outside Latin America and has had to depend primarily on domestic markets and policies, tung

TABLE 12

Crop Production in Misiones, 1888, 1925, 1965

Crop	Acreage (ha)		
	1888	1925	1965
Yerba Mate	—	8,500	130,000
Tung	—	—	58,000
Tea	—	—	32,000
Maize	2,956	15,000	30,000
Manioc	—	—	14,000
Citrus	1,534	2,380	12,000
Tobacco	152	3,481	11,000
Sugar cane	2,033	1,250	3,000
Rice	43	2,608	2,500
Soya	—	—	1,210
Sweet Potatoes	608	—	—
Peanuts	50	600	—
Essential oils	—	—	2,000
Totals	7,376	33,819	295,710

Source: Gustav Niederlien, "Mis exploraciones en el Territorio de Misiones," *Boletín, Instituto Geográfico Argentino* 2 (1890):216; Republic of Argentina, "Mapa económico de la República Argentina" (Buenos Aires, 1925); "Suplemento especial de Misiones," *Analisis* 4 (1965):207–220.

oil has been in demand both at home and abroad. Actually, until the 1950s, the United States imported almost 50 per cent of its supply of this valuable paint product from Misiones. Protection of home products and competition from synthetic substances manufactured in the United States have caused a decline of sales to this country, but Europe continues to import the natural oil.

The diversification process also includes tobacco, cultivation of which now accounts for one-fourth of Argentine production, citrus (mostly oranges), now about 8 per cent of Argentine production, and wood.

In the latter field Misiones supplies over 50 per cent of the national consumption of plywood, and over 20 per cent of Argentina's logs and posts. In fact, over 500 sawmills and 15 plywood factories have been established in Misiones. One of Argentina's two paper mills has been built at Puerto Piray just north of Monte Carlo. Reforestation therefore represents the largest sizeable investment activity in Provincial agriculture and is favored by the rapid growth of trees in the mild climate. Araucaria pine grows 2 meters in height and 3 cm in diameter per year, for example. Since Argentina must import over $200,000,000 of wood products annually, Misiones pioneers, many of whom are expert foresters, have set their goals on the new marketing possibilities, and at a pace of 3,000 ha per year have already transformed both the Campo, which changed from an open to a wooded (eucalyptus) landscape between 1960 and 1965, and the Upper Paraná region, which has begun to look like a replica of the Schwarzwald with its thousands of ha of dark pines.

The spectacular growth of agricultural production in Misiones has been achieved largely by cooperative methods about which much has already been said. The cooperative spirit has entered practically every phase of commercial life in Misiones and has even been employed to organize such sophisticated commodities as rural electrification and crop insurance, making this region unique in the interior of Latin America. The achievements of the cooperative movement may be summarized briefly by pointing to the successful federation of these organizations since 1939. By 1949, 20 cooperatives had joined the Federation, and by 1969 the number had increased to over 30, with a membership of approximately 16,000 and an active capital exceeding 100,000,000 pesos.[2]

POPULATION GROWTH

Rate of Increase.   The rapid economic growth rate since the period of modern colonization in Misiones has been accompanied by an equally rapid rate of population increase. Whereas less than 2,000 scattered families were reported living in Misiones at the time of federalization in 1881, by 1914 the total population had risen to 55,000. The growth rate reached 3.9 per cent per year at this time — a figure which was maintained until 1947. From 1947 to 1967 the growth rate averaged 3.5 per cent per year. This is not only one of the highest rates in Latin America, but it is especially significant in Argentina where the national rate of population increase between 1914 and 1967 averaged only 2 per cent per year. Moreover, in most provinces of the interior the migration of rural population toward Buenos Aires is very high. But in Misiones, average census data indicate that for every 100 people who leave, 195 arrive from other provinces. Thus, Misiones has become one of the few agricultural areas in the country to attract more people than leave, and this in spite of being remote. These are the reasons for an estimated population of over 500,000 in the Province for 1970. Nor has the rural nature of the population of Misiones changed rapidly: 87 per cent in 1895, 81 per cent in 1914 and in 1947, 77 per cent in 1957.[3] A more detailed statement about the population is given in Table 13.

TABLE 13

Rural and Urban Population in Misiones, 1957

Population Categories	No. of Agglomerated Settlements	Population	% of Population
Total Urban	*10*	*82,000*	*23*
50,000 or more	1	52,000	15
20,000–49,999	0	—	0
10,000–19,999	0	—	0
5,000–9,999	1	7,000	2
2,000–4,999	8	23,000	6
Total Villages	*59*	*21,000*	*6*
1,000–1,999	3	5,000	1
500–999	11	7,000	2
less than 499[a]	45	9,000	3
Total Dispersed	—	*257,000*	*71*
Totals	*69*	*360,000*	*100*

[a] Author's estimate from the source; does not include lumber camps.

Source: Misiones Province, *Planeamiento de la Provincia de Misiones,* 2 vols. (Buenos Aires, 1961), 2:73.

Government Colonies. The growth of population in Misiones is plainly marked by the appearance of numerous colonies (some with urban and semi-urban settlements) since the end of the nineteenth century. The earliest of these were concentrated on public lands, mostly at the abandoned Jesuit mission sites. They are listed below with dates of founding:

1. Posadas, 1872 (capital)
2. Candelaria, 1877
3. San José, 1877
4. Apóstoles, 1877
5. Concepción, 1877 (with port of Barra De Concepción)

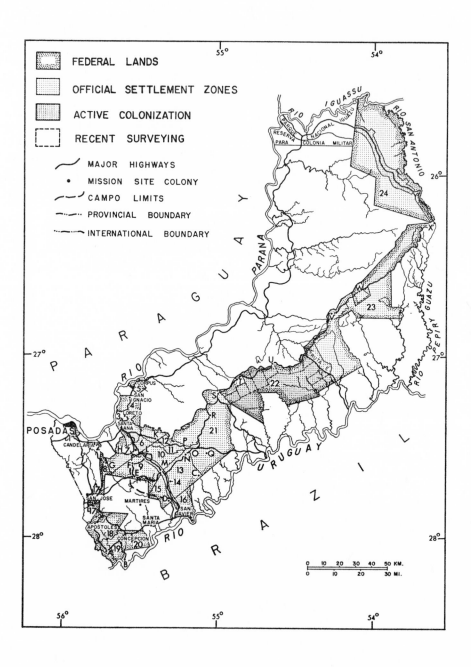

FEDERAL LANDS

OFFICIAL SETTLEMENT ZONES

ACTIVE COLONIZATION

RECENT SURVEYING

MAJOR HIGHWAYS

MISSION SITE COLONY

CAMPO LIMITS

PROVINCIAL BOUNDARY

INTERNATIONAL BOUNDARY

6. San Javier, 1877   9. Corpus, 1877
7. Santa Ana-Loreto, 1877   10. Bonpland, 1894
8. San Ignacio, 1877   11. Cerro Corá, 1894
                                      12. Azara, 1900

These colonies grew slowly at first, but all the choice land had been entirely claimed by the turn of the century when the Selva was actively opened to settlement. An especially rapid period of growth occurred between 1920 and 1930 when the following villages appeared on government land in the interior:

13. Leandro N. Alem   18. Villa Svea
14. Almafuerte   19. Oberá
15. Mártires   20. Campo Viera
16. Caá Yarí   21. Campo Grande
17. Campo Ramón   22. Aristóbulo del Valle

A sizeable number of smaller settlements also emerged on federal lands during this period; they are listed below:

23. Ameghino   29. Guaraní
24. Villa Rural   30. Dos de Mayo
25. Cerro Azul   31. Fracrán
26. O.V. Andrade   32. San Pedro
27. Profundidad   33. B. de Irigoyen
28. Colonia Finlandesa   34. San Antonio

By far the greatest number of colonists on public lands settled in damero colonies (Fig. 19).

Private Colonies.   Growth of private colonies has been rapid

Fig. 19 (*facing page*). Federal colonies in Misiones. *Settlement Centers*: A. Azara; B. Barra Concepción; C. Florentino Ameghino; D. Villa Rural; E. Cerro Azul; F. Olegario V. Andrade; G. Profundidad; H. Cerro Corá; J. Bonpland; K. Colonia Finlandesa; L. Almafuerte; M. Leandro N. Alem; N. Guaraní; O. Oberá; P. Yerbal Viejo; Q. Campo Ramón; R. Campo Viera; S. Campo Grande; T. Aristóbulo del Valle; U. 2 de Mayo; V. Fracrán; W. San Pedro; X. Bernardo de Irigoyen; Y. San Antonio. *Official Settlement Zones*: 1. Posadas; 2. Candelaria; 3. Santa Ana; 4. San Ignacio; 5. Corpus; 6. Bonpland; 7. Cerro Corá; 8. Colonia Profundidad; 9. Ensanche Cerro Corá; 10. Ensanche Colonia Bonpland; 11. Picada de Bonpland a Yerbal Viejo; 12. Yabebiry; 13. Guaraní; 14. Picada de Cerro Corá a San Javier; 15. Caá Guazú; 16. San Javier; 17. San José; 18. Apóstoles; 19. Azara; 20. Concepción de la Sierra; 21. Yerbal Viejo; 22. Aristóbulo del Valle; 23. San Pedro; 24. Manuel Belgrano.

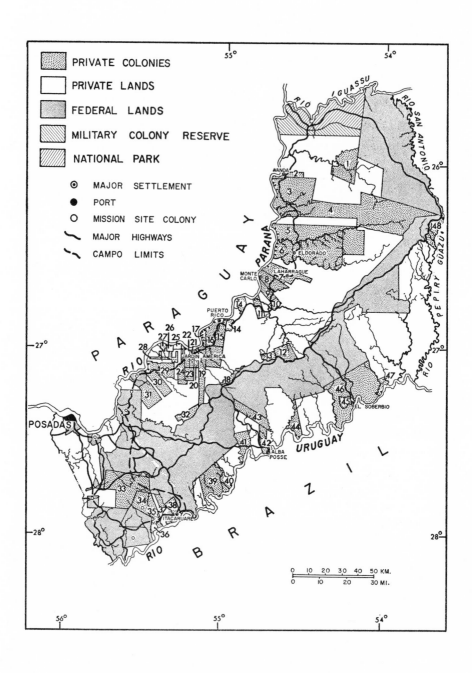

PRIVATE COLONIES

PRIVATE LANDS

FEDERAL LANDS

MILITARY COLONY RESERVE

NATIONAL PARK

⊙ MAJOR   SETTLEMENT

● PORT

○ MISSION   SITE   COLONY

〰 MAJOR   HIGHWAYS

〰 CAMPO   LIMITS

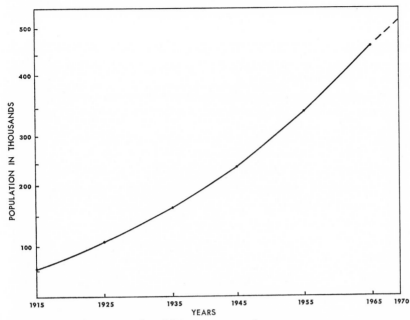

Fig. 21. Population growth in Misiones, 1914–1967.

although early starts failed and real success was not achieved until after 1919 when C. Culmey and A. J. Schwelm avoided the major pitfalls of government settlement forms by adopting the extraordinarily successful Waldhufen type for opening Puerto Rico, Monte Carlo, and Eldorado. Many private colonies have been planned since the opening of the first three, all but several of which have adopted the Waldhufen settlement form. The forty-eight private colonies and their locations are presented on the map in Fig. 20. Overall population increase in all settlements is summarized in Fig. 21.

Fig. 20 (*facing page*). Private colonies in Misiones. 1. Gdor. Lanusse; 2. Wanda; 3. Pto. Irigoyen; 4. Delicia; 5. Victoria; 6. Eldorado; 7. Laharrague; 8. Monte Carlo; 9. Caraguatay; 10. Tarumá; 11. El Alcazar; 12. B. Rivadavia; 12. 2 de Mayo; 14. Garuhapé; 15. San Alberto; 16. Puerto Rico; 17. Oro Verde; 18. Salto Encantado; 19. J. U. Martín; 20. Flora; 21. La Otilia; 22. San Pedro de Tabay; 23. Sol de Mayo; 24. Jardín de América; 25. Oasis; 26. Polana; 27. Guapoy; 28. Juan Pablo Palacios; 29. Nacanguazú; 30. Santo Pipó; 31. Gobernador Roca; 32, Chapa; 33. Félix Ortiz de Taranco; 34. San Juan de la Sierra; 35. Sta. María la Mayor; 36. Santa María; 37. Sta. María la Mayor; 38. Itacaruaré; 39. Buena Vista; 40. Panambí; 41. Acaragua; 42. Alba Posse; 43. 25 de Mayo; 44. Aurora; 45. Ongay; 46. El Soberbio; 47. El Paraíso; 48. Bernardo de Irigoyen.

The Capital City of Posadas.   The status of settlement growth in Misiones is well illustrated by the emergence of Posadas, the capital, as a major city in the Argentine interior. The population of this center has kept pace with rapid growth in the rest of the region. In 1935 the number of inhabitants of the Capital District of Posadas reached approximately 28,000 and the city had already grown large enough to support numerous businesses and industries which dealt with yerba mate, lumber and tobacco processing and shipping. There were also four banks, two hospitals, and one specialized agricultural school. By 1955, the number of inhabitants had increased to 60,000. Streets immediately around the central square in Posadas had been paved and the plaza itself adorned with a few shrubs and trees. Ten years later, according to local estimates, the Capital District had 75,000 people and boasted the first high-rise construction on the plaza. Trees in the square had reached majestic heights and provided ample shade. Several more blocks of streets had been paved around this park-like center. Expanded movement of people and businesses in Posadas both within the city and on its edges indicated that growth would reach 100,000 in the Capital District during the 1970s.

Daily life in Posadas reflects the energetic growth of the city. Residents arise early in the morning in order to take advantage of the cool temperature. By 7:00 A.M., bicycles and motorbikes are everywhere, the latter making an almost intolerable racket. Within the next few hours automobiles of almost every vintage from 1926 Chevrolets to brand new Fiats and Jeeps travel the streets. At noon the daily siesta, only reminder of a less active era, begins. At 4:00 P.M. businesses reopen and the hum of the city proceeds unabated until late in the cool evening. Cabarets open for business after sundown and at 9:00 P.M. a handful of small movie houses begin to show old United States westerns like "Tierra de los Valientes" starring Hoot Gibson, as well as the latest film imports from Europe in Spanish, German, and Swedish. Finally, by midnight, most activities have ceased and residents retire to prepare for another active day.

The personality of Posadas as a gateway to pioneer lands of the interior is everywhere evident. A number of the well-stocked downtown stores advertise map making and map copying. The Oficina de Tierras y Bosques is open on Saturdays and Sundays along with other offices and supply stores for new colonists or for those who take time to come in for weekend purchases and entertainment. Advertisements in the local newspaper sometimes are half-page announcements of land sales in freshly opened settlements in the still remote Selva. Real estate promoters sell and resell improved *chacras*, or small farms, in many parts of Misiones. Airport taxis announce light plane departures for Monte Carlo, Eldorado, Oberá, and Iguazú, while dusty buses leave for the interior by roads carved like red veins out of the now famous tierra colorada soils. Only a few blocks beyond the plaza red dust and mud from these soils contrast sharply with the smudged white of paved streets. Here, on the edge of the settlement, mules, horses, and wagons may be seen along with increasing numbers of metal-roofed wooden shacks. Sprinkled among them along the main roads out of town are occasional buildings made of modern glass and steel which are harbingers of expansion toward the interior.

A short walk northeast from the central plaza takes one to the harbor on the left bank of the Paraná River. This is the site of shipping facilities for less perishable products of Misiones such as yerba mate and lumber. Numerous small cargo boats reminiscent of Rhine barges even to the living quarters dot the harbor. They assist large log rafts downstream and beach them at points where lumber mills have been built or tow them to other downstream ports. The city power plant is likewise located on the banks of the river. At one point of the harbor there is a dock with launch service every fifteen minutes to and from Encarnación, Paraguay. A steady stream of women arrives daily from that country with heavy baskets balanced carefully on top their heads. These important ladies bring vegetables and eggs for the markets of Posadas, delicate lace items for the stores, and cheap, hand-rolled cigars of various sizes and shapes for Argentine smokers. Their Indian appearance and language add flavor to the international scene.

On the streets of Posadas one hears not only the Guaraní of the Paraguayans, but Spanish and Portuguese, German, English, Japanese, and even Ukrainian. In fact, the obviously high percentage of foreign-born in Posadas reflects the frontier nature of this city and of its hinterland. The international atmosphere portrays, along with other traits, the economic potential and vigor of the entire region.

Government Recognition of Misiones Achievements. The unquestioned achievement of pioneer settlement in Misiones was officially recognized as early as 1953 by the federal government in Buenos Aires. The measure of success was indicated by the change in status of the region from that of National Territory to independent Province. In 1956 even the remaining federal lands were turned over to the new Province which is now managing a growing push of descendants of original pioneers toward the Río Uruguay and the Altiplano de Irigoyen.

> A country is not made of rocks and desert expanses
> but of human beings and their homes.
>
> Mark Jefferson, *Peopling the Argentine Pampa*

In drawing conclusions about the results of colonization efforts two of the most important considerations — both from the point of view of the host country and of the colonists themselves — are the manner of adjustment by settlers in a new region and the speed with which sizeable commercial quantities of food and other useful items can be produced. The Misiones investigation generally leads to the conclusion that viable colonization results have been achieved in each of these areas and that success has depended largely on the following factors: location of the colonization area; settlement form and size; choice of settlers; methods of land titling and inheritance; formalized systems of resource utilization; and governmental attitudes toward colonization. The observations in the concluding paragraphs of this investigation are based on these factors as they apply to Misiones in particular, and to marginal regions of Latin America in general.

LOCATION OF THE COLONIZATION AREA

The decision to colonize Misiones in the face of many physical geographical obstacles was prompted originally by the need of the Jesuits to find a safe area in which they could build reducciones and protect their Indian charges. Through trial and error the Society's priests selected the best village sites, worked out the most economical crops for the new locations, such as manioc, yerba mate, citrus fruit, and tobacco, and developed effective methods of raising and processing these crops and of transporting them to the large markets. Jesuit knowledge of mineral resources and of the use of native woods in manufacturing was as advanced as that found anywhere in the world at that time. Fortunately, most of the mission colonization experiences were published and were available in modern times when settlers entered and developed Misiones.

More than a century and a half following the termination of the colonial mission period, the new Argentine government also found reasons for opening land in Misiones. The attempts of foreigners to invade this border area could not be prevented since the region was covered by a dense rainforest which was difficult if not impossible to police. Illegal exploitation of forest products, smuggling, and the development of an undesirable population of itinerant squatters all added to the need for land settlement. Moreover, the swift appearance of latifundismo in 1881 made it urgent that Misiones be settled by bona fide farmers. When the government established its colonization program the damero settlement form was transferred to the Campo by orders from Buenos Aires. The federal officials never understood that most of Misiones was hilly if not mountainous and that the popular damero settlement form was not suited to this area. In fact, the damero system became less and less efficient as pioneers moved from the Campo inland to the more rugged Selva. Fortunately hilly topography was a familiar problem to large numbers of pioneers who came from adjacent Brazil, from Germany's Schwarzwald, Erzgebirge, and the Bayerischen Wald, from Austria's Mühlviertel, and from parts of Switzerland and Poland. On some public lands the influence of these foreign pioneers caused the government to permit alterations in the damero survey method and various Waldhufen-like settlement types were established. European and ethnic European settlers from every area mentioned above were also acquainted with a method of land division dating from medieval times which provided more equitable distribution of farm property and surface water resources in rough terrain. They recognized the appropriateness of their model to the Misiones landscape and were able to introduce the so-called Waldhufen settlement form on private holdings as well as on some parts of federal lands. This type of colonization was possible on federal lands because the government failed to keep up damero surveys in remote and difficult areas of the Selva. Thus, the locational peculiarities of the Misiones landscape played an important role in the creation of damero and various long-lot forms, all of which have become permanent settlement features.

The remote location of Misiones has also been a major contributing factor toward preventing demoralization of pioneers, which sometimes occurs because of excessive governmental zeal to force a rapid breakdown in the cultural identity of foreigners. Both colonial and modern experience in Misiones have demonstrated that isolated pioneer settlements operate best when homogeneous groups are only broadly supervised while being permitted to adjust in difficult landscapes. Under such circumstances, and even in less isolated areas, if there is too much supervision, or if colonists of sharply differing nationalities or regions are interspersed by design (or by chance), linguistic, religious, economic, and other cultural differences and outright suspicion prevent naturally conservative farm people from working harmoniously. The time and energy lost by intracommunal arguments can be disastrous to the formation and progress of cooperatives, and at best the loss detracts from productive land use by adding to the numerous dangers already inherent in pioneer settlement. This is not to say, however, that broadly supervised, homogeneous groups cannot be placed in juxtaposition, as has happened so successfully in parts of modern Misiones. This Swiss method seems to act as a favorable stimulus to colonization progress both in the initial stages and later and has produced excellent results in isolated colonies like Monte Carlo (private) and Oberá (government).

It would seem probable, all things considered, and quite aside from the necessity of overcoming poor transportation to market areas, that remoteness itself is a factor which may be less disadvantageous under some circumstances than is generally presumed in modern pioneer settlement. In other words, the greater social stability fostered by relative isolation of homogeneous settlement groups (the military "buddy" principle) helps promote the pioneering process during critical early stages in difficult landscapes.[1] Knowledge of this fact should provide a measure of encouragement toward increasing land opening activities in other parts of the more remote interior of Latin America.

In spite of the decision to colonize an area where invaluable services had been performed by successful earlier pioneers — the

Jesuits — superimposition of modern settlements on former colonial lands has led to another important consideration, namely that previous erosive use of transitional or marginal areas like Misiones may trigger disastrous consequences in modern times. The formation of the "Poor Zone" in northeast Argentina illustrates the fact that early settlement practices must be carefully studied and the results remedied by the employment of *correct* agricultural techniques in reopening these lands. Although early attempts to open remote and unused lands in Latin America have been made by various other organizations less well known than the Jesuits, the old records are too frequently neglected by modern groups. This is just as true of land settlement documents in Europe and the rest of the Old World. Successful employment in Misiones of experience gained from earlier settlements suggests that historical information about older settlement projects should prove as useful in the location of other modern pioneering areas as it has in Argentina where selection of appropriate crops, establishment of farm practices based on sound ecological principles, and choice of proper transport routes and settlement sites and forms were all facilitated by Jesuit colonial experiments.[2]

Another conclusion which may be drawn from investigation of the Misiones landscape is that comparative studies of difficult settlement projects should be of exceptional value to anyone engaged in colonization planning. In Misiones most uninitiated modern settlers were able to learn about appropriate settlement forms, sizes, etc., from more experienced neighbors because of the juxtaposition of pioneer colonies — a feature abetted by location of the colonization area between two close rivers. Additionally, colonists successfully exchanged comparative knowledge of settlement forms employed in similar American and European landscapes. Even though the Misiones example demonstrates the value of comparative studies, recent records of pioneer settlements in widely separated areas of this hemisphere are, like the colonial ones, not easily accessible to those engaged in the important task of land opening. Consequently, not a single Spanish- or English-language effort has been made to integrate knowledge already accumulated by numerous, modern colonization agencies or by nonorganized groups which have experimented within remote parts of Latin America. A comparative study, complete with bibliography, text, and detailed maps of both rural and urban settlements would be of major assistance to the life of new colonies, especially if information were gathered from the earliest or most critical moments of land opening in difficult locations. By making comparisons on an international basis and by keeping them up to date, much wasted effort could be avoided and the repetition of failures minimized at a time when unjustifiable risks can no longer be afforded. Indeed, a more careful attitude toward the location of new settlements might not only help bring about the transfer of more appropriate settlement forms and sizes, but might thereby make it possible for any Latin American planning agency to eliminate settlement failure.[3]

SETTLEMENT FORM AND SIZE

Settlement Form. The importance of settlement form to the success of land opening is well illustrated in Misiones Province where the damero and the Waldhufendorf types have a close spatial relationship. Since variations of such major physical geofactors in Misiones as vegetation, soil, drainage, and landform characteristics are relatively minor, the comparison of colonies using the damero and Waldhufendorf settlement forms has been facilitated. It has likewise been possible to compare the two settlement forms when they have been undertaken by people of the same as well as of different cultural backgrounds, thus enabling more accurate interpretation of the role of major cultural geofactors such as language, religion, and settlement techniques. The results of the field studies strongly indicate that the advantages of the Waldhufendorf to the success of settlement are very impressive under certain circumstances, and that any disadvantages which might accrue from this line village form are far outweighed by those of the damero type.[4] A summary of these features is made below:

ADVANTAGES OF THE WALDHUFENDORF
SETTLEMENT FORM

Transportation

1. Greater accessibility of colonists to main road.
2. Greater accessibility to neighbors, then to urban facilities when they appear.
3. Lower cost of bridges and road construction.

4. Better working facilities for formation of cooperatives, for electrification, and for use of mechanized equipment requiring gasoline supplies and repairs.
5. Greater ease in fighting forest fires.
6. Greater ease in fighting epidemics.
7. Cheaper well costs (hired driller can service far more farms per day).
8. Easier tax assessment and collection.
9. Easier police protection from squatters.
10. Greater ease of expansion of colonization, especially along frontier (linear) zones.

Agricultural Land Use

1. Fairer exposure of (north) slopes and of protection from undesirable (south and southeast) winds.
2. Possibility of raising cattle and other livestock because fresh, running water is present on each lot.
3. Equitable distribution of different kinds of land in rough terrain.
4. Greater incentive for developing permanent agriculture. Colonists *see* each other's progress.
5. Promotes efficient, compact settlement instead of stray bits and pieces of isolated farmlands. Thus, forest opening is maintained on a broad front and farms are more effectively maintained.
6. Original lots can be made large (i.e., long) enough for future mechanization without detracting from any of the advantages noted above.

Other

1. More harmonious adjustment of settlement features to terrain.
2. Promotes more stable settlement, thus enabling pioneer settlement to become rapidly established during the early phases.

Of the numerous disadvantages in the damero system, lack of water and local isolation of settlers are the most severe. As has been pointed out, lack of access to fresh water even in the rainiest areas results in the undesirable stagnation of the primitive system of hack farming on only part of the land instead of the expected progression of more efficient plow agriculture over all of it, irrespective of the training and education of the pioneers. The damero form offers no possibility of incorporating the drainage system into the settlement plan in rolling terrain and is therefore ill advised unless it is known that wells can easily be dug everywhere. Because the damero plan can easily be employed independently of the water system, it is inherently associated with settlement schemes in which the basic details of other physical geofactors in a region are apt to be overlooked prior to colonization. This may save money at first, but in the long run is more costly and may contribute to the rapid decline of settlement.

Settlers who receive square damero lots are often isolated from main lines of communication. If they are not to be cut off, roads have to be so numerous that costs are unreasonably high. Since damero roads are all surveyed in straight rows, they must be re-surveyed when they are actually built and this process not only represents a hidden cost, but creates much subsequent hardship for individual colonists who have to make property available for road deviations. Furthermore, the extra energy expended on the difficult task of clearing land for the numerous roads required would be better spent on preparing land for farms. The extent of this wasted energy may be seen from the fact that the minimum number of roads in a damero colony, or the amount required for the boundary of each lot to be adjacent to a road, and for all lots to be linked to the market road, requires the clearing of ap-proximately three times as much forest as a Waldhufendorf of the same size. Moreover, a minimum of some 10 per cent of the da-mero colonists, and possibly more, depending on which roads are left out of the system to save money, will always be at least one-half km from the nearest road. This means that a long path must be opened and constantly maintained through the Selva by each of these families over some of the most difficult conditions imagin-able at the very beginning of the pioneer process when time is needed for other things. Experience likewise shows that damero colonists are rarely closer than 1 km to the nearest neighbor. There-fore, settlers are so isolated that they have little or no social inter-course during the initial colonization period — a factor of consid-erable importance which is nearly always lacking in damero colo-nies. This neighbor-distance factor further militates against the formation and operation of cooperatives, efficient maintenance of roads and of bridges, of which many more are required, and even the combating of forest fires, disease, and the like. In addition, successful marketing, electrification of farms, agricultural control, improved medical assistance, and the education of children are all hampered by the lack of accessibility. The inescapable conclu-sion to be drawn from these observations is that a relatively high percentage of damero settlement failures is related to the distance of farms from roads and neighbors. When added to the significantly high percentage of failures from unfair soil, slope, and water distribution in this system, it raises to over 35 per cent the failures likely from the start and explains why damero colonies have a much slower initial rate of development.

There is still another aspect of the settlement form which has nothing to do with colonists' preferences, but which may be the reason for continued employment of the damero in Misiones. Argentine surveyors, used to working in the level, treeless areas of Patagonia and the Pampa, or in the Chaco, do not like surveying along Misiones rainforest water routes as is required by the Waldhufen system. Culmination points for determining latitudes by star fixes should be made at night and there is often fog on streams and rivers at just that time. Glass instruments constantly steam over and it is sometimes uncomfortably cold and difficult to get around in the dark of the dense Selva. The task of surveying straight damero lines irrespective of topographic features is considerably less troublesome than the more variable boundaries and angles found in the typical Waldhufendorf. Although the damero is not so expensive to survey initially, its selection on state and some private lands has been influenced less by financial reasons than by the facts that: settlements in nearly level Argentina have traditionally been of the damero type, and there is a natural tendency to reject other forms; the surveyors have only been trained in the damero system and have had almost complete operating discretion in the field, particularly on state lands; colonization agencies have not generally considered that the type of settlement form is important to the success of land opening in hilly, forested regions.

The emergence of different settlement forms in Misiones points clearly toward some functional variations which are related to two distinctive parts of the Province: the public lands, and estate holdings settled by private companies. Although there has been a minor amount of overlap of the damero and Waldhufen settlements in both areas, by and large the public lands have been surveyed according to the former, and the private lands according to the latter form. This separation of forms enables some interesting comparisons of rural versus urban development. In the federal lands, which extend in a narrow band through the center of Mi-

siones, the government surveyors generally laid out damero colonies which had land reserved for the development of central urban facilities. They even put aside urban land in the Waldhufen-
like village types which emerged. As soon as any village had 1,000
people, it became the seat of a municipio, or local administrative
region. Financial aid and land grants were then awarded which
hastened the formation of the quadrate grid pattern common to
most Argentine townscapes, thus obliterating initial Waldhufen
settlement forms and standardizing the grid pattern. Village centers created during the period from 1920 to 1930, some of which
have since become municipios, were numerous on public lands.
The most important of these are Oberá, Leandro N. Alem, and
a group of nine located at old Jesuit mission sites. By far the largest of these is that of Oberá, now the second city of Misiones with
over 15,000 residents.

Private estate owners in Misiones were intrigued by the initial
colonization success on federal lands and decided to capitalize
on these results by engaging in competition of their own. Some
rented out land contiguous to public holdings at exorbitant prices,
knowing that colonists would pay to be near friends. Others began to subdivide or sell their property to colonization companies
at prices often starting 15 to 20 times higher than those charged
for federal land. In 1919 private colonization was organized on
some 250,000 ha of latifundium holdings in the first large-scale
efforts of this type. Eldorado, Monte Carlo, and Puerto Rico, the
most sizeable and successful of the private colonies, were begun
by construction of long picadas inland from landings on the Alto
Paraná River. Colonists were sold small Waldhufen lots along
these roads. Crops such as tobacco, yerba mate, tung, and tea were
produced on all of them and easily shipped with the aid of cooperative societies in river boats, on the railroad, and later by
truck. By the 1930s agricultural production from these colonies
had already surpassed that from the older damero settlements on
federal lands. Yet unlike many farmers in the damero colonies who
had access to modern urban centers, prosperous residents of the
Waldhufendörfer had to do their shopping by means of buses
which travelled through "business districts" built up in line fashion
along several kilometers of the main colony road. These colonies
were not designated as municipios until much later than the da-

mero settlements, and long after surpassing the limit of 1,000 inhabitants established by the government on public lands. The private municipios could not be formed until privately organized urban facilities were built; furthermore, they were never given land grants since there was no federal property available in them.

Herein lie two significant functional differences between the damero and Waldhufendorf settlement systems: namely that the dameros grow very slowly at first because of the disadvantages already enumerated, whereas the Waldhufendörfer have so many favorable features that they advance rapidly in the first years of colonization. However, after the land is cleared in successful damero colonies, the increasing need for urban facilities is quickly and satisfactorily fulfilled so that their growth rate is given a fast push. On the other hand, in the Waldhufendörfern, whose initial agricultural growth rates have been rapid, there is much frustration and only slow growth with respect to urban facilities which are not normally planned. Awkward, kilometer-long business districts emerge with wasteful duplication of facilities. Furthermore, the rising cost of land makes it ever more difficult to convert the midsection of a linear Waldhufendorf into the efficient grid pattern required by modern urban centers. All of the Waldhufendörfer of Misiones still suffer from lack of proper urbanization and have lagged behind the thriving government colony centers in this respect.

It is evident from analysis of the Misiones landscape that a more satisfactory settlement form for future application in this and similar areas of Latin America would result from a combination of the most desirable features of both the damero and the Waldhufendorf. In other words, long-lot, linear settlements which follow the natural landscape features but which have centralized reserve areas for future urban expansion should simultaneously permit the most rapid initial agricultural progress and subsequent urbanization as soon as land is needed for this important function. The nearest thing to this combined settlement form in the Province of Misiones is the government Colonia Picada de Cerro Corá a San Javier with its planned urban center at Leandro N. Alem. It is important to note that ultimately only the Waldhufendörfer have the possibility of approaching this idealized form, but they cannot do so until sufficient wealth has been amassed in order to purchase expensive farmland along the main road for making a grid street pattern. Even with good offers for land, some long-lot farmers always resist this process so that urbanization is slow and spotty. It should also be kept in mind that in the damero settlements both the urban and the rural facilities will suffer from a permanent want of harmony between topographic features and this inflexible settlement form — a point well illustrated in Misiones by the slow rate of agricultural growth and by the frustration of the urban community on very sloping land in the colony of Caraguatay. In spite of the fact that some damero settlements may eventually achieve the same degree of intensive agricultural land use found in the Waldhufendörfern, this will take so much longer that the economic contribution will generally remain less significant.

The rate of development of agricultural land is closely related to the form of settlement and is more rapid when colonists work close to each other, i.e., less than 500 meters apart along a road, instead of in isolated openings scattered over a difficult landscape (Pls. 7 and 8). Although statistics are not available which would permit a detailed analysis of production differences between the colonies on the federal strip of land and the surrounding private settlements, some general data are indicative of the major digression between them. They are presented in Table 14.

TABLE 14

Private and Federal Land Use in Misiones[a]

Type of Use	Area (ha)	% of Total	Used Land (ha)	% of Total	Unused Land (ha)	% of Total
Private	2,057,843	69.1	852,655	41.5	1,205,188	58.6
Federal	922,257	30.9	184,822	20.0	737,435	80.0

[a] Sums of more than 100.0 are the result of rounding of figures.

Source: Misiones Province, *Planeamiento de la Provincia de Misiones*, 2 vols. (Buenos Aires, 1961), 2:105.

Yerba mate statistics for 1933 indicate that divergence of production between private and federal lands had already taken place.[5] At that time, 64.4 per cent of the total production was from private lands, whereas government colonies produced only

35.6 per cent. However, the latter possessed 75.5 per cent of the farms in Misiones, and only 32.4 per cent of the farmed land. Private colonies on the other hand had 24.5 per cent of the total farms and 67.6 per cent of the farmed land. Since farm holdings have always averaged 25 ha in both areas, the indication is that a much more rapid rate of initial land clearing and planting characterized the private colonies. By 1947 a survey showed that of all the land in Misiones employed for agricultural purposes, 27 per cent was in private hands, whereas only 6 per cent belonged to the government.[6]

It is evident from these statistics that once a land-use system is well established in an area all subsequent development is influenced along similar lines, since expansion tends to conform to the original model. If a system for the spatial arrangement of farms is employed which does not foster rapid initial growth, then it is to be expected that little will happen over the years and that the countryside will remain heavily forested much to the detriment of everyone. Although graduated land-use taxes have never been applied in Misiones to hasten farm progress in damero settlements, this method might work. In any case, speed is of the essence in the success of pioneer settlement so that appropriate methods of stimulation should always be employed once it is known that initial development momentum has begun to lag. At a later date in the development of Waldhufendörfer, when urbanization is essential, tax refunds to farmers willing to sell land for urban purposes might help maintain good initial momentum.

Settlement Size.   The question of the size of pioneer settlement has not yet received sufficient attention by those opening new lands in the Americas. Nevertheless, the investigation of this phenomenon in Misiones leads to the conclusion that size itself is one of the essential ingredients for the favorable outcome of colonization. The importance of this factor appears to be directly proportional to the degree of isolation, keeping in mind that isolation reflects *overland time* rather than *actual distance* from markets and supply centers. Settlers are generally agreed that the failure of the colony of Victoria, only 10 km from the center of Eldorado, was due at least partly to excessive isolation of a small group.

For a time at the beginning of colonization it was easier to get medical help in Victoria from much more distant places than Eldorado which had a doctor but no road connection with the new colony. Although in some circumstances the lack of a physician might not be critical in the success of a colony, in this case it was, and it serves as an illustration of the magnification of some service needs among pioneers when isolation is great and settlement size small. Victoria also suffered from a lack of regular shipping service on the Paraná River because it was so much smaller than Eldorado and Monte Carlo. Consequently supplies and contacts with the outside were inadequate in the beginning when they were sorely needed. Only 51 families settled in Victoria colony in the first few years compared with 85 in Garuhapé, 400 in Monte Carlo, and over 700 in Eldorado. In addition, the overland connection between Monte Carlo and Eldorado has been adequate almost from the beginning and has always been good between Garuhapé and the other colonies. Finally, the favored colonies have benefited not only from the greater number of colonists in each settlement, meaning that more services were available from the start in any one of them, but from the total number of original colonies. The amount of land accessible in all three — Puerto Rico, Monte Carlo, and Eldorado — was so great that colonists could go where it was most suitable for their religious background, financial means and abilities, and personal contacts with friends and relatives. The importance of internal and overall size in the success of colonization may also be seen in the federal colonies of Apóstoles and Azara, and Colonia Picada de Cerro Corá a San Javier and Oberá.

It would appear from the Victoria example in Misiones that under severe conditions of isolation 50 families are too few to provide internal stability and steady growth. The nearly 100 Japanese families at Garuhapé, on the other hand, rapidly achieved much success, although it must be kept in mind that they have had both good road connections with nearby markets and some assistance from the Japanese government. Certainly a size of 100 families appears minimal under difficult conditions, assuming that outside help is available. Otherwise a total number of between 400 and 500 families would be a far safer starting size. Perhaps the best general statement on size relationships has been made by Christopher Turner, an administrator for A. J. Schwelm, who reported from the experiments in Misiones that "unsuccessful group settlement is costly, but where it is successful it is the most economic form of settlement. Once it has reached a certain size it is its own best advertisement, and acquires the magnetic power of attracting new settlers to the area."[7] One need only add that the sooner the appropriate size threshold is reached in the life of the colony, the greater its assurance of success.

Still another aspect of size is important to future growth of a pioneer colony: that of the areal dimension of individual lots. Farm lots which are too small seriously detract from permanent settlement success. There are two reasons for this: future mechanization is inhibited or even precluded by overly small lot sizes; and an undesirable type of branch settlement results. Moreover, the latter process fosters repetition of the original problems as more branch settlements are produced. In both damero and Waldhufen settlement systems, the first problem may be easily solved by increasing the original lot size. However, only in the Waldhufendorf form can lot size easily be increased without causing settlers to be severely isolated. Judging from the Misiones example, it would appear that an optimum minimal lot size would be 50 ha, or double that used most frequently in the Province. Lot widths should be well below 500 meters since this dimension characterizes the 25-ha damero squares which force isolation on settlers. A long-lot size of 300 × 1,500 meters would produce approximately the desired area without restrictive separation of colonists, since all would be in contact along the same road. It would foster repetition of more desirable features in the branch expansion process, provided that sufficient acreages of accessible land exists around the mother colony, and that succeeding generations of children remain in the area of colonization. It is concluded that these land conditions are minimal for bringing about a process of line settlement along a river or road which will be successful in the long run, that is, be productive of original and branch settlements with inherently successful traits. It is perhaps superfluous to add that better results from initial as well as future, or branch, colonization processes, are possible with smaller numbers of pioneers in the Waldhufen settlement than in the damero. In comparing the two systems it becomes quite clear that both *settlement form and size* are necessarily related to the whole colonization process and are probably its most important ingredients.

THE CHOICE OF SETTLERS

Field studies in Misiones indicate that the pioneer settler should fulfill at least three requirements if a colony is to succeed with a minimum number of people and only a modest amount of outside assistance. First, the individual should be an adult in excellent health; second, he should have had some agricultural experience; and third, he should be the head of a family. The health of settlers is vital to the arduous tasks of land clearing, and to withstanding the peculiar problems that may arise in the tropics and semi-tropics, especially from disease and insects. It is highly probable that the failure of Victoria stemmed partly from illness among colonists who, because of poor selection, were not healthy enough to withstand the life of a pioneer. When the colony is small, and no doctor appears as a settler, each illness is magnified out of proportion to its true significance and the general morale may be rapidly lowered.

Agricultural experience is another sine qua non; however, it should not be assumed that urban residents cannot qualify as pioneers. Many of them have horticultural backgrounds or experience working with cooperatives or other businesses which may satisfy this requirement. A high percentage of the most successful colonists in Misiones are those who have had former experience raising vegetables and flowers. The probable explanations for this correlation are that: garden agriculture is an intensive form which requires devoted personal attention, just as is required in warm climates where year-around farm work is a must; and that urban residents with agricultural training are apt to be both highly sensitive to market demands and innovative. It appears that special efforts should be made toward attracting colonists of this type for pioneer settlement projects. Settlers with little or no agricultural experience who fulfill the other colonization standards suggested as essential should be given agricultural orientation and should probably not become more than a small percentage of the initial number of colonists.

Pioneer heads of families are especially desirable colonists because they are the kind who are stable enough to withstand the usually worst initial hardships. The psychological urge to leave before immunity to insects is acquired (about 5 per cent never become immunized), or while combating ants and dry weather spells, or while waiting for more comfortable living quarters, is very great. Adverse factors have been responsible for a real exodus at some early stage of almost every colony in Misiones. The exodus appears to have been started most frequently by young single men. Even if it is true that some bachelors make good pioneers, as a general rule they are the most anxious to leave a colony when the going becomes difficult. If their numbers are proportionately great, the spirit of departure can and will extend to the rest of the settlement.

In addition to these primary requirements there are several of a secondary nature which bear on the stability of pioneer settlement. One is the family structure which among some people produces efficient attitudes toward labor and its organization, as may be seen in the example of the Japanese at Garuhapé. A second is a highly developed tradition of money saving which may help produce better cooperative results — one of the strong features of colonists in places like Eldorado and Monte Carlo. Finally, the attitude of colonists toward religion and education is most significant as it goes hand in hand with high standards of community organization and productivity in any successful colony.

It is likely that the primary and secondary requirements for successful colonists are to be found among certain kinds of people whose qualifications culturally predispose them to adjust to difficult environments, and that these people should be sought out from within a nation attempting to colonize or from outside its borders as the most suitable types.

METHODS OF LAND TITLING AND INHERITANCE

Although some progressive titling practices have been carried out on federal holdings in Misiones, it is on these same government lands that delayed titling, or total lack of it, has caused widespread ill effects and is still common. The creation of large numbers of squatters, and even of *intrusos a los intrusos*, i.e., squatters on squatters' land, is well known and has created extra legal expenses for both colonists and governing authorities. The squatter problem has also produced the need for private police systems on the large estates and in private colonies. Unfortunately, when squatter populations are sizeable in densely forested areas, little can be done about policing either the smallest holdings or the uncolonized areas, especially in damero settlements, unless pioneers take up arms. This is a procedure curiously reminiscent of the medieval Wehrbauern in European Waldhufendörfern and requires time and energy in addition to an armed populace. Another major problem is that where settlers have no titles they treat the land badly and after a few years would not accept legal ownership under any circumstances. Since there is always more federal land, they expect to move on to some other part of the forest whenever the authorities arrive or soils wear out. Certainly the lack of locally granted titles adds to the lack of stability in such pioneer areas. Unfortunately for the shifting population involved, there will always be problems of obtaining credit and obvious restrictions of land sales. Actually the general social unrest and lack of confidence created by squatters has often caused the departure of bona fide colonists or has militated against steady progress, especially in the government colonies. Figure 11 illustrates the seriousness of the problem by portraying the status of titled and nontitled property on public lands as of 1966.

The inheritance system has also affected the stability of pioneer settlement in Misiones, especially on privately colonized lands. Lands has often been sold to meet inheritance expenses, and a risky subdivision of 25-ha farm lots has already begun in some places. Under the circumstances, there is no guarantee that *minifundismo* will not eventually occur in the poorer colonies of Misiones. Moreover, another type of land splintering has resulted from the desire to provide children with land of their own. This is the purchase of land at some distance from mother settlements made necessary because of small original holding sizes. The original size of farms and the inheritance practices can thus combine to produce inefficient land holdings which will eventually lower the productivity of a settlement and increase the desire of young people to leave. The logical conclusion is that the 25-ha farms which once were adequate in Misiones are in reality too small for long-term mechanized development and probably should have been doubled in size from the outset.

There are two other ways of insuring against minifundismo and the uneconomical breakup of colonies as soon as the children of original pioneers are grown. One is to make illegal the subdivision of minimum-sized farms and to educate settlers about such legal requirements; the other is to assist farm mechanization in every possible way so that individual farmers can hasten the forest clearing process and bring more land into production before their children decide to leave. If mechanization is to be a goal, as it should be, then the 25-ha farm is too small to permit a growth sequence which would preserve the initial successes of a colony. Larger farms have, moreover, a greater opportunity for raising cattle for milk and beef sales because there is sufficient land for extensive use. Reconsolidation of splintered holdings can still prevent a decline of the agricultural situation in Misiones because the problem is still in the earliest stages. Delay can only produce steady extension of the "Poor Zone" to other parts of the Province.

FORMALIZED SYSTEMS OF RESOURCE UTILIZATION

Two of the most important aspects of resource utilization in the opening of new lands are the marshalling of financial reserves, and the system of tilling the soil. In both of these areas the colonists in Puerto Rico, Eldorado, Monte Carlo, Picada de Cerro Corá a San Javier, Oberá, Colonia Liebig, Garuhapé, and other settlements have demonstrated that good organization and close coordination can favorably accelerate the pioneer settlement phenomenon, especially in the important initial stages.

The most significant formalized method yet devised of organizing and coordinating finances and farming is that of the cooperative. Judging from the experience in the colonies of Misiones, 400 to 500 pioneer families must have already had a number of successful harvest years before there are sufficient financial reserves for beginning a small cooperative with a loan bank. If there were 1,000 or more families the monetary resources could be organized much sooner in the life of a colony. In any case, where settlers are poor to begin with, as most are apt to be, it is imperative that a fair source of money be made available at once if the colony is to succeed rapidly. Moreover the source should be local since interest earned may then remain in the settlement and be used for making more loans or for improvements in the future urban system. If a branch bank is established in the colony, money earned does not necessarily remain in the area and the structure of any local cooperative may be weakened. Organizations of the

Raiffeisen-type are therefore admirably suited to pioneer settlement since they provide at the outset both a cooperative and a locally organized credit institution. It is significant that even the Japanese in Misiones have adopted cooperative methods of this kind.

Another important contribution of the cooperative movement is its spirit of innovation and experimentation in agriculture. Because of this there has been a steady pressure exerted toward high standards, i.e., ultimate agricultural diversification in the case of the Europeans, and an immediate diversification of crops in the Japanese colony. Although temptation to engage in the traditional yerba mate monoculture of Misiones has been felt by the Japanese, the cooperative has stood firmly for diversified efforts. As a consequence, the Japanese at Garuhapé marketed successfully a broad variety of items in record time and did not have to go through the financial crises and subsequent forced diversification processes which once characterized the economies of Monte Carlo, Puerto Rico, Colonia Picada de Cerro Corá a San Javier, Victoria, and others, and which continue to characterize new and relatively unplanned pioneer settlements. The Japanese, who themselves are good innovators, have learned from their own experiences as well as from those of other colonists in Misiones. Fortunately, they have not come to Misiones with the idea of directly transplanting their society, but rather have studied what has evolved in the new area. They have realized that the hope of directly recreating a social system usually results in failure; but their combination of the best features of three systems has set a good example of how newcomers to pioneer settlement can succeed in a minimum of time even in a marginal landscape.

GOVERNMENTAL ATTITUDES TOWARD COLONIZATION

The federal government of Argentina initiated colonization of Misiones by establishing a narrow strip of public land through the middle of the Province. This was accomplished by gaining a foothold on the reserved lands of the old Jesuit missions and extending government holdings to the interior by reclaiming land from large estates. The latter were in some cases improperly surveyed; in others the owners had not fulfilled the conditions of the original land grants and were forced to give up some territory. Through a gradual process of litigation which is still under way, the government has acquired a strip of land which amounts to almost one-third of the provincial area. That this has been a sufficiently large proportion of the total area to set an official example of colonization and to attract widespread subdivision and settlement of adjacent private estates is evident from the successful land opening that emerged in Misiones. The government program has thus set in motion a colonization program which consists of both federal and private types competing in a friendly and beneficial manner. Each has learned from the other and an example of peaceful land tenure change has occurred here without any use of massive expropriation schemes involving great expense and loss of political prestige by the government. That this so-called método extremo has not been employed is a tribute to the sensibility of many Argentine legislatures over the years. Besides, the generous attitude of the government in assisting transport of pioneers to the area and of making land easily available to them without imposing a divisive or unrealistic set of rules and regulations during the formative years made for high initial morale and continued arrival of settlers — both essential to any successful colonization program. Lastly, it should be remembered that the achievements of colonization in Misiones have been made possible by permitting both foreign and national groups to open land, both of which have contributed new ingredients to the economic success for which the region is now justly noted. It is, of course, to be expected that such a major undertaking, which was carried out in a completely different type of landscape from that found in the rest of the country, would have suffered from its share of frustrations and mistakes. Yet it is from the solution to these problems that others stand to learn most so that future colonization programs can be instigated more rapidly and effectively.

It goes almost without saying that the intelligent approach employed by the Argentine government in Misiones has pointed a new way toward solving simultaneously the serious problems of latifundismo and unproductive, empty border zones which characterize so much of Latin America today.

THE ARGENTINE APPROACH IN THE REST OF LATIN AMERICA

The essential ingredients of the Misiones system of agricultural colonization should be applicable to other marginal areas in Latin

America. The presence of vast regions with physical conditions reasonably similar to those in Misiones is clearly recognizable in parts of Brazil, Paraguay, Bolivia, and Peru, as well in other parts of Latin America. The presence in these same places of extensive latifundium holdings is likewise recognized. If applied at the outset, the purchase (or expropriation if necessary) of at least a third of the latifundia in strategic swaths of land throughout their extent, sufficient attention to previous colonization efforts, experimental investigations to assure good land use, application of a settlement form whose general orientation is topographic rather than schematic, attention to the proper magnitude of settlement, and one good access road for each strip of land — all should offer a major impulse toward successful land opening. When bona fide land titles, appropriate selection of colonists, multifaceted cooperative financial organization, and educational facilities corresponding to the standards of the settlers are added to the basic settlement elements, success should be achieved even where colonization has previously failed. The Misiones investigation leads to the conclusion that if only half of the latter items are added to the basic settlement elements, success may still be achieved, assuming that favorable government attitudes are maintained. According to the Misiones experience, it is highly likely that if success is achieved on such government lands, and if the government encourages colonization outside its holdings by offering inducements such as lowered taxes, that latifundium holders will be motivated to subdivide their own properties along the federal strips of land by establishing private colonies.

Application of these ingredients to other settlement programs in Latin America will undoubtedly take time and energy. Education of colonization agencies must take place before that of colonists themselves who are generally very malleable. The need for change is everywhere evident and experimentation with new methods is already encouraging. The official adoption during the 1960s of a long-lot system in the rural settlement program of Venezuela, its use in the Yapacaní-Puerto Grether-Moile area of eastern Bolivia, and the initial success of the same settlement form in the Tingo María area of Peru and in the Caquetá region of Colombia are examples of the growing acceptance of this workable settlement type outside Argentina and Brazil. Indications are that the system can be so adjusted as to be workable with proper supervision, even when native peoples alone are involved and when a variety of physical landscapes is encountered. It is to be hoped that adaptations of some aspects of the Misiones cooperative program by the Venezuelans, Colombians, and others points toward more rapid progress in land opening. It is also to be hoped that such programs, whether they fail or succeed, will be carefully investigated at all stages and publicized for the purposes of maintaining the important record of landscape change and of developing a deeper understanding of pioneer settlement processes.

REFERENCE MATTER

NOTES

CHAPTER 1: INTRODUCTION

1 Isaiah Bowman, *The Pioneer Fringe* (New York, 1931). See also Wolfgang Louis Gottfried Joerg, ed., *Pioneer Settlement* (New York, 1932), esp. pp. 80–145.

2 Misiones Province, *Planeamiento de la Provincia de Misiones*, 2 vols. (Buenos Aires, 1961), 1:54.

3 William C. Thiesenhusen, *Chile's Experiments in Agrarian Reform* (Madison, Wis., 1966), p. 33.

4 Craig L. Dozier, "Northern Paraná, Brazil: An Example of Organized Regional Development," *Geographical Review* 46 (1956): 318–33.

5 Sanford A. Mosk, *Industrial Revolution in Mexico* (Berkeley, Cal., 1954), pp. 219–22. See also Alfonso González, "Problems of Agricultural Development in a Pioneer Region of Southwestern Coastal Mexico," *Revista Geográfica* 64 (1966):29–52; and José Rogelio Alvarez, ed., *Noticia de Jalisco: 1953–1959* (Guadalajara, 1959), pp. 301–322.

6 Felix Monheim, *Junge Indianerkolonisation in den Tiefländern Ostboliviens* (Braunschweig, 1965); J. Valerie Fifer, "Bolivia's Pioneer Fringe," *Geographical Review* 57 (1967):1–23; and Raymond E. Crist, "Bolivians Trek Eastward," *Américas* 15 (1963):33–38.

7 Emilio A. Conforti, "Colonización, reforma agraria, migraciones internas: Consideraciones, sugerencias, propuestas," mimeographed (Quito, 1960), p. 41.

8 Wolfgang Brücher, *Die Erschließung des tropischen Regenwaldes am Ostrand der kolombianischen Anden. Der Raum zwischen Río Ariari und Ecuador* (Tübingen, 1968); Raymond E. Crist and Ernesto Guhl, "Pioneer Settlement in Eastern Colombia," *Smithsonian Institution Annual Report for 1956* (Washington, D.C., No. 4282, 1957), pp. 391–414.

9 Norman R. Stewart, "Recent Trends in Paraguayan Immigration and Pioneer Settlement," *Geographical Review* 51 (1961):431–33.

See also his *Japanese Colonization in Eastern Paraguay* (Washington, D.C., 1967).

10 Craig L. Dozier, *Land Development and Colonization in Latin America: Case Studies of Peru, Bolivia, and Mexico* (New York, 1969); Republic of Peru, *Inventario, evaluación e integración de los recursos naturales de la zona del Río Pachitea* (Lima, 1966), esp. pp. 209–233.

11 Christoph Borcherdt, "Junge Wandlungen der Kulturlandschaft in Venezuela," *Geographische Zeitschrift* 55 (1967):142–61; H. David Davis, ed., *The Economic Development of Venezuela* (Baltimore, 1961), esp. pp. 246–80.

12 Craig L. Dozier, "Northern Paraná, Brazil: Settlement and Development of a Recent Frontier Zone" (Ph.D. dissertation, Johns Hopkins University, 1954); Roland E. Chardon, "Changes in the Geographic Distribution of Population in Brazil — 1950–1960," in Eric N. Baklanoff, ed. *New Perspectives of Brazil* (Nashville, 1966), pp. 155–78; Henry J. Bruman, "Post-War Agricultural Colonization in Brazil," mimeographed (Washington, D.C., Nonr 233(03), 1958).

13 William H. Jeffrey, *Mitre and Argentina* (New York, 1952), pp. 201–5.

14 Faustino R. Berrondo Guiñazú, "Estudios de antecedentes de las adjudicaciones realizadas por la legislatura de la Provincia de Corrientes, por la ley de 21 de junio de 1881 en el Territorio Nacional de Misiones," manuscript (Buenos Aires, 1947), p. 35.

15 Robert E. Dickinson, *Germany: A General and Regional Geography* (New York, 1953), pp. 142–46.

16 Misiones was made a Province by Law 14,294, Dec. 10, 1953. Decreto 12,012 of July 5, 1956, placed all federal lands (*tierras fiscales*) available for colonization in the hands of the new Province.

CHAPTER 2: THE PHYSICAL SURROUNDINGS

1 Alberto Carlos Muello, *Misiones: las cataratas del Iguazú, el Alto Paraná y el cultivo de la yerba mate* (Buenos Aires, ca. 1930), pp. 32–35.

2 Misiones Province, *Planeamiento de la Provincia de Misiones*, 2 vols. (Buenos Aires, 1961), 2:51; Glieb Grüner, *La erosión en Misiones*, 2nd ed. (Buenos Aires, 1955), pp. 37, 41–43.

3 This phenomenon appears to occur more frequently in the Campo than in the Selva, but requires further study (ibid., p. 45).

4 See also, Federico Prohaska, "Regímenes estacionales de precipita-

ción de Sudamérica y mares vecinos (desde 15°s hasta Antártida)," *Meteoros* 2 (1952):66–100.

5 Alejo Peyret, *Cartas sobre Misiones* (Buenos Aires, 1881), p. 109.

6 H. Wilhelmy records a 5,000-ha fire loss in Campo Grande in 1935. Herbert Wilhelmy, and Wilhelm Rohmeder, *Die La Plata Länder: Argentinien-Paraguay-Uruguay* (Braunschweig, 1963), p. 369. See also Wilhelmy's "Zur Klimatologie und Bioklimatologie des Alto Paraná-Gebietes in Südamerika," *Petermanns Geographische Mitteilungen* 94 (1950):130–39.

7 Misiones Province, *Planeamiento*, climatic charts for several stations opp. 2:46.

8 Every six or seven years minimum temperatures drop to −5°c or −6°c. A frost during which the minimum temperature of the vegetation is below the dew point is called locally an *helada blanca*. If the minimum frost temperature is above the dew point an *helada negra* results, during which leaves usually turn black.

9 In addition to diabase and melaphyre, theoleiites, spilites, diabaseporphyres, and other materials are present. These various forms are interwoven and exist in layers sometimes referred to by the name trap or Trapp do Paraná in the literature. Use of the vague term basalt has been intentionally avoided in this discussion. See Misiones Province, *Informe geológico* (Buenos Aires, 1964), pp. 1–25; Reinhard Maack, "Neue Forschungen in Paraguay und am Río Paraná. Die Flußgebiete Monday und Acaray," *Die Erde* 93 (1962):4–48; Herbert Wilhelmy, "Aufbau und Landformen des Alto Paraná-Gebietes," *Petermanns Geographische Mitteilungen* 92 (1948):32–38; and Victorio Angelelli, *Reconocimiento geológico del territorio de Misiones en busca de bauxita* (Buenos Aires, 1936).

10 Misiones Province, *Informe geológico*, pp. 7–8; and Grüner, *La Erosión*, pp. 20–22.

11 See, for example, Juan B. Ambrosetti, "Un viaje a Misiones," *Anales de la Sociedad Científica Argentina* 38 (1894):32, and his other articles listed in the Bibliography.

12 Misiones Province, *Informe geológico*, p. 59.

13 Carlos Burmeister, *Memoria sobre el Territorio de Misiones* (Buenos Aires, 1899), pp. 55–57; Ramón Lista, *El territorio de las misiones* (Buenos Aires, 1883), pp. 38–39.

14 Interview with J. Rubén Olmo, Geologist, Universidad del Noreste, Posadas, Misiones, Nov. 10, 1965.

15 Moisés S. Bertoni, *Descripción física y económica del Paraguay* (Puerto Bertoni, 1918), p. 132.

16 Franz Kühn, *Argentinien* (Breslau, 1927), p. 214. See also V.
Koutché, *Vegetación forestal del parque nacional del Iguazú*
(Buenos Aires, 1948), preface.

17 The following list of plant types and uses may serve as a guide to
the exploitable flora of the Selva Misionera:

Popular Name	Botanical Name	Use
Curiy, or Paraná pine	*Araucaria angustifolia*	Laminated wood, construction
Cedro misionero	*Cedrela fissilis*, v. *macrocarpa*	Furniture, marine construction
Lapacho negro	*Tabebuia ipe*	Cabinets, marine construction
Incienso	*Myrocarpus frondosus*	Furniture
Peteribí (*loro negro*)	*Cordia trichotoma*	Furniture, musical instruments
Timbó	*Enterolobium contortisiliquum*	Furniture, doors
Curupay	*Piptadenia rigida*	Bridges, fencing

Several tree types are used for extracting resins and dyes. Among
them are the *aquaray-guazú* (*Stinacacia* ?), *aquaraibai* (*Schinus
molle*) from which *bálsamo de las misiones* was prepared by the
Jesuits (Lista, *El territorio*, pp. 63–65) and *incienso* (*Myrocarpus
frondosus*). The *ñandipá* (*Sorocea ilicifolia*) produces fruit which
is used to make a blue dye. *Sangre de Drago* (*Croton succirubrum*)
yields red dye; *urubú-retimá* (?), indigo; and *tatyiba* (?), yellow.

Among numerous recognized textile plants are the *palma negra*
(*Copernicia cerifera*), whose fiber is employed in baskets and hat
weaving; *guembé* (*Bromelia caraguata*) with a fiber long used for
clothing and rope (ibid., p. 70, for ex.).

Many plants are available which are reputed to have medicinal
qualities. The roots from *yurupebá* (*Solanum paniculatium*) produce a tonic for anemia and fevers, *yerba de la víbora* (*Asclepiades
campestris*) supplies a snake bite antitoxin, and *Citrus aurantium*
buds provide a heart remedy.

18 Burmeister, *Memoria*, p. 65.

19 Adolfo C. Furnus, with A. A.Obloblin, and J. Tarabanoff, *La yerba
mate* (Buenos Aires, 1930), p. 18.

20 Ibid., p. 20.

21 Campo soils are also too acid for alfalfa and must be neutralized. See ibid., pp. 27–28.

CHAPTER 3: COLONIAL LAND OPENING IN MISIONES

1 Cabot was the Venetian who had explored North America for Henry VII of England. Pedro Francisco Javier de Charlevoix, *Historia del Paraguay*, 5 vols. (Madrid, 1910–14), see esp. 1:58–65.
2 Wilhelm Lütge, "Die ersten Deutschen in Argentinien," *Auslands-warte* 32 (1952):34–36.
3 Charlevoix, *Historia*, 1:64.
4 Ibid., p. 69. See also the description in Albert B. Martínez and Maurice Lewandowski, *Argentinien im zwanzigsten Jahrhundert*, 4th ed. (Gotha, 1912), p. 19.
5 Charlevoix, *Historia*, 1:79–85.
6 Mendoza is reported to have brought 2,500 men on his expedition. Among them were approximately 150 German settlers. One of the Germans was Ulrich (Utz) Schmidl whose account of Spanish activities between Buenos Aires and Asunción in his *Reise nach Süd-amerika in den Jahren 1534 bis 1554* (Stuttgart, 1889), is one of the earliest detailed records of European settlement in this part of Latin America. A useful Spanish version of this work is, Edmundo Wernicke, trans., *Ulrico Schmidl: derrotero y viaje a España y las Indias*, 2nd ed. (Buenos Aires, 1947).
7 Charlevoix, *Historia*, 1:85–91.
8 Ibid., p. 100.
9 Cabeza de Vaca had accompanied the Pánfilo de Narváez expedition to Florida in 1528. See ibid., p. 105.
10 Ibid., pp. 105–9.
11 Ibid., 2:113, 121–42.
12 Herbert Wilhelmy, *Südamerika im Spiegel seiner Städte* (Hamburg, 1952), pp. 223–24. Guillermo Furlong, *Misiones y sus pueblos de Guaraníes* (Buenos Aires, 1962), p. 18, records the founding date as 1554.
13 Nicolás del Techo, *Historia de la Provincia del Paraguay de la Compañía de Jesús*, 5 vols. (Madrid, 1897), 1:77, 2:97. See also Charlevoix, *Historia*, 2:167, 231.
14 The Caingang were less numerous than the Guaraní and inhabited a part of Misiones along the Uruguay River. For a discussion of native peoples in this part of South America see Salvador Canals Frau,

Las poblaciones indígenas de la Argentina: Su orígen, su pasado, su presente (Buenos Aires, 1953); and Ricardo Levene et al., *Historia de la nación Argentina*, 10 vols. (Buenos Aires, 1935–42), 1, esp. Ch. 7, pp. 473–548.

15 The Crown sent six Franciscan missionaries to Buenos Aires in 1539 (Charlevoix, *Historia*, 1:89). The first missionaries in the Asunción region were Franciscans from Peru. For an account of their activities east of the Andes, see P. Fray Bernardino Izaquirre, *Misiones franciscanas y narración de los progresos de la geografía en el Oriente del Perú: 1619–1921*, 14 vols. (Lima, 1922); and Magnus Mörner, *The Political and Economic Activities of the Jesuits in the La Plata Region: The Hapsburg Era* (Stockholm, 1953), pp. 66, 72–73.

16 Pablo Hernández, *Misiones del Paraguay: Organización social de las doctrinas de la Compañía de Jesús*, 2 vols. (Barcelona, 1913), 1:3–39.

17 Furlong, *Misiones*, p. 148.

18 Charlevoix, *Historia*, 2:131–32.

19 Mörner, *Political and Economic Activities*, p. 67.

20 Charlevoix, *Historia*, 2:131–33.

21 Karl Andree, *Buenos Ayres und die argentinischen Provinzen* (Leipzig, 1856), p. 35.

22 See Antonio Ruiz de Montoya, *Conquista espiritual hecha por los religiosos de la Compañía de Jesús en las provincias del Paraguay, Paraná, Uruguay y Tape* (Bilbao, 1892), pp. 154, 296, and Juan P. Gay, *Historia da república jesuítica do Paraguai desde o descobrimento do Rio da Prata até aos nossos dias, ano de 1861*, 2nd ed. (Rio de Janeiro, 1942), p. 240. If these 60,000 are added to the 40,000 the Spanish themselves captured, the result is 100,000 Indians lost. This figure is less than the total since there is no record of how many were lost in El Tape. In a report by King Philip IV dated Sept. 16, 1639, he claims that over 300,000 Indians from "Paraguay" had been kidnapped by the Paulistas alone. See P. Bernhard Nusdorfer, *Beytrag zur Geschichte von Paraguay, und denen Missionen der Jesuiten daselbst* (Frankfurt and Leipzig, 1768), pp. 12–13.

23 Charlevoix, *Historia*, 2:321.

24 Ruiz de Montoya, *Conquista espiritual*, p. 154.

25 Ibid. See also "Consulta a la Junta de Guerra," May 31, 1641, regarding arming mission Indians, in Republic of Argentina, *Catálogo de documentos del archivo de Indias en Sevilla referentes a la historia de la República Argentina*, 3 vols. (Buenos Aires, 1901), 1,

Item No. 1641; Mörner, *Political and Economic Activities*, pp. 74, 77, 128, 200; Charlevoix, *Historia*, 2:372–79.

26 See the useful comparison of original founding dates for the reducciones given by various authors in Diego A. de Santillán, *Gran Enciclopedia Argentina*, vol. 5 (Buenos Aires, 1959), pp. 300–5. See also Hernández, *Misiones*, 2:272–77.

27 Ricardo Piccirilli, Francisco L. Romay, and Leoncio Gianello, *Diccionario histórico argentino*, vol. 5 (Buenos Aires, 1959), pp. 252–64; Furlong, *Misiones*, p. 134. Dates given are for establishment of reducciones in Misiones, not necessarily original founding dates elsewhere.

28 Three other missions were founded after 1745 in order to link the Misiones del Paraguay with the northern route to Alto Perú (Bolivia). These, however, never became as important as the other missions, partly because of remoteness and partly because of difficulties with natives in the region. See Hernández, *Misiones*, 1:19–20.

29 The Crown legalized the practice of arming the Indians in 1644 and thereafter used them regularly in military and construction services. Ibid., pp. 495–96. See also Furlong, *Misiones*, pp. 391–96.

30 See the careful account by Bruno Garsch, a priest and well-trained geographer, in *Der Einfluß der Jesuiten-Missionen auf den Wandel der Naturlandschaft zur Kulturlandschaft im Stromgebiet des Paraguay-Paraná während des 17. und 18. Jahrhunderts* (Breslau, 1934), p. 53.

31 Hernández, *Misiones*, 1:280.

32 The Jesuits disliked the classification of doctrina which was imposed upon them by Philip IV in 1650 and 1652 (Charlevoix, *Historia*, 2:49). They may have felt that it lessened their ability to protect the natives and opened the way to settlement by secular colonists who invariably demanded native labor.

33 A summary of mission locations and moves is given in Estanislao S. Zeballos, *Arbitration Upon a Part of the National Territory of Misiones Disputed by the United States of Brazil* (New York, 1893), pp. 384–88.

34 The rectangular grid was intentionally brought to America approximately three decades after the Conquest. Dan Stanislowski, "The Origin and Spread of the Grid Pattern Town," *Geographical Review* 36 (1946):105. See also his "Early Spanish Town Planning in the New World," *Geographical Review* 37 (1947):94–105.

35 Hernán Busaniche, *La arquitectura en las misiones jesuíticas guaraníes* (Santa Fe, 1955), p. 36.

36 Furlong, *Misiones*, p. 187.

37 Burmeister, *Memoria*, p. 18.

38 Furlong, *Misiones*, p. 253.

39 These were the so-called Jesuit mines in Misiones. An example of Jesuit copperware is the large bowl on display in the Sala Misiones Jesuíticas at the Museo Histórico Nacional in Buenos Aires. Original church bells of copper are still in position at the mission of Trinidad (opposite San Ignacio) in Paraguay. Some copper was also imported from Chile according to Charlevoix, *Historia*, 2:67.

40 John Constanse Davie, *Letters from Paraguay* (London, 1805), pp. 176–224; William L. Powell, *Diary of the Water Witch Expedition, from Asunción to the Yerbales of San Estanislao, Returning by Way of Misiones, 1854* (Washington, D.C., 1966), p. 74.

41 Hernández, *Misiones*, 2:618. This number is substantially the same as that given for 1732 by Furlong, *Misiones*, opp. p. 631, although the later data are less complete.

42 Ibid., p. 152.

43 Juan de Escandón, and Bernhard Nusdorfer, *Geschichte von Paraguay aus spanischen Handschriften übersetzt nebst dem Criminal-Prozess wider die Jesuiten in Spanien* (Frankfurt, 1769), esp. pp. 80–83.

44 Ibid., pp. 80–81. See also L. A. Muratori, *Relation des Missions du Paraguai* (Paris, 1754), pp. 196–98. This is a translation from Italian; a German translation was made in Vienna in 1758.

45 Hernández, *Misiones*, 2:525–27; Charlevoix, *Historia*, 2:65–66.

46 Escandón and Nusdorfer, *Geschichte*, pp. 80–85.

47 Muratori, *Relation*, p. 198; Furlong, *Misiones*, pp. 398–99.

48 Muratori, *Relation*, p. 198.

49 Anton Sepp, and Anton Böhm, *Reisebeschreibung: Wie nemlichen dieselbe auss Hispanien in Paraquariam kommen; und kurzer Bericht der denckwürdigsten Sachen selbiger Landschafft/Völkern und Arbeitung der sich alldort befinden* (Ingolstatt, 1712), pp. 153, 180–81. See also Escandón and Nusdorfer, *Geschichte*, pp. 80–85.

50 Ibid., pp. 84–85.

51 See, for example, the description by José Cardiel, *Declaración de la verdad* (Buenos Aires, 1947), quoted in Furlong, *Misiones*, p. 416.

52 A description of the yerba mate commerce is given by Escandón and Nusdorfer, *Geschichte*, pp. 88–89.

53 Ibid., p. 88.

54 Ibid.

55 Ibid., pp. 88–90. The tribute established in 1649 was one silver peso per male Indian between the ages of 18 and 50, with the exception

of *caciques* (chiefs) and their first-born sons. If we assume that men in this age group were married, and that there were five members per family, $5 \times 25,116 = 125,580$ Indians at the time the Escandón-Nusdorfer report was written (1760). This figure corroborates the population accounts of Hernández and Zeballos cited on page 42.

56 Escandón and Nusdorfer, *Geschichte*, pp. 86–87.

57 Ibid., pp. 88–90.

58 Garsch, *Der Einfluß der Jesuiten-Missionen*, p. 109.

59 Ibid., p. 111; Muratori, *Relation*, pp. 198, 201.

60 Garsch, *Der Einfluß der Jesuiten-Missionen*, p. 110.

61 Ibid., p. 112.

62 Sepp and Böhm, *Reisebeschreibung*, pp. 180–81; Garsch, *Der Einfluß der Jesuiten-Missionen*, p. 113.

63 Escandón and Nusdorfer, *Geschichte*, pp. 84–87.

64 Charlevoix, *Historia*, 1:41. See also A. Mutinelli, *El cultivo del algodón en Misiones* (Buenos Aires, 1936).

65 Sepp and Böhm, *Reisebeschreibung*, pp. 232, 236.

66 Garsch, *Der Einfluß der Jesuiten-Missionen*, p. 110. Large numbers of livestock were raised in the grasslands far to the south of the Misiones region.

67 Ibid.

68 Hernández, *Misiones*, 1:544.

69 Sepp and Böhm, *Reisebeschreibung*, p. 233.

70 Garsch, *Der Einfluß der Jesuiten-Missionen*, p. 120.

71 Zeballos, *Arbitration*, p. 280.

72 Sepp and Böhm, *Reisebeschreibung*, pp. 233, 254–57.

73 Héctor José Tanzi, "Breve historia de la imprenta en el Río de la Plata, que trata de esclarecer el orígen de la existente en el Museo Histórico Nacional," *Historia, Revista de Historia Argentina, Americana y Española* 25 (1961):22–23; Vicente Gambón, *A través de las misiones guaraníticas* (Buenos Aires, 1904), p. 108.

74 Garsch, *Der Einfluß der Jesuiten-Missionen*, p. 123.

75 Mörner, *Political and Economic Activities*, p. 210. The Jesuits were accorded special shipping privileges to Buenos Aires by the Crown.

76 Hernández, *Misiones*, 1:385; See also Maria Faßbinder, *Die "Jesuitenstaat" in Paraguay* (Halle [Saale], 1926), pp. 96, 109.

77 These calculations are based on the following assumptions: for yerba mate, an 80 per cent yield of 1.5 kg per plant, or 12,000 plants; for cotton, 200 kg per ha; for livestock, 2 head per ha. San José's population is approximately the same as the average figure for reducciones at this time, and therefore the report gives a representative view of land use at any one of the missions. Harvest data are

from a letter by Nusdorfer, published in 1768 in *Neue Nachrichten,* reprinted in Hernández, *Misiones,* 1:279. The yerba mate yields are consistent with calculations made from another report by Escandón and Nusdorfer, *Geschichte,* p. 88, and by Bonpland for Candelaria in Wilhelm Schulz, *Aimé Bonpland. Alexander von Humboldts Begleiter auf der Amerikareise, 1799–1804. Sein Leben und Wirken, besonders nach 1817 in Argentinien* (Wiesbaden, 1960), p. 23.

78 These calculations are in fair agreement with those for other missions whose plantations are listed in Furlong, *Misiones,* p. 687.

79 Garsch, *Der Einfluß der Jesuiten-Missionen,* p. 110.

80 There is some evidence that the Jesuits planted Araucaria pines which were used both for lumber and edible seeds. The practice was probably not extensive judging from the paucity of information on the topic. See Gay, *Historia,* p. 603.

81 In this regard, see Glieb Grüner, *La erosión en Misiones,* 2nd ed. (Buenos Aires, 1955), p. 51.

82 Santillán, *Gran Enciclopedia Argentina,* 5:303–5.

83 Zeballos, *Arbitration,* p. 269.

84 Escandón and Nusdorfer, *Geschichte,* pp. 25–30.

85 Furlong, *Misiones,* pp. 646–74.

86 Ibid., p. 674.

87 Piccirilli, Romay, and Gianello, *Diccionario histórico argentino,* 5:254–57.

88 A detailed treatment of the end of the mission period is given in Pablo Hernández, *El extrañamiento de los jesuitas del Río de la Plata y de las Misiones del Paraguay, por decreto de Carlos III* (Madrid, 1908). See also Furlong, *Misiones,* esp. pp. 675–93.

89 Misiones did not become part of Argentina until 1876.

90 Juan Queirel, *Las ruinas de Misiones* (Buenos Aires, 1901), p. 32.

91 Hernández, *Misiones,* 2:275.

92 Paraguayan troops captured the mission and removed everything they could. Misiones Province, *Planeamiento de la Provincia de Misiones,* 2 vols. (Buenos Aires, 1961), 2:22–23.

93 These may be seen in such works as Ramón Lista, *El territorio de las misiones* (Buenos Aires, 1883); Rafael Hernández, *Cartas misioneras* (Buenos Aires, 1887); and Jean Antoine Victor Martin de Moussy, *Description Géographique et Statistique de la Confédération Argentine,* 3 vols. (Paris, 1860–64), which contain numerous encouraging references to settlement possibilities in Misiones.

94 Wilhelm Lütge, Werner Hoffmann, and Karl W. Körner, *Geschichte des Deutschtums in Argentinien* (Buenos Aires, 1955), p. 276.

CHAPTER 4: CORRIENTES PROVINCE AND LATIFUNDISMO

1 See especially, Ricardo Levene et al., *Historia de la Nación Argentina,* 10 vols. (Buenos Aires, 1935–42), 9:566–67.
2 Misiones Province, *Planeamiento de la Provincia de Misiones,* 2 vols. (Buenos Aires, 1961), 2:16.
3 Ibid.
4 Guillermo Furlong, *Misiones y sus pueblos de guaraníes* (Buenos Aires, 1962), pp. 675–93.
5 Misiones Province, *Planeamiento,* 2:16.
6 The percentage was calculated from data in Pablo Hernández, *Misiones del Paraguay: organización social de las doctrinas de la Compañía de Jesús,* 2 vols. (Barcelona, 1913), 2:195, and elsewhere. That this decline is a conservative estimate may be inferred from the fact that by 1775 there were only 564 Indians registered in the Pueblo of Corpus. See Estanislao S. Zeballos, *Arbitration Upon a Part of the National Territory of Misiones Disputed by the United States of Brazil* (New York, 1893), p. 289.
7 Misiones Province, *Planeamiento,* 2:16.
8 Republic of Argentina, "Informe al Consejo del Contador General, Conde de Casa-Valencia," Nos. 125-6-7, Archivo General de Indias, in *Catálogo de documentos del archivo de Indias en Sevilla referentes a la historia de la República de Argentina,* 3 vols. (Buenos Aires, 1910), vol. 3.
9 Zeballos, *Arbitration,* p. 301.
10 Ibid., p. 304.
11 See Levene, *Historia,* 10:566–67; Furlong, *Misiones,* p. 704.
12 Mardoquéo Navarro, *El Territorio Nacional de Misiones* (Buenos Aires, 1881), p. 22.
13 Misiones Province, *Planeamiento,* 2:17.
14 Levene, *Historia,* 10:567–69.
15 Zeballos, *Arbitration,* pp. 456–57.
16 Hernán F. Gómez, *Corrientes en la guerra con el Brasil* (Corrientes, 1928), esp. p. 47.
17 Various accounts are given in Navarro, *El Territorio Nacional,* p. 70; Levene, *Historia,* 10:573; and Alejo Peyret, *Cartas sobre Misiones* (Buenos Aires, 1881), p. 28.
18 On the important role played by the few remaining Indians in the formation of boundaries in Misiones, see Levene, *Historia,* vol. 10.
19 Peyret, *Cartas sobre Misiones,* p. 39.
20 Navarro, *El Territorio Nacional,* pp. 92–96.
21 Levene, *Historia,* 10:576–83.

22 Ibid., 9:326.

23 Corrientes Province, *Colección de datos y documentos referentes a Misiones como parte integrante del territorio de la Provincia de Corrientes hecha por una comisión nombrada por el gobierno de ella* (Corrientes, 1877), p. 355.

24 Misiones Province, *Planeamiento*, 2:21.

25 Ibid., p. 22.

26 Ibid.

27 Ibid., pp. 22, 25.

28 Article 25 of this Constitution, which is still in force, states: "The Federal Government shall encourage European immigration; and may not restrict, limit or burden with any tax whatsoever, the entrance into Argentine territory of foreigners who arrive for the purpose of tilling the soil, improving industries, and introducing and teaching the arts and sciences." "Constitution of the Argentine Nation," *Inter-American Juridical Yearbook* (Washington, D.C., 1949), p. 366.

29 This law was in force until 1903. Augusto da Rocha, *Colección completa de leyes nacionales sancionadas por el Honorable Congreso durante los años 1852 a 1917*, vols. 4 and 5 (Buenos Aires, 1918), 4:227–52.

30 Corrientes Province, *Colección*, pp. 427–32. This record does not account for all settlers, the majority of whom were undoubtedly squatters.

31 Ibid., p. 355.

32 Ibid., p. 357.

33 Ituzaingó is approximately 100 km downstream from Posadas (see Fig. 4).

34 Republic of Argentina, *Primer censo de la República Argentina, 1869* (Buenos Aires, 1872), pp. 607–8.

35 Corrientes Province, *Colección*, p. 358.

36 Ibid.

37 Ibid., pp. 380–82.

38 Ibid., p. 356.

39 Ibid., pp. 340–41. Note that, although copies of the original decree indicate that the area reserved for animal breeding was to be all the land between "the Uruguay (River) and the Cordillera to the East which divided the land next to the Paraná River . . . ," it is assumed that since there is no Cordillera east of the Uruguay dividing it from the Paraná, the word "East" is in error and should have been "North."

40 The disease is *Tripanosoma equinum*, and was described by Carlos

Burmeister, *Memoria sobre el Territorio de Misiones* (Buenos Aires, 1899), p. 40. At intervals it destroyed whole horse herds, thus making mule raising essential because of the resistance of these animals. The malady may be similar to the tsetse disease of Africa.

41 There are still buildings in which old mission tiles and bricks have been used.

42 Peyret, *Cartas sobre Misiones*, pp. 87–88.

43 Statistics from Corrientes Province, *Colección*, p. 419.

44 Peyret, *Cartas sobre Misiones*, p. 87.

45 Ibid., p. 109.

46 Misiones Province, *Planeamiento*, 2:24, 30.

47 Corrientes Province, *Colección*, pp. 427–32.

48 Misiones Province, *Planeamiento*, 2:24.

49 Industrial data compiled from Corrientes Province, *Colección*, p. 421, unless otherwise specified.

50 Rafael Hernández, *Cartas misioneras* (Buenos Aires, 1887), p. 57.

51 Corrientes Province, *Colección*, p. 421.

52 Details of the regulation were based on suggestions made by the French naturalist Aimé Bonpland, who first came to South America with his friend Alexander von Humboldt. Bonpland eventually settled in Latin America and carried on investigations in Argentina. Although Bonpland recorded some of his observations on yerba mate, most of his work was never published. Francia, dictator of Paraguay, was afraid that the investigations would lead to competition from Argentina, and imprisoned Bonpland late in 1821 for his efforts. After being released in 1831 Bonpland spent the rest of his life in the old Jesuit region. He died near the mission of San Borja in 1858 and is buried in Paso de los Libres, Argentina. For accounts of his work see Juan P. Gay, *Historia da república jesuítica do Paraguai desde o descobrimento do Rio da Prata até aos nossos dias, ano de 1861*, 2nd ed. (Rio de Janeiro, 1942), pp. 448–58; and Henri M. Cordier, *Papiers inédites du Naturaliste Aimé Bonpland conservés à Buenos Aires* (Buenos Aires, 1914); Wilhelm Schulz, *Aimé Bonpland. Alexander von Humboldts Begleiter auf der Amerikareise 1799–1804. Sein Leben und Wirken, besonders nach 1817 in Argentinien* (Wiesbaden, 1960). See also Florenzio de Basaldúa, *Pasado-presente-porvenir del territorio nacional de Misiones* (La Plata, 1901), p. 199.

53 Corrientes Province, *Colección*, pp. 389–92.

54 Carlos R. Gallardo, *La industria yerbatera en Misiones* (Buenos Aires, 1898), p. 38.

55 Misiones Province, *Planeamiento*, 2:25.

56 Rocha, *Colección*, 5:293, Ley 1,246, for ex. See also Hernández, *Cartas misioneras*, p. 57.

57 Ibid.

58 Peyret, *Cartas sobre Misiones*, p. 151.

59 Misiones Province, *Planeamiento*, 2:25.

60 Corrientes Province, *Recopilación completa de códigos, leyes y decretos reglamentarios vigentes de la Provincia de Corrientes*, 2 vols. (Corrientes, 1904), 2:22–23.

61 According to Estanislao S. Zeballos, *Descripción amena de la República Argentina*, 2 vols. (Buenos Aires, 1881–83), 1:314, U.S. Statutes of May 18, 1796, May 10, 1800, and March 3, 1877, all served as guides for surveying by the Federal Department of Immigration, Colonization and Agriculture in Argentina.

62 Corrientes Province, *Colección*, pp. 364–67.

63 The Argentine government granted 250,000 pesos on Oct. 5, 1877, to pay for ocean passages and to give aid to the *Ruso-alemanes*, as they were called (see Rocha, *Colección*, 5:350). The Brazilian government took similar action in 1877–79 and *Wolgadeutsche*, i.e., Russian-German, colonists went to the state of Paraná. Some of them ultimately made their way to Argentina after finding they could not raise wheat on the poor soils of the Brazilian campos. They established colonies at María Luisa, Celia, Santa María, and Mandisoví in Entre Ríos, not far from Misiones. See Juan A. Alsina, *La inmigración europea en la República Argentina*, 3rd ed. (Buenos Aires, 1898), esp. pp. 233–34; Leo Waibel, "European Colonization in Southern Brazil," *Geographical Review* 40 (1950):529–47.

64 Peyret, *Cartas sobre Misiones*, pp. 32–33.

65 Burmeister, *Memoria*, p. 33.

66 Faustino R. Berrondo Guiñazú, "Estudios de antecedentes de las adjudicaciones realizadas por la legislatura de la Provincia de Corrientes, por la ley de 21 de junio de 1881 en el Territorio Nacional de Misiones," manuscript (Buenos Aires, 1947), pp. 206–7. This important work is basic to the legislation now employed to increase the extent of the narrow strip of federal lands, and could well serve as a model for similar investigations elsewhere.

67 Rocha, *Colección*, 4:227–52 (text of National Colonization Law of Oct. 19, 1876).

68 Corrientes Province, *Colección*, pp. 510–15. See also Republic of Argentina, Congreso Nacional, *Cámara de Diputados*, vol. 5, 1919 (Buenos Aires, 1920), pp. 202, 204.

69 Benjamín T. Solari, "Restitución del territorio de Misiones a la Provincia de Corrientes," *Cámara de Diputados*, pp. 191–218.

70 Corrientes Province, *Colección*, pp. 368–71.

71 Corrientes Province, *Recopilación*, 2:23–28.

72 Presumably this law was amended to include the formation of a farm colony at Trincheras de San José by the Corrientes legislature in 1879. The amount of land granted is not stated. See Republic of Argentina, *Cámara de Diputados*, p. 193.

73 See, for example, Wilhelm Lütge, Werner Hoffman, and Karl W. Körner, *Geschichte des Deutschtums in Argentinien* (Buenos Aires, 1955), pp. 276–80.

74 Peyret, *Cartas sobre Misiones*, p. 275.

75 Corrientes Province, *Colección*, p. 347.

76 Corrientes Province, *Recopilación*, 2:28.

77 Ibid., p. 35.

78 Ibid., p. 37.

79 Antonio Sánches Negrete, *Cuestión-Misiones: Refutación del presidente con el manifiesto de la H. Legislatura de la Provincia de Corrientes* (Corrientes, 1881), pp. 1–5, text of the address.

80 Corrientes Province, *Recopilación*, 2:39.

81 Ibid., p. 42.

82 Berrondo Guiñazú, "Estudios de antecedentes," p. 14.

83 D. G. de la Fuente, *Tierras, colonias y agricultura. Recopilación de leyes, decretos y otras disposiciones nacionales* (Buenos Aires, 1894), p. 85. See Art. 2 of the law. As late as 1913 it was reported that 18 of the landowners in Misiones still owned 68 per cent of the entire Territory. Adolph N. Schuster, *Argentinien, Land, Volk, Wirtschaftsleben und Kolonisation*, 2 vols. (Diessen vor München, 1913), 2:264–66.

84 Peyret, *Cartas sobre Misiones*, p. 33.

85 Ibid., p. 162. Peyret gives no reason for this statement. Either his was the first observation of a phenomenon which had existed without being recorded earlier, or possibly an outbreak appeared at the time of his trip just as has occurred in the modern settlement period, especially at times of low water on the Alto Paraná and its tributaries.

86 Hernández, *Cartas misioneras*, p. 100.

87 Ibid., p. 99.

88 Peyret, *Cartas sobre Misiones*, pp. 127–28.

89 Ramón Lista, *El territorio de las misiones* (Buenos Aires, 1883), pp. 33–34.

CHAPTER 5: PUBLIC LANDS AND GOVERNMENT COLONIZATION

1 D. G. de la Fuente, *Tierras, colonias y agricultura. Recopilación de leyes, decretos y otras disposiciones nacionales* (Buenos Aires, 1894), p. 87.

2 Ibid., pp. 95, 120.

3 The terms sección (10,000 ha) and lote (100 ha) were employed especially for Misiones. See Art. 10 of Law 1,265 in Augusto da Rocha, *Colección completa de leyes nacionales sancionadas por el Honorable Congreso durante los años 1852 a 1917*, vols. 4 and 5 (Buenos Aires, 1918), 5:357. In the rest of Argentina, i.e., Patagonia, the Pampa, and the Chaco, the word sección meant a unit of 1,000,000 ha; this unit was subdivided into four *fracciones* of 250,-000 ha each, and these into square lotes of 10,000 ha. The discrepancy in terminology is not explained and may be an oversight. In subsequent legislation the lote of 10,000 ha is also referred to in Misiones. See, for example, colonization Law 2,857 of Nov. 18, 1891. In this chapter the word lote will be used to refer to a land unit of 10,000 ha.

4 See Rafael Hernández, *Cartas misioneras* (Buenos Aires, 1887), and his "Informe sobre la fundación de las primeras colonias en Misiones," *Revista de la Sociedad Geográfica Argentina* 2 (1884):142–64. R. Hernández was the brother of José Hernández who was also interested in rural life in Argentina and wrote *Martín Fierro*, a classic of Argentine literature which deals with life on the Pampa.

5 Michael George Mulhall, and E. T. Mulhall, *Handbook of the River Plate: 1885* (Buenos Aires, 1885), p. 224.

6 D. G. de la Fuente, *Tierras, colonias y agricultura*, p. 250.

7 Misiones Territory, *La tierra pública y su colonización: Yerbales* (Buenos Aires, 1894), p. 12.

8 Data compiled by the author from topographic maps of the colonies prepared by Hernández, *Cartas misioneras*.

9 D. G. de la Fuente, *Tierras, colonias y agricultura*, p. 253. Unless otherwise stated, hereafter texts of laws and decretos are from Rocha, *Colección*; and Rocha, *Decretos reglamentarios de leyes nacionales clasificadas*, 4 vols. (Buenos Aires, 1935).

10 Nicasio Oroño, *Informe sobre colonización de tierras nacionales* (Buenos Aires, 1890), pp. 36–40; Oroño, *Informe del Director de Tierras, Inmigración y Agricultura a S.E. El Sr. Ministro del Interior sobre las denuncias del diario "La Prensa"* (Buenos Aires, 1892), p. 88.

11 Misiones Territory, *La tierra pública*, p. 31.

12 Faustino R. Berrondo Guiñazú, "Estudios de antecedentes de las adjudicaciones realizadas por la legislatura de la Provincia de Corrientes, por la ley de 21 de junio de 1881 en el Territorio Nacional de Misiones," manuscript (Buenos Aires, 1947), p. 14.

13 Brazil was awarded an area as large as Misiones itself by the arbitration of President Grover Cleveland. The Brazilian claim to eastern Misiones dated back to the treaty of 1750 under which Portugal relinquished all claims to the Philippine Islands in exchange for Spanish approval of a westward extension of the Brazilian frontier. See Estanislao S. Zeballos, *Arbitration Upon a Part of the National Territory of Misiones Disputed by the United States of Brazil* (New York, 1893), on this question.

14 Juan Queirel, *Misiones* (Buenos Aires, 1897), p. 368.

15 Misiones Territory, *La tierra pública*, p. 11.

16 Queirel, *Misiones*, p. 440.

17 The colony was named after Aimé Bonpland.

18 Author's analysis of colony maps in Oficina de Tierras y Bosques, Posadas, Misiones, Nov., 1965.

19 Queirel, *Misiones*, p. 372.

20 Republic of Argentina, Departamento de Tierras, Colonias y Agricultura, "Mesa de entradas y salidas, expediente No. 2,438, P," Unpublished archival report, 1895.

21 Queirel, *Misiones*, p. 372.

22 Ibid., p. 401. Private rental prices in these areas soon exceeded the value of the land itself. Settlers complained to the government and probably helped to harden the official attitude toward land reclamation proceedings against the terratenientes of Misiones.

23 As early as Sept. 3, 1877, Argentina began accepting Volga Germans directly from Bremen, Germany, after they had decided not to go to Brazil. See *Der deutsche Auswanderer* 33 (1937):86. Germans first began to colonize southern Brazil in 1824. Descendants of these early pioneers had already opened land close to the Misiones border by the late 19th century.

24 Misiones Province, *Planeamiento de la Provincia de Misiones*, 2 vols. (Buenos Aires, 1961), 2:30. See also Jean Roche, *La Colonisation Allemand et le Rio Grande do Sul* (Paris, 1959).

25 Queirel, *Misiones*, pp. 331–33.

26 Francisco Latzina, *La Argentina considerada en sus aspectos físico, social y económico*, 2 vols. (Buenos Aires, 1902), 1:450.

27 Misiones Province, *Planeamiento*, 2:32–33.

28 Colony maps in Oficina de Tierras y Bosques, Posadas.

29 The so-called Poor Zone is defined by Misiones Province, Ministerio

de Asuntos Agrarios, "Registro: Decreto 859, Expediente No. 336/61, April 5, 1961," Unpublished archival report, 1961. Article 2 of the decree states that the *Zona Pobre* consists of: Cerro Corá and expansions NE, SW, and Secciones A,B,C,F; Colonia Bonpland and expansions I, II, III; Picada Bonpland a Yerbal Viejo and Secciones Ia and IIa; Picada San Javier a Cerro Corá, Secciones N and S; Expansión N of the Colony of San Javier; Caá-Guazú, Secciones I, II, III; Colonias Profundidad, Sierra de San José, Santa Ana, and San Ignacio.

30 Yssouribehere, *Investigación agrícola*, p. 58.

31 "Suplemento especial de Misiones," *Analysis* 4 (1965):166.

32 See, for example, Francisco Manzi, *Breves apuntes sobre el Territorio de Misiones* (Corrientes, 1910), pp. 161–62.

33 Carlos D. Girola, *Monografía sobre la yerba mate* (Buenos Aires, 1926), pp. 4–7.

34 Antonio Gómez Langenheim, *Colonización en la República Argentina* (Buenos Aires, 1906), p. 422; text of the Decreto Reglamentario of Nov. 2, 1903 appears on pp. 414–36.

35 Rocha, *Colección*, 5:356.

36 Yssouribehere, *Investigación agrícola*, p. 200.

37 Republic of Argentina, Dirección General de Tierras: Geodesia, "Archivo de Mensuras: Folder 49, May 23, 1902," Unpublished archival report, 1902.

38 Ibid., "Folder 51, Aug. 10, 1903."

39 Decreto of Nov. 2, 1903, Article 10, regulating Law 4,176.

40 Republic of Argentina, Dirección General de Tierras: Geodesia, "Archivo de Mensuras: Duplicado No. 142: Profundidad (No. 54)," Unpublished archival report, 1906.

41 Misiones Province. Oficina de Tierras y Bosques, "Colonias: Asesoría de topografía y mensuras," Unpublished archival report, 1963, p. 1.

42 Republic of Argentina, Dirección General de Tierras: Geodesia, "Archivo de Mensuras, Folder 56, 1906," esp. pp. 1–6. The urban center of Bonpland was also mapped by Fouilland on lot 143 in Colonia Bonpland as part of the same project.

43 Ibid.

44 V. Lunnasvaara, "Colonia Finlandesa: Misioneksen suomalaissiirtola," *Terra* 44 (1932):5.

45 Information from *El Noticiero* (Posadas), May 16, 1906, No. 1,387, a copy of which appears in Republic of Argentina, Dirección General de Tierras: Geodesia, "Archivo de Mensuras, Folder 56, 1906."

46 Lunnasvaara, "Colonia Finlandesa," p. 6.

47 Yssouribehere, *Investigación agrícola*, pp. 85–86.

48 Ibid., p. 87.
49 Carlos Burmeister, *Memoria sobre el Territorio de Misiones* (Buenos Aires, 1899), pp. 34–35. The Neumann technique involved soaking the hard seeds for many hours.
50 P. Allain, *Proyecto de una plantación de yerba mate en Misiones* (Buenos Aires, 1910).
51 Gustav Niederlein, *Reisebriefe von der deutsch-argentinischen Expedition zur Prüfung der Colonisationsfähigkeit der Lezama'schen Misionesländereien* (Berlin, 1883).
52 Herrmann F. Hassel, "Los alemanes en Misiones," *El Territorio* (Posadas), June 2, 1965, pp. 11–12.
53 Republic of Argentina, Dirección General de Tierras: Geodesia, "Archivo de Mensuras, Mapoteca C, No. 86: Amojonamiento de chacras en la Picada San Javier a Cerro Corá," Unpublished archival report, 1915. See esp. map of colony.
54 Ibid.
55 Ibid., p. 3.
56 Ibid., p. 95. For further information on the problem of the mensú, see J. A. Solari, *Miseria de la riqueza argentina* (Buenos Aires, 1932); Alberto Carlos Muello, *Misiones: Las cataratas del Iguazú, el Alto Paraná y el cultivo de la yerba mate* (Buenos Aires, ca. 1930), pp. 73–77.
57 Villa Svea is located 3 km southwest of the modern city of Oberá. Swedish settlers are still there, as is a Swedish consulate in Oberá.
58 Herbert Wilhelmy, *Siedlung im südamerikanischen Urwald* (Hamburg, 1949), pp. 21–25.
59 Republic of Argentina, Dirección General de Tierras: Geodesia, "Archivo de Mensuras, Mapoteca C, No. 86," pp. 4–11.
60 Ibid., map of colony.
61 Th. Fuhrmann, "Leandro N. Alem, wie es wurde," in Herrmann F. Hassel, ed., *Deutscher Kalender für den Alto Paraná* (Buenos Aires, 1939), pp. 49–53.
62 Lisandro de la Torre, *El Territorio de Misiones: La industria yerbatera* (Buenos Aires, 1924), p. 84.
63 Francisco Suaiter Martínez, *Problemas sociales y económicos de Misiones* (Buenos Aires, 1928), p. 120.
64 Hassel, ed., *Deutscher Kalender* (1934), p. 42.
65 Misiones Province. Oficina de Tierras y Bosques, "Colonias: Asesoría de topografía y mensuras (Aprobación de pueblos)," Unpublished archival report, 1963, pp. 1–2.
66 Hassel, *Deutscher Kalender* (1940), p. 114.

67 Republic of Argentina, Dirección General de Tierras: Geodesia, "Archivo de Mensuras, Acta No. 102," Unpublished archival report, 1923.
68 Interview with Atilio Fernández de la Puente, former head, Oficina de Tierras y Bosques, Posadas, Aug. 22, 1965.
69 Misiones Province, Oficina de Tierras y Bosques, "Colonias," p. 2.
70 Land title maps, Oficina de Tierras y Bosques, Posadas.
71 Title records, Oficina de Tierras y Bosques, Posadas.
72 Republic of Argentina, Dirección General de Tierras: Geodesia, "Archivo de Mensuras, Folder No. 170, Buenos Aires, 1939," pp. 1–2.
73 Ibid.
74 Some pioneers of different nationality and religion have had gun battles over lot boundaries, according to local accounts. Similar serious difficulties are reported among colonists in Israel when they come from very different backgrounds and must work together in *moshavim* settlements. See Werner Richter, "Der Moshav Ovdim. Entwicklung und Probleme einer typischen kooperativen ländlichen Siedlungsform in Israel," *Geographische Rundschau* 22 (1970):175–85, esp. p. 181.
75 Lack of urban facilities is a major problem in modern colonization efforts elsewhere in forested regions. See, for example, Robert C. Eidt, "Pioneer Settlement in Colombia," *Geographical Review* 58 (1968):298–300.
76 Misiones Province, Oficina de Tierras y Bosques, "Colonias," p. 1.

CHAPTER 6: FOREIGN COLONIZATION COMPANIES
IN MISIONES

1 Information about the Compañía Introductora was kindly furnished by C. Jauch, formerly administrative secretary to A. J. Schwelm.
2 Information about Santa Rosa may be obtained from Nilo Bernardes, "A colonização no município de Santa Rosa, estado do Rio Grande do Sul," *Revista Brasileira de Geografía* 12 (1950):33–42.
3 See, for example, Werner Emmerich, "Das mittelalterliche Siedelwerk (Landesausbau und Rodung)," in Hans Scherzer, ed., *Gau Bayreuth, Land, Volk und Geschichte*, 2nd ed. (München, 1942), pp. 276–300.
4 Hans Fehn, "Siedlungsrückgang in den Hochlagen des Oberpfälzer und Bayerischen Waldes," in *Erlanger Geographische Arbeiten* (*Festschrift für Otto Berninger*) 10 (1963):155–67.

5 In addition to possessing linear fields, the farmyards in some Drubbel settlements are also arranged in linear form.

6 Interview with O. Berninger, Erlangen, Feb. 3, 1965.

7 Hans Fehn, "Waldhufendörfer im Hinteren Bayerischen Wald," *Mitteilungen und Jahresberichte der Geographischen Gesellschaft Nürnberg* 6 (1937):5–61.

8 Rudolf Käubler, "Die erzgebirgischen Waldhufendörfer zur Zeit ihrer Entstehung," *Wissenschaftliche Zeitschrift der Martin Luther-Universität* (Halle-Wittenburg, Math. Nat. XII/10, 1963), p. 729.

9 Waldhufen settlements, including closely related forms such as the Hagenhufendorf, occur in many parts of Germany. In the north they are found along the lower Rhine near the international border, and in the Schaumburg-Lippe, Bückeberg, Aller-Leine, and Mecklenburg-Pommern districts. In central Germany they exist in the northern Schwarzwald, Odenwald, Spessart, southern Rhön, Thüringer Wald, Frankenwald, Fichtelgebirge, Bayerischen Wald, Vogtland, Erzgebirge, and in the areas of Sudetenland and Schlesien, occupied by Poland since World War II. Numerous different linear settlement forms exist in other parts of Germany (*Reihendörfer*) as do a variety of long-lot field forms (*Streifenfluren*).

For the reader who is interested in pursuing further the study of the origins of Waldhufen settlements, the following references are especially important: August Meitzen, *Siedlung und Agrarwesen der Westgermanen und Ostgermanen, der Kelten, Römer, Finnen und Slaven*, 4 vols. (Berlin, 1895: Republished in 4 vols. Aalen, 1963); Otto Schlüter, *Die Siedlungen im nordöstlichen Thüringen, Ein Beispiel für die Behandlung siedlungsgeographischen Fragen* (Berlin, 1903); Rudolf Martiny, *Die Grundrißgestaltung der deutschen Siedlungen* (Gotha, 1928); W. Bernard, *Das Waldhufendorf in Schlesien* (Breslau, 1931); Johannes Leipoldt, "Die Flurformen Sachsens," *Petermanns Geographische Mitteilungen* 82 (1936):341–45; R. Blohm, *Die Hagenhufendörfer in Schaumburg-Lippe* (Oldenburg i.O., 1943); Wilhelm Müller-Wille, "Die Hagenhufendörfer in Schaumburg-Lippe," *Petermanns Geographische Mitteilungen* 90 (1944):245–47; Hans Mortensen, "Zur Entstehung der deutschen Flurformen, insbesondere des Waldhufendorfes," *Nachrichten der Akademie der Wissenschaft* (Göttingen, Phil.-Hist. Klasse 1946/47), pp. 76–80; Georg Niemeier, "Frühformen der Waldhufen," *Petermanns Geographische Mitteilungen* 93 (1949):14–27; Franz Engel, "Rodungskolonisation und Vorformen der Hagenhufen im 12. Jahrhundert," *Die schaumburgisch-lippische Heimat* 11 (1951):125–46;

Edgar F. Warnecke, *Engter und seine Bauerschaften* (Hannover, 1958); Walther Manshard, "Afrikanische Waldhufen und Wald-streifenfluren — wenig bekannte Formenelemente der Agrarland-schaften in Oberguinea," *Die Erde* 92 (1961):246–58; Hans-Jürgen Nitz, *Die Ländlichen Siedlungsformen des Odenwaldes* (Heidel-berg, 1962); Karl Albert Habbe, "Die 'Waldhufensiedlungen' in den Gebirgen Südwestdeutschland als Problem der systematischen Siedlungsgeographie," *Berichte zur deutschen Landeskunde* 37 (1966):40–52; Rainer Krüger, "Das 'eigentliche' Waldhufendorf Begriffsbestimmung-Formaltypologische Einordnung-Formgenese," *Berichte zur deutschen Landeskunde* 39 (1967):273–80; R. Krüger, *Typologie des Waldhufendorfes nach Einzelformen und deren Ver-breitungsmustern* (Göttingen, 1967); Harald Uhlig, and Cay Lie-nau, eds., *Materialien zur Terminologie der Agrarlandschaft: Flur und Flurformen* (Gießen, 1967), vol. 1.

10 Interview with E. Bischoff, Monte Carlo, Aug. 25, 1965. Bischoff ar-rived April 17, 1919, at Puerto Rico and was the colony's first settler. He and his wife now reside in Monte Carlo.

11 Ibid.

12 Pedro J. Yssouribehere, *Investigación agrícola en el Territorio de Misiones* (Buenos Aires, 1904), pp. 204–5.

13 N. R. Engwald, *Eldorado: 20 Aar i Sydamerika* (Copenhagen [?], 1938), pp. 95–110.

14 Interview with Schwelm's Eldorado Colony manager, C. Jauch, Monte Carlo, Aug. 22, 1965. Most of the factual information in this section comes from interviews with E. Bischoff, H. Helm, C. Jauch, and J. Wipfel of Monte Carlo, and J. Fausch, Caraguatay.

15 Kenneth Lindsay, *Eldorado, an Agricultural Settlement. A Brief History of its Origin and Development* (Birmingham, Eng., 1931), p. 13. It is to be noted, however, that, in densely forested areas like this, the strips of land must not be so wide as to isolate pioneers, or the conditions of the damero form will be repeated.

16 See, for example, Schwelm's (Compañía Eldorado, Colonización y Explotación de Bosques, S.A., Ltda.) *Die Entwicklung der Eldo-rado-Kolonien: 1919–1929* (Buenos Aires, ca. 1929); and, by the same Company, *La Colonia Eldorado, Río Alto Paraná, Misiones* (Buenos Aires, 1931); *Some Thoughts on Colonization* (London, 1932); *Avantages qu'offre la Colonie San Alberto, Río Alto Paraná, Misiones, Argentine* (Buenos Aires, 1933); and *Colonias de la Com-pañía Eldorado, S.A., Eldorado, Monte Carlo, Puerto Rico* (Buenos Aires, 1934).

17 Approximately 300 such agencies blossomed between 1919 and

1924. Among those directing colonists to Latin America were Die Auskunftsstelle für Auswanderer in Dresden, Der Sankt Raphael Verein in Limburg a.d. L. (Catholic), Der Evangelische Verein für deutsche Auswanderer in Witzenhausen a.d. W. (Protestant), and Die Siedlungs- und Handelsgesellschaft Neu-Karlsruhe (Eingetragener Verein) in Karlsruhe.

18 See the undivided land just east of Puerto Monte Carlo, Fig. 15.

19 One colonist interviewed in Monte Carlo stated that he had come from the medieval Waldhufendorf of Nassau in the Erzgebirge where it took him one hour and a half to walk the length of the village section. Others report complete sympathy and familiarity with the Monte Carlo development and would not like to see it changed.

20 "Suplemento especial de Misiones," *Analysis* 4 (1965):282.

21 Wilhelm Ernst von Jungenfeld, *Ein deutsches Schicksal im Urwald* (Berlin, 1933), pp. 124–37.

22 See Reglamento de la Ley de Tierras of Nov. 8, 1906, Article 66, which states "The state is not responsible for the condition of the land. It is assumed that land will be inspected by the purchaser before buying." Augusto da Rocha, *Decretos reglamentarios de leyes nacionales clasificadas*, 4 vols. (Buenos Aires, 1935), 1:11.

23 Héctor Barreyro, *Ideas de gobierno* (Buenos Aires, 1919), p. 26.

24 See E. A. Pérez Llana, *Derecho agrario*, 3rd ed., 2 vols. (Santa Fe, 1959), p. 462.

25 See articles 798, 824–829, of the decree of Jan. 19, 1927. A copy of this decree is on file at the Comisión Reguladora de la Yerba Mate in Posadas, Misiones.

26 See Ernesto Daumas, "El problema de la yerba mate," *Revista de la Economía Argentina* 25 (1930):49.

27 Héctor Barreyro, "Censo de las plantaciones de yerba mate en el Territorio de la Gobernación de Misiones," *Revista de Ciencias Económicas* 16 (1928):1,627.

28 Daumas, "El problema de la yerba mate," pp. 24–25.

29 Data supplied by C. Jauch, Monte Carlo, Aug. 1965.

30 Daumas, "El problema de la yerba mate," pp. 33–34.

31 Cooperativa Agrícola Eldorado, *Memoria, balance general y cuenta de pérdidas y excedentes* (Eldorado, 1968).

32 Cooperativa Agrícola Mixta de Monte Carlo, *Memoria y balance general* (Monte Carlo, 1969).

33 Gustav Klusak, *Die Raiffeisen-Kreditgenossenschaften* (Frankfurt a. M., 1964), p. 14.

34 A published call had been made as early as 1912 for the *Cajas* Raif-

feisen as the best solution to Argentina's agricultural credit problem. M. de Campo Mendivil, *Una nueva forma de cooperativa agrícola* (Buenos Aires, 1912).

35 Federico Puerta, *Misiones: Sus cooperativas, su campo, sus industrias* (Apóstoles, 1957), p. 33.

36 Norman R. Stewart, "Tea — A New Agricultural Industry for Argentina," *Economic Geography* 36 (1960):267–76.

37 Law 3,831, Misiones Province.

38 Nevertheless, only five Monte Carlo families left for Germany during the Hitler regime. According to other colonists, two of these returned after the war at Argentine government expense.

39 Data from J. Wipfel, Secretary, Cooperativa Agrícola Mixta de Monte Carlo.

40 A small tractor costs approximately five times the US price.

41 Ludwig Holzner, "The Role of History and Tradition in the Urban Geography of West Germany," *Annals of the Association of American Geographers* 60 (1970):315–39, esp. p. 335.

42 Karl Albert Habbe, *Das Flurbild des Hofsiedlungsgebiets im mittleren Schwarzwald am Ende des 18. Jahrhunderts* (Bad Godesberg, 1960).

43 Leo Waibel, *Die europäische Kolonisation Südbrasiliens* (Bonn, 1955), esp. p. 94.

44 Leo Waibel, "Princípios da Colonização Europeia no Sul do Brasil," *Revista Brasileira de Geografía* 11 (1949):159–222, esp. p. 197.

45 Alfred Hettner, "Das Deutschtum in Südbrasilien," *Geographische Zeitschrift* 8 (1902):609–626, esp. pp. 612–14.

46 Ibid., p. 614.

47 Paul Langhans, "Die mittlern Serra-Kolonien in Rio Grande do Sul," *Petermanns Mitteilungen* 35, (1889):185–87.

48 Herlig Zschocke, *Die Waldhufensiedlungen am linken deutschen Niederrhein* (Wiesbaden, 1963).

49 Alfred Hettner, "Das südlichste Brasilien," *Zeitschrift der Gesellschaft für Erdkunde* 26 (1891):85–144, esp. p. 86; H. von Jhering, and Paul Langhans, "Das südliche Koloniengebiet von Rio Grande do Sul," *Petermanns Mitteilungen* 33 (1887):328–43, esp. p. 330.

50 Karl-Alexander Wettstein, *Brasilien und die deutsch-brasilianische Kolonie Blumenau* (Leipzig, 1970), esp. pp. 142–46; and Stuart Clark Rothwell, *The Old Italian Colonial Zone of Rio Grande do Sul, Brazil* (Pôrto Alegre, 1959), esp. sketch opp. p. 48.

51 Orlando Valverde, "Excursão à região colonial antiga do Rio Grande do Sul," *Revista Brasileira de Geografía* 10 (1948):477–534, esp. pp. 504–6; Rothwell, *The Old Italian Colonial Zone.*

52 Comissão de Festejos, *Centenário de Blumenau: 1850–1950* (Rio de Janeiro, 1950), esp. pp. 145–46. The new form of settlement was by no means immune to Indian attacks. In this regard see Gerhard Kohlhepp, "Die deutschstämmigen Siedlungsgebiete im Südbrasilianischen Staate Santa Catarina," in *Heidelberger Studien zur Kulturgeographie: Festgabe zum 65. Geburtstag von Gottfried Pfeifer* (Wiesbaden, 1966), pp. 219–44, esp. p. 232.

53 Orlando Valverde, "Excursão à região colonial antiga do Rio Grande do Sul."

54 Other useful references to these matters may be found in: Robert Avé-Lallement, *Reise durch Südbrasilien im Jahre 1858*, 2 vols. (Leipzig, 1859); Adalbert Jahn, *Die Kolonien von São Leopoldo in der Provinz Rio Grande do Sul* (Leipzig, 1871); Hugo Zöllner, *Die deutschen im brasilischen Urwald*, 2 vols. (Berlin, 1883); Wilhelm Breitenbach, *Die Provinz Rio Grande do Sul Brazilien und die deutsche Auswanderung dahin* (Heidelberg, 1885); Ernst Wagemann, *Die deutschen Kolonisten im brasilianischen Staate Espírito Santo* (München, 1915); Siegfried Endreß, *Blumenau. Werden und Wesen einer deutschbrasilianischen Landschaft* (Öhringen, 1938); Lourival Câmara, "Estrangeiros em Santa Catarina," *Revista Brasileira de Geografía* 10 (1948):51–253; G. Neufeldt, "Das neu erschloßene Siedlungsgebiet in Nord Paraná," *Erdkunde* 5 (1951): 233–37; Leopoldo Petry, *São Leopoldo berço da colonização alemã do Rio Grande do Sul*, 2d ed. (São Leopoldo, 1964); Jean Roche, *A colonização alemã no Espírito Santo* (São Paulo, 1968).

55 Walter Ostermann, "Neu-Karlsruhe: Monografie einer deutschen Kolonie," *Südamerika* 4 (1954):657–60.

56 Herbert Wilhelmy, "Neu-Karlsruhe (Liebig): Ein warnendes Beispiel gescheiterter Genossenschaftssiedlung in nördlichen Argentinien," *Festschrift für Karl Maßman* (Kiel, 1954), pp. 240–62, esp. p. 244. See also Hermann Lamm, *Auswanderungsmöglichkeiten in Argentinien* (Dresden, 1929), p. 80.

57 Ostermann, "Neu-Karlsruhe," p. 658. The estancia was La Merced; it belonged to the South American Cattle Farms, Ltd., a branch organization of Liebig's.

58 Ibid., p. 659.

59 Wilhelmy, "Neu-Karlsruhe," p. 253.

60 Herrmann Hassel, "Los Alemanes en Misiones," *El Territorio* (Posadas), June 2, 1965, pp. 11–12.

61 Reginald William Thompson, *Voice From the Wilderness* (London, 1947), p. 165.

62 The Victoria Colonization Company, Ltd., *Victoria: Colony for British Settlers in Paraná River, Argentina* (London, 1935), p. 7.
63 Thompson, *Voice From the Wilderness*, p. 180.
64 A well costs as much as 1 ha of land in Misiones. If the required construction insurance were added, the cost could run to five times the cost of 1 ha of virgin forest.
65 In 1964 the price was 45,000 pesos per ton when delivered in Candelaria.
66 The Japanese claim successful experimentation with lupine (*Lupinus*, sp.), a legume which appears to give good ground cover for up to six months in Misiones. See Robert C. Eidt, "Japanese Agricultural Colonization: A New Attempt at Land Opening in Argentina," *Economic Geography* 44 (1968):15.

CHAPTER 7: SETTLEMENT AND POPULATION GROWTH
IN MISIONES

1 Unless otherwise stated, statistical data for tables in this chapter are taken from Republic of Argentina, *Cuarto censo nacional* (Buenos Aires, 1947).
2 Federación de Cooperativas Agrícolas de Misiones, Ltda., *Boletín Mensual* 11 (1949):1; Federación de Cooperativas Agrícolas de Misiones, Ltda., *Memoria y balance general* (Posadas, 1960).
3 Misiones Province, *Planeamiento de la Provincia de Misiones*, 2 vols. (Buenos Aires, 1961), 2:73.

CHAPTER 8: CONCLUSION

1 An example of the achievements of isolated foreign groups which are allowed to remain together long enough to become socially and economically stabilized is that of the Mennonites in northwestern Paraguay. Increasing contacts with the rest of Paraguay are now rather smoothly bringing about the process of assimilation with this respected community after approximately a half century of independent adjustment. See esp. Joseph Winfield Fretz, *Immigrant Group Settlements in Paraguay* (North Newton, Kansas, 1962), "An Attitude Survey," pp. 135–40.
2 In a related example, construction of the final transportation link between Lima and Pulcallpa along a now well-known trans-Andean route was halted in 1938 by the Padre Abad mountains. One of the

road engineers eventually found a description of the only feasible pass through the range by reading the detailed accounts left by the Franciscan Order of its colonization activities in eastern Peru. Air reconnaissance methods had not revealed the pass because of heavy forest vegetation and almost continuous cloud cover. Only after the Franciscan records were investigated was it possible to finish the road. Settlement activity then began which has resulted in an economic boom in these tropical lowlands as well as in the gradual integration of the region with the rest of Peru. See Robert C. Eidt, "Pioneer Settlement in Eastern Peru," *Annals of the Association of American Geographers* 52 (1962):255–78.

3 See Leo Waibel's concern about better mapping of Brazilian pioneer settlements in his "European Colonization in Southern Brazil," *Geographical Review* 40 (1950):529–47.

4 See, as well, the discussion of Waldhufendorf disadvantages on pages 202–4.

5 See p. 145 and Table 10.

6 Misiones Province, *Planeamiento de la Provincia de Misiones*, 2 vols. (Buenos Aires, 1961), 2:91. Since most holdings on government lands were untitled, it is assumed that most of the "privately owned land" reported in 1947 was outside the narrow strip of federal land in Misiones.

7 Christopher Turner in Adolph Julius Schwelm, *Some Thoughts on Colonization* (London, 1932).

BIBLIOGRAPHY

Aigner, Gerhard. "Der Jesuitenstaat in Paraguay und seine Wirtschaft." Ph.D. Dissertation, Hochschule für Welthandel, Wien, 1959.

Allain, P. *Proyecto de una plantación de yerba mate en Misiones.* Buenos Aires, 1910.

Alsina, Juan A. *La inmigración europea en la República Argentina.* 3rd ed. Buenos Aires, 1898.

Ambrosetti, Juan B. "Rápida ojeada sobre el Territorio de Misiones." *Boletín del Instituto Geográfico Argentino* 13 (1892):168–80.

————. "Segundo viaje a Misiones por el Alto Paraná e Iguazú." *Boletín del Instituto Geográfico Argentino* 15 (1894):18–114, 247–304.

————. "Tercer viaje a Misiones." *Boletín del Instituto Geográfico Argentino* 16 (1895):391–523.

————. "Viaje a las misiones argentinas y brasileras por el Alto Uruguay." *Revista del Museo de la Plata* 3 (1892):419–48.

————. "Viaje a las misiones argentinas y brasileras por el Alto Uruguay." *Revista del Museo de la Plata* 5 (1893):225–50.

————. "Un viaje a Misiones." *Anales de la Sociedad Científica Argentina* 38 (1894):31–52.

Andree, Karl. *Buenos Ayres und die argentinischen Provinzen.* Leipzig, 1856.

Angelelli, Victorio. *Reconocimiento geológico del Territorio de Misiones en busca de bauxita.* Buenos Aires, 1936.

Aparicio, Francisco de, and Difrieri, Horacio A., eds. *La Argentina: Suma de geografía.* 9 vols. Buenos Aires, 1958–63.

Asociación Rural Yerbatera Argentina, and Federación de Cooperativas Agrícolas de Misiones, Ltda. *La producción de tung en Misiones y sus aspectos diversos.* Posadas, 1944.

Augelli, John P. "Agricultural Colonization in the Dominican Republic." *Economic Geography* 38 (1962):15–27.

————. "Cultural and Economic Changes of Bastos, a Japanese Colony on Brazil's Paulista Frontier." *Annals of the Association of American Geographers* 48 (1958):3–19.

Avé-Lallement, Robert. *Reise durch Südbrasilien im Jahre 1858.* 2 vols. Leipzig, 1859.

Azara, Félix de. *Descripción e historia del Paraguay y Río de la Plata.* 2 vols. Asunción, 1896.

———. *Geografía física y esférica de las provincias del Paraguay y Misiones Guaraníes.* Montevideo, 1904.

———. *Viajes por la América Meridional.* 2 vols. Madrid, 1934.

Baker, Charles Laurence. "The Lavafield of the Paraná Basin." *Journal of Geology* 31 (1923):66–79.

Baklanoff, Eric N., ed. *New Perspectives of Brazil.* Nashville, 1966.

Balestra, Juan. *Informe de la Dirección General de Tierras y Colonias.* Buenos Aires, 1894.

Barnes, C. P. "Economies of the Long-Lot Farm." *Geographical Review* 25 (1935):298–301.

Barreyro, Héctor. "Censo de las plantaciones de yerba mate en el Territorio de la Gobernación de Misiones." *Revista de Ciencias Económicas* 16 (1928): 1624–29.

———. *Ideas de gobierno.* Buenos Aires, 1919.

Basaldúa, Florenzio de. *Pasado-presente-porvenir del Territorio Nacional de Misiones.* La Plata, 1901.

Beltrame, Alfredo. "Industria y cultivo de la yerba mate en la Argentina." *Revista de Economía Argentina* 10 (1923):162–66.

Beltrán, Juan G. *Centenario de Corrientes. Reintegración de Misiones al territorio correntino.* Buenos Aires, 1915.

Bernabe, Farina, R., and Canteros Bauna, T., eds. "La hormiga minera," *Mundo Misionero* 1 (1960):15.

Bernard, W. *Das Waldhufendorf in Schlesien.* Breslau, 1931.

Bernardes, Lysia Maria Cavalcanti. "O problema das 'frentes pioneiras' no estado do Paraná." *Revista Brasileira de Geografía* 15 (1953):355–84.

Bernardes, Nilo. "Caracteristicas gerais da agricultura brasileira em meados do século XX." *Revista Brasileira de Geografía* 23 (1961): 363–420.

———. "A colonizãço no município de Santa Rosa, estado do Rio Grande do Sul." *Revista Brasileira de Geografía* 12 (1950):33–42.

Berninger, Otto. "Der Anteil des Deutschtums an der Bildung eines bodenständigen Bauerntums in Chile." *Lebensraumfragen europäischen Völker III.* Teil 2: *Süd America.* Liepzig [1944—never published; author consulted galley proofs].

Berrondo Guiñazú, Faustino R. "Estudios de antecedentes de las adjudicaciones realizadas por la legislatura de la Provincia de Corrientes, por la ley de 21 de junio de 1881 en el Territorio Nacional de Misiones." Manuscript. Buenos Aires, 1947. On file at Dirección de Catastro, Geodesia y Topografía, Posadas.

Bertoni, Moisés Santiago. *Descripción física y económica del Paraguay.* Puerto Bertoni, 1918.

Blohm, R. *Die Hagenhufendörfer in Schaumburg-Lippe.* Oldenburg i. O., 1943.

Blume, Helmut, and Schröder, Karl Heinz, eds. *Beiträge zur Geographie der Tropen und Subtropen. Festschrift zum 60. Geburtstag von Herbert Wilhelmy.* Tübingen, 1970.

Borcherdt, Christoph. "Junge Wandlungen der Kulturlandschaft in Venezuela." *Geographische Zeitschrift* 55 (1967):142–61.

Borea, Domingo. *La colonización oficial y particular en la República Argentina. La tierra en la República Argentina, inmigración y colonización. Nueva ley de tierras.* Buenos Aires, 1923.

Bowman, Isaiah. *The Pioneer Fringe.* New York, 1931.

————, ed. *The Limits of Land Settlement.* New York, 1937.

Breitenbach, Wilhelm. *Die Provinz Rio Grande do Sul Brasilien und die deutsche Auswanderung dahin.* Heidelberg, 1885.

Brinkmann, Th. "Der Yerba-Mate-Bau im argentinischen National Territorium Misiones als Grundlage bäuerlicher Siedlung." *Berichte über Landwirtschaft* n.F. 11 (1930):403–442.

Brücher, Wolfgang. *Die Erschließung des tropischen Regenwaldes am Ostrand der kolumbianischen Anden. Der Raum zwischen Río Ariari und Ecuador.* Tübingen, 1968.

Bruman, Henry J. "Post-War Agricultural Colonization in Brazil." Mimeographed. ONR Report Nonr 233(03). Washington, D.C., 1958.

Brünger, W. *Einführung in die Siedlungsgeographie.* Heidelberg, 1961.

Bürger, Otto. *Argentinien. Land, Volk, und Wirtschaft.* 2 vols. Leipzig, 1924.

Burgos, Juan Jacinto. *Las heladas en la Argentina.* Buenos Aires, 1963.

Burmeister, Carlos. *Memoria sobre el Territorio de Misiones.* Buenos Aires, 1899.

Busaniche, Hernán. *La arquitectura en las misiones jesuíticas guaraníes.* Santa Fe, 1955.

Câmara, Lourival. "Estrangeiros em Santa Catarina." *Revista Brasileira de Geografía* 10 (1948):51–253.

Campo Mendivil, M. de. *Una nueva forma de cooperativa agrícola.* Buenos Aires, 1912.

Campolieti, Roberto. *La Colonizazione Italiana nell'Argentina.* Buenos Aires, 1902.

Canals Frau, Salvador. *Las poblaciones indígenas de la Argentina: su origen, su pasado, su presente.* Buenos Aires, 1953.

Cárcano, Miguel Angel. *Evolución histórica del régimen de la tierra pública: 1810–1916.* 2nd ed. Buenos Aires, 1925.

Carlevari, Isidro J. *La Argentina.* 2nd ed. Buenos Aires, 1964.

Charlevoix, Pedro Francisco Javier de. *Historia del Paraguay.* 5 vols. Madrid, 1910–14.

Colonia Caraguatay, Misiones. Eigentum der Doctoren Nicolás A. Avellaneda und Alfredo Echagüe. Buenos Aires, ca. 1930.

Comissão de Festejos. *Centenário de Blumenau: 1850–1950.* Rio de Janeiro, 1950.

Compañía Eldorado, Colonización y Explotación de Bosques, S.A. Ltda. *Avantage qu'offre la Colonie San Alberto, Río Alto Paraná, Misiones, Argentine.* Buenos Ayres, 1933.

———. *La Colonia Eldorado Río Alto Paraná, Misiones.* Buenos Aires, 1931.

———. *Colonias de la Compañía Eldorado, Eldorado, Monte Carlo, Puerto Rico.* Buenos Aires, 1934.

———. *Eldorado.* Buenos Aires, 1934.

———. *Die Entwicklung der Eldorado-Kolonien: 1919–1929.* Buenos Aires, ca. 1929.

———. *Das kolonisatorische Werk der Eldorado-Gesellschaft.* Buenos Aires, 1929.

———. *Leben und Treiben in Eldorado.* Buenos Aires, 1931.

———. *Some Thoughts on Colonization.* London, 1932.

Conforti, Emilio A. "Colonización, reforma agraria, migraciones internas: Consideraciones, sugerencias, propuestas." Mimeographed. Quito, 1960.

Cooperativa Agrícola Eldorado. *Memoria, balance general y cuenta de pérdidas y excedentes.* Eldorado, 1968.

Cooperativa Agrícola Mixta de Monte Carlo. *Memoria y balance general.* Monte Carlo, 1969.

Cordier, Henri M. *Papiers inédites du Naturaliste Aimé Bonpland conservés à Buenos Aires.* Buenos Aires, 1914.

Corrientes Province. *Colección de datos y documentos referentes a Misiones como parte integrante del territorio de la Provincia de Corrientes hecha por una comisión nombrada por el gobierno de ella.* Corrientes, 1877.

———. *Recopilación completa de códigos, leyes y decretos reglamentarios vigentes de la Provincia de Corrientes.* 2 vols. Corrientes, 1904.

Cozzo, D. "Breve cartilla forestal para los productos de Misiones." *Mundo Misionero* 2 (1961):20–21.

Crist, Raymond E. "Bolivians Trek Eastward." *Américas* 15 (1963): 33–38.

Crist, Raymond E. and Guhl, Ernesto. "Pioneer Settlement in Eastern Colombia." In *Smithsonian Institution Annual Report for 1956*. Washington, D.C., No. 4282 (1957):391–414.

Daumas, Ernesto. "El problema de la yerba mate." *Revista de la Economía Argentina* 25 (1930):15–66.

Daus, Federico A., and García Gache, Roberto. *Fisonomía regional de la República Argentina*. Buenos Aires, 1959.

————. *Geografía física de la Argentina*. 4th ed. Buenos Aires, 1950.

————. *Geografía de la República Argentina*. Buenos Aires, 1954.

Davidson, Hunter. *Informe de una expedición al Alto Paraná para estudiar las mejoras necesarias en el Salto Grande de Apipé, agosto y setiembre de 1882*. Buenos Aires, 1882.

Davie, John Constanse. *Letters from Paraguay*. London, 1805.

Dickinson, Robert E. *Germany: A General and Regional Geography*. New York, 1953.

Dozier, Craig. L. *Land Development and Colonization in Latin America: Case Studies of Peru, Bolivia, and Mexico*. New York, 1969.

————. "Northern Paraná, Brazil: An Example of Organized Regional Development." *Geographical Review* 46 (1956):318–33.

————. "Northern Paraná, Brazil: Settlement and Development of a Recent Frontier Zone." Ph.D. dissertation, Johns Hopkins University, 1954.

————. "Problemas para la colonización efectiva de tierras nuevas en América Latina: Algunos ejemplos actuales." In *Unión Geográfica Internacional: Conferencia Regional Latinoamericana*, vol. 1. Mexico D.F., 1966, pp. 229–46.

Drewes, Wolfram U. "Die Bedeutung der modernen Verkehrserschließung für die wirtschaftliche Nutzung und dauernde Besiedlung eines tropischen Waldlandes." *Geographische Rundschau* 11 (1958):395–404.

————. "The Economic Development of the Western Montaña of Central Peru as Related to Transportation." *Andean Air Mail and Peruvian Times Supplement*. Lima, 1958.

————. "Die Erweiterung des Lebensraumes im südlichen Peru." *Geographische Rundschau* 15 (1963):55–60.

Eidt, Robert C. "Comparative Problems and Techniques in Tropical and Semi-Tropical Pioneer Settlement: Colombia, Peru and Argentina." *Yearbook of the Association of Pacific Coast Geographers* 26 (1964):37–42.

————. "Japanese Agricultural Colonization: A New Attempt at Land Opening in Argentina." *Economic Geography* 44 (1968):1–20.

————. "Modern Colonization as a Facet of Land Development in

Colombia, South America." *Yearbook of the Association of Pacific Coast Geographers* 29 (1967):21–42.

———. "A Note on Japanese Farmers in the Cauca Valley, Colombia." *Revista Geográfica* 18 (1956):41–51.

———. "Pioneer Settlement in Colombia." *Geographical Review* 58 (1968):298–300.

———. "Pioneer Settlement in Eastern Peru." *Annals of the Association of American Geographers* 52 (1962):255–78.

———. "Die Staatliche und Private Besiedlung von Misiones (Argentinien)." *Geographische Rundschau*, 17 (1965):464–70.

———. "Economic Features of Land Opening in the Peruvian Montaña." *The Professional Geographer* 18 (1966):146–50.

Eggers, Heinz. *Schwarzwald und Vogesen. Ein vergleichender Überblick.* Braunschweig, 1964.

Emmerich, F. *Leitfaden für Auswanderer.* München, 1920.

Endreß, Siegfried. *Blumenau. Werden und Wesen einer deutschbrasilianischen Landschaft.* Öhringen, 1938.

Engel, Franz. "Rodungskolonisation und Vorformen der Hagenhufen im 12. Jahrhundert." *Die schaumburgisch-lippische Heimat* 11 (1951):125–46.

Engwald, Nina Raben. *Eldorado. 20 Aar i Sydamerika.* Copenhagen [?], 1938.

Escandón, Juan de, and Nusdorfer, Bernhard. *Geschichte von Paraguay aus spanischen Handschriften übersetzt nebst dem Criminal-Prozess wider die Jesuiten in Spanien.* Frankfurt, 1769.

Evangelischer Verein für deutsche Ansiedler und Auswanderer. *Der deutsche Auswanderer* 33 (1937).

Ezcurra, Mariano de. *Cuestión social, cuestión rural.* Buenos Aires, 1923.

Faßbinder, Maria. *Der "Jesuitenstaat" in Paraguay.* Halle (Saale), 1926.

Federación de Cooperativas Agrícolas de Misiones, Ltda. *Boletín Mensual 11.* Posadas, 1949.

———. *Memoria y balance general.* Posadas, 1960.

Fehn, Hans. "Waldhufendörfer im Hinteren Bayerischen Wald." *Mitteilungen und Jahresberichte der Geographischen Gesellschaft* (Nürnberg) 6 (1937):5–61.

———. "Siedlungsrückgang in den Hochlagen des Oberpfälzer und Bayerischen Waldes." In *Erlanger Geographische Arbeiten (Festschrift für Otto Berninger)* 10 (1963):155–67.

Fernández Ramos, Raimundo. *Apuntes históricos sobre Misiones.* Madrid, 1929.

Fienup, Darrell Fischer, Brannon, Russell H., and Fender, Frank A. *The Agricultural Development of Argentina. A Policy and Development Perspective.* New York, 1969.

Fifer, J. Valerie. "Bolivia's Pioneer Fringe." *Geographical Review* 57 (1967):1–23.

Fina, Armando L. de, and Garbosky, Arturo J. *Difusión geográfica de cultivos índices en la Mesopotamia Argentina y sus causas.* Buenos Aires, 1948.

Fretz, Joseph Winfield. *Immigrant Group Settlements in Paraguay.* North Newton, Kansas, 1962.

Fuente, D. G. de la. *Tierras, colonias y agricultura. Recopilación de leyes, decretos y otras disposiciones nacionales.* Buenos Aires, 1894.

Fuentes Godo, Pedro M. and Roth, Alberto. "Problemas del manejo de suelos de Misiones." *IDIA* (Suplemento No. 1, 1960):218–21.

Fuhrmann, Th. "Leandro N. Alem. wie es wurde." In *Deutscher Kalender für den Alto Paraná.* Buenos Aires, 1939, pp. 49–53.

Furlong, Guillermo. "La acción de los jesuitas alemanes en la Argentina." *Mitteilungen. Institut für Auslandsbeziehungen* 11 (1961): 106–9.

———. *Misiones y sus pueblos de Guaraníes.* Buenos Aires, 1962.

Furnus, Adolfo C., with Obloblin, A. A., and Tarabanoff, J. *La yerba mate.* Buenos Aires, 1930.

Gabrialdo, A. *Enslingen i urskogen. Reseskildring fran Argentinas urskogar (Misiones, Bompland).* Helsingfors, 1911.

Gaignard, Romain. "L'économie de la République Argentine. L'utilisation du sol." *Les Cahiers d'outre-Mer* (Bordeaux) 13 (1960):59–103.

———. "La faillite de l'expérience de colonisation agricole des "Pieds-Noirs" en Argentine." *Les Cahiers d'Outre-Mer* (Bordeaux) 21 (1968):308–317.

Galharretborde, J. O. *Té argentino: Proyección de la demanda.* Informe Técnico de la Estación Experimental Agropecuaria de Misiones, No. 9, Cerro Azul (Misiones), 1967.

Gallardo, Carlos R. *La industria yerbatera en Misiones.* Buenos Aires, 1898.

Galli Pujato, J. M. *El problema de la tierra y la colonización nacional.* Santa Fe, 1950.

Gambón, Vicente. *A través de las misiones guaraníticas.* Buenos Aires, 1904.

Garsch, Bruno. *Der Einfluß der Jesuiten-Missionen auf den Wandel der Naturlandschaft im Stromgebiet des Paraguay-Paraná während des 17. und 18. Jahrhunderts.* Breslau, 1934.

Gay, Juan P. *Historia da república jesuítica do Paraguai desde o descobrimento do Rio da Prata até aos nossos dias, ano de 1861.* 2nd ed. Rio de Janeiro, 1942.

Geer, J. S. *Der Jesuitenstaat in Paraguay. Staats-, Wirtschaftsform und Entwicklungsgeschichte.* Nürnberg, 1928.

Gelodi, Alfredo. "Misiones: Sus cultivos de yerba mate y tabaco." *Anales de la Sociedad Científica Argentina* 101 (1926):155–215.

Gernhard, Robert. *Dona Francisca, Hansa und Blumenau. Drei Mustersiedlungen im südbrasilischen Staate Santa Catharína.* Breslau, 1901.

Giordano, Guglielmo. "Misiones: una region d'avvenire." *L'Universo* 47 (1967):115–32.

Girola, Carlos D. *Cultivo de la yerba mate en la República Argentina.* Buenos Aires, 1929.

———. *Monografía sobre la yerba mate.* Buenos Aires, 1926.

Gómez, Hernán F. *Corrientes en la guerra con el Brasil.* Corrientes, 1928.

Gómez Langenheim, Antonio. *Colonización en la República Argentina.* Buenos Aires, 1906.

Gori, Gastón. *Inmigración y colonización en la Argentina.* Buenos Aires, 1964.

Gradmann, Robert. *Süddeutschland.* 2 vols. Stuttgart, 1931.

Grüner, Glieb. *La erosión en Misiones.* 2nd ed. Buenos Aires, 1955.

Grüter, P. Ludger, ed. *Festschrift zum Fünfzig-Jahr-Jubiläum (1878–1928) der Einwanderung der Wolga-Deutschen in Argentinien.* Buenos Aires, 1928.

Haabe, Karl Albert. *Das Flurbild des Hofsiedlungsgebiets im mittleren Schwarzwald am Ende des 18. Jahrhunderts.* Bad Godesberg, 1960.

———. "Die 'Waldhufensiedlungen' in den Gebirgen Südwestdeutschland als Problem der systematischen Siedlungsgeographie." *Berichte zur deutschen Landeskunde* 37 (1966):40–52.

Hassel, Herrmann F., ed. *Deutscher Kalender für den Alto Paraná.* Buenos Aires, 1934–1961.

———. *Guía provincial de turismo de Misiones.* Posadas, 1965.

———. "Los alemanes en Misiones." *El Territorio* (Posadas), June 2, 1965, pp. 11–12.

———. "Reisbau in Misiones." In *Deutscher Kalender für den Alto Paraná.* Buenos Aires, 1934, pp. 97–98.

Heer, E. J., et al. *La producción de tung en Misiones: sus aspectos diversos.* Posadas, 1944.

Hegen, Edmund Eduard. *Highways into the Upper Amazon Basin. Pioneer Lands in Southern Colombia, Ecuador, and Northern Peru.* Gainesville, Fla., 1966.

Heppner, Julius. "Aus den Uranfängen der Kolonie Leandro N. Alem (Mecking) 1905–1935." In *Deutscher Kalender für den Alto Paraná.* Buenos Aires, 1936, pp. 133–34.

Hernández, Pablo. *El extrañamiento de los Jesuitas del Río de la Plata y de las Misiones del Paraguay, por decreto de Carlos III.* Madrid, 1908.

————. *Misiones del Paraguay: Organización social de las doctrinas guaraníes de la Compañía de Jesús.* 2 vols. Barcelona, 1913.

Hernández, Rafael. *Cartas misioneras.* Buenos Aires, 1887.

————. "Informe sobre la fundación de las primeras colonias en Misiones." *Revista de la Sociedad Geográfica Argentina* 2 (1884):142–64.

Hettner, Alfred. "Das Deutschtum in Südbrasilien." *Geographische Zeitschrift* 8 (1902):609–626.

————. "Das südlichste Brasilien (Rio Grande do Sul)." *Zeitschrift der Gesellschaft für Erdkunde* 26 (1891):85–144.

Holmberg, Eduardo L. *Viaje a Misiones.* Buenos Aires, 1887.

Holzner, Lutz. "The Role of History and Tradition in the Urban Geography of West Germany." *Annals of the Association of American Geographers* 60 (1970):315–39.

Humboldt, Alexander von. *Kosmos. Entwurf einer physischen Weltbeschreibung. Gesammelte Werke,* vols. 1, 2. Stuttgart, 1889.

Isacovich, Marcelo. *Argentina económica y social.* 2nd ed. Buenos Aires, 1965.

Izaquirre, P. Fray Bernardino. *Misiones franciscanas y narración de los progresos de la geografía en el Oriente del Perú: 1619–1921.* 14 vols. Lima, 1922.

Jahn, Adalbert. *Die Kolonien von São Leopoldo in der Provinz Rio Grande do Sul.* Leipzig, 1871.

James, Preston. *Latin America.* 4th ed. New York, 1969.

Jefferson, Mark. *Peopling the Argentine Pampa.* New York, 1926.

Jeffrey, William H. *Mitre and Argentina.* New York, 1952.

Joerg, Wolfgang Louis Gottfried, ed. *Pioneer Settlement.* New York, 1932.

Jordan, Terry G. "Aspects of German Colonization in Southern Brazil." *Southwestern Social Science Quarterly* (1962):346–53.

Jungenfeld, Wilhelm Ernst von. *Ein Deutsches Schicksal im Urwald.* Berlin, 1933.

Käubler, Rudolf. "Die erzgebirgischen Waldhufendörfer zur Zeit ihrer Entstehung." *Wissenschaftliche Zeitschrift der Universität Halle* (Halle-Wittenburg, Math. Nat. XII/10, 1963):729–34.

Kempski, Carlos E. "El cultivo del algodón en Misiones." *El Territorio* (Posadas), 1937: May 3, 4, 5.

————. *Die Yerba Kultur in Argentinien.* Buenos Aires, 1926.

Kochwasser, Friedrich. "Ulrich Schmidel aus Straubing — Der erste Geschichtsschreiber Argentiniens." *Mitteilungen des Instituts für Auslandsbeziehungen* 11 (1961):109–117.

Klute, Fritz, ed. *Die ländlichen Siedlungen in verschiedenen Klimazonen.* Breslau, 1933.

Klusak, Gustav. *Die Raiffeisen-Kreditgenossenschaften.* Frankfurt a.M., 1964.

Kohlhepp, Gerhard. "Neue Forschungen über die deutsch-brasilianische Bevölkerung." *Geographische Zeitschrift* 53 (1965):61–73.

————. "Types of Agricultural Colonization on Subtropical Brazilian Campos Limpos." *Revista Geográfica* 70 (1969):131–55.

Kopp, Thomas. *Die Siedlung im Walde. Deutsches Schaffen am oberen Paraná.* Buenos Aires, 1949.

Koutché, Vsevolod. *Vegetación forestal del parque nacional del Iguazú.* Buenos Aires, 1948.

Kreisel, W. "Structures agraires de Waldhufendorf dans le Jura." *Revue de Géographie de Lyon* 44 (1969):85–113.

Krüger, Rainer. *Typologie des Waldhufendorfes als Einzelformen und deren Verbreitungsmustern.* Göttingen, 1967.

Kühn, Franz. *Argentinien.* 2 vols. Breslau, 1927.

Lahitte, Emilio. *La cooperación rural.* Buenos Aires, 1912.

————. *El crédito agrícola: Sociedades cooperativas.* Buenos Aires, 1907.

Lamm, Herrmann. *Auswanderungsmöglichkeiten in Argentinien.* Dresden, 1929.

Lange, Henry. *Südbrasilien: Die Provinzen São Pedro do Rio Grande do Sul, Santa Catharina und Paraná mit Rücksicht auf die deutsche Kolonisation.* 2nd ed. Leipzig, 1888.

Lanusse, Juan José. *Colonización en Misiones: 1897–1901.* Posadas, 1902.

Lasserre, Santiago R. "Los suelos de Misiones y su capacidad de uso para plantaciones de coníferas." *IDIA* (Suplemento forestal No. 5, 1968/69):40–50.

————, and Galharretborde, J. O. *Reordenamiento de la economía yerbatera: Plan integral.* Informe Técnico de la Estación Experimental Agropecuaria de Misiones No. 4, Cerro Azul (Misiones), 1966.

Latzina, Francisco. *La Argentina considerada en sus aspectos físico, social y ecónomico.* 2 vols. Buenos Aires, 1902.

Lehmann, Edgar. "Historische Züge der Landesentwicklung im südlichen Brasilien." *Wissenschaftliche Veröffentlichungen des deutschen Instituts für Länderkunde.* n.F. 15/16(1958):51–93.

Leipoldt, Johannes. "Die Flurformen Sachsens." *Petermanns Geographische Mitteilungen* 82 (1936):341–45.

Levene, Ricardo, et al. *Historia de la nación Argentina.* 10 vols. Buenos Aires, 1935–42.

Lindsay, Kenneth. *Eldorado, an Agricultural Settlement. A Brief History of its Origin and Development.* Birmingham, England, 1931.

Lista, Ramón. *El territorio de las misiones.* Buenos Aires, 1883.

Lunnasvaara, V. "Colonia Finlandesa: Misioneksen suamalaissiirtola." *Terra* 44 (1932):1–29.

Lütge, Wilhelm. "Die ersten Deutschen in Argentinien." *Auslandswarte* 32 (1952):34–36.

Lütge, Wilhelm, Hoffmann, Werner, and Körner, Karl W. *Geschichte des Deutschtums in Argentinien.* Buenos Aires, 1955.

Maack, Reinhard. "Neue Forschungen in Paraguay und am Río Paraná. Die Flußgebiete Monday und Acaray." *Die Erde* 93 (1962):4-48.

Maass, Alfredo. *Entwicklung und Perspektiven der wirtschaftlichen Erschließung des tropischen Waldlandes von Peru, unter besonderer Berücksichtigung der verkehrsgeographischen Problematik.* Tübingen, 1969.

Manshard, Walther. "Afrikanische Waldhufen und Waldstreifenfluren—wenig bekannte Formenelemente der Agrarlandschaft in Oberguinea." *Die Erde* 92 (1961):246–58.

Manzi, Francisco. *Breves apuntes sobre el Territorio de Misiones.* Corrientes, 1910.

Märtens, Paul. *Süd-Amerika unter besonderer Berücksichtigung Argentiniens.* Berlin, 1899.

Martínez, Albert B., and Lowandowski, Maurice. *Argentinien im zwanzigsten Jahrhundert.* 4th ed. Gotha, 1912.

Martiny, Rudolf. *Die Grundrißgestaltung der deutschen Siedlungen.* Gotha, 1928.

Meitzen, August. *Siedlung und Agrarwesen der Westgermanen* . . . *der Kelten, Römer, Finnen und Slaven.* 4 vols. Aalen, 1963.

Métraux, A. "Jesuit Missions in South America." In *Handbook of South American Indians,* vol. 5. Washington, D.C., 1949, pp. 645–53.

Misiones Province. *Anteproyecto del plan regulador.* Posadas (?), 1957.

————. *Informe edafológico.* Buenos Aires, 1964.

————. *Informe geológico.* Buenos Aires, 1964.

————. *Informe sobre los recursos forestales.* Buenos Aires, 1964.

————. *Planeamiento de la provincia de Misiones.* 2 vols. Buenos Aires, 1961.

Misiones Province, Ministerio de Asuntos Agrarios. "Registro: Decreto 859, Expediente No. 336/61, April 5, 1961." Unpublished archival report, 1961.

Misiones Province, Oficina de Tierras y Bosques. "Colonias: asesoría de topografía y mensuras (Aprobación de pueblos)." Unpublished archival report, 1963.

Misiones Territory. *La tierra pública y su colonización: Yerbales.* Buenos Aires, 1894.

Molinari, Antonio Manuel. *La ley de colonización y la enmienda Palacios.* Buenos Aires, 1940.

Monbeig, Pierre. *Pionniers et Planteurs de São Paulo,* Paris, 1952.

Monheim, Felix. *Junge Indianerkolonisation in den Tiefländern Ostboliviens.* Braunschweig, 1965.

Moreno, Ruis. *Nociones de geografía histórica, física, económica y política de los territorios nacionales.* Buenos Aires, 1916.

Mörner, Magnus. *The Political and Economic Activities of the Jesuits in the La Plata Region: The Hapsburg Era.* Stockholm, 1953.

Mortensen, Hans. "Zur Entstehung der deutschen Flurformen, insbesondere des Waldhufendorfes." *Nachrichten der Akademie der Wissenschaft* (Göttingen, Phil.-Hist. Klasse 1946/47), pp. 76–80.

Mosk, Sanford A. *Industrial Revolution in Mexico.* Berkeley, Cal., 1954.

Moussy, Jean Antoine Victor Martin de. *Description Géographique et Statistique de la Confédération Argentine.* 3 vols. Paris, 1860–64.

Muello, Alberto Carlos. *Misiones: Las Cataratas del Iguazú, el Alto Paraná y el cultivo de la yerba mate.* Buenos Aires, ca. 1930.

————. *Yerba mate — su cultivo y explotación.* Buenos Aires, 1946.

Mulhall, Michael G., and Mulhall, E. T. *Handbook of the River Plate: 1885.* Buenos Aires, 1885.

Müller-Wille, Wilhelm. "Die Hagenhufendörfer in Schaumburg-Lippe," *Petermanns Geographische Mitteilungen* 90 (1944):245–47.

————. "Langstreifenflur und Drubbel. Ein Beitrag zur Siedlungsgeographie Westgermaniens." *Deutsches Archiv für Landes- und Volksforschung* 8 (1944):9–44.

Muratori, L. A. *Relation des Missions du Paraguai.* Paris, 1754.

Mutinelli, A. *El cultivo del algodón en Misiones.* Buenos Aires, 1936.

Navarro, Mordoquéo. *El Territorio Nacional de Misiones.* Buenos Aires, 1881.

Negrete, Antonio Sanches. *Cuestión-Misiones: Refutación del mensaje del Presidente con el manifiesto de la H. Legislatura de la Provincia de Corrientes.* Corrientes, 1881.

Neufeldt, G. "Das neu erschloßene Siedlungsgebiet in Nord Paraná."
    Erdkunde 5 (1951):233–37.
Neugebauer-Pfrommer, Ursula L. *Die Siedlungsformen im Nordöst-
    lichen Schwarzwald und ihr Wandel seit dem 17. Jahrhundert.* Tü-
    bingen, 1969.
Neumeyer, Max. "Misiones." *Anales de la Sociedad Científica Argentina*
    67 (1909):229, 248.
Newton, Jorge. *Misiones: Oro verde y tierra colorada.* Buenos Aires,
    1951.
Niederlein, Gustav. *Argentinien als deutsches Siedlungsland.* Berlin,
    1922.
————. "Mis exploraciones en el Territorio de Misiones." *Boletín del
    Instituto Geográfico Argentino,* 11 (1890):211–37.
————. *Gutachten für Herrn Baron v. Hirsch über die Colonisations-
    fähigkeit Paraguays und der Argentinischen Territorium Misiones,
    Formosa und Chaco Austral.* Buenos Aires, 1892.
————. *Reisebriefe von der deutsch-argentinischen Expedition zur
    Prüfung der Colonisationsfähigkeit der Lezama'schen Misioneslän-
    dereien.* Berlin, 1883.
————. "La riqueza florestal de la República Argentina en la Exposición
    Universal de París de 1889." In D. Santiago Alcorta, *Colección de in-
    formes.* Buenos Aires, 1889, pp. 1–6.
Nielsen, Roger. *Til Argentina Rejsen dertil paa tredje Klasse. Forhal-
    dene.* Copenhagen, 1912.
Niemeier, Georg. "Frühformen des Waldhufen." *Petermanns Geo-
    graphische Mitteilungen* 93 (1949):14–27.
————. *Siedlungsgeographie.* 2nd ed. Braunschweig, 1969.
Nieves, R. *Los problemas del tung en nuestro país.* Buenos Aires, 1948.
Nitz, Hans-Jürgen. *Die ländlichen Siedlungsformen des Odenwaldes.*
    Heidelberg, 1962.
Noellenburg Alverdes, H. "Misiones und seine Wirtschaft." *Boletín de
    la Cámara de Comercio Argentino-Alemana* (1964):134–38.
El Noticiero (Posadas). May 16, 1906, No. 1, p. 387.
Nusdorfer, Bernhard. *Beytrag zur Geschichte vom Paraguay, und denen
    Missionen der Jesuiten daselbst.* Frankfurt, 1768.
Oddone, Jacinto. *La burguesía terrateniente argentina.* Buenos Aires,
    1930.
Ogrissek, Rudi. *Dorf und Flur in der DDR.* Leipzig, 1961.
Oroño, Nicasio. *Informe del director de tierras, inmigración y agricul-
    tura a S.E. el Sr. Ministro del Interior sobre las denuncias del diario
    "La Prensa."* Buenos Aires, 1892.

Ostermann, Walter. "Neu-Karlsruhe: Monografie einer deutschen Kolonie." *Südamerika* 4 (1954):657–60.

———. "Tung-Oel." In *Deutscher Kalender für den Alto Paraná*. Buenos Aires, 1937, pp. 87–88.

Parsons, James J. *Antioqueño Colonization in Western Colombia.* 2nd ed. Berkeley, 1968.

———. *Antioquia's Corridor to the Sea: An Historical Geography of the Settlement of Urabá.* Berkeley, 1967.

Papadakis, Juan. "Posibilidades agrícolas de Misiones." *IDIA* 82(1954): 4–16.

Pérez Llana, E. A. *Derecho Agrario.* 2 vols. 3rd ed. Sante Fe, Argentina, 1959.

Petry, Leopoldo. *São Leopoldo berço da colonização alemã do Rio Grande do Sul.* 2nd ed. São Leopoldo, 1964.

Peyret, Alejo. *Cartas sobre Misiones.* Buenos Aires, 1881.

Piccirilli, Ricardo, Romay, Francisco L., and Gianello, Leoncio. *Diccionario histórico argentino.* Buenos Aires, 1954. Vol. 5.

Pigretti, Eduardo A., and Santesteban, Joaquín. *Recopilación de leyes agrarias.* 2 vols. Buenos Aires, 1960.

Powell, William L. *Diary of the Water Witch Expedition, from Asuncion to the Yerbales of San Estanislao, Returning by Way of Misiones, 1854.* Washington, D.C., 1966.

Prohaska, Federico. "Regímenes estacionales de precipitación de Sudamérica y mares vecinos (desde 15°s hasta Antártida)." *Meteoros* 2 (1952):66–100.

Queirel, Juan. "Apuntes de viaje sobre el Territorio de Misiones." *Boletín del Instituto Geográfico* 14 (1894):469–88.

———. *Misiones.* Buenos Aires, 1897.

———. *Las ruinas de Misiones.* Buenos Aires, 1901.

Quelle, O. "Das Problem des Jesuitenstaates Paraguay." *Ibero-Amerikanisches Archiv* 8 (1934):260–82.

Quevedo, Casiano V. and Bellón, Carlos A. "Reconocimiento para conservación del suelo en la Estación Experimental Agropecuaria de Loreto (Misiones)." *IDIA* (Suplemento No. 1, 1960):162–64.

Rademacher, Federico. "Misiones — die neue Heimat." In *Deutscher Kalender für den Alto Paraná*. Buenos Aires, 1937, pp. 30–32.

Republic of Argentina. *Catálogo de documentos del Archivo de Indias en Sevilla referentes a la historia de la República Argentina.* 3 vols. Buenos Aires, 1901–1910.

———. *Código civil.* 19th ed. Buenos Aires, 1964.

———. *Cuarto censo nacional.* Buenos Aires, 1947.

———. "Mapa económico de la República Argentina." Buenos Aires, 1925.

———. *Misiones: La tierra pública y su colonización. Yerbales.* Buenos Aires, 1894.

———. *Primer censo de la República Argentina, 1869.* Buenos Aires, 1872.

Republic of Argentina, Comisión Reguladora de la Producción y Comercio de la Yerba Mate. *Memorias.* Posadas, 1944–68.

Republic of Argentina, Congreso Nacional. *Cámara de Diputados. Vol. 5, 1919.* Buenos Aires, 1920.

Republic of Argentina, Consejo Federal de Inversiones. *Acaray-Misiones Interconnection Feasibility Report.* Buenos Aires, 1965.

Republic of Argentina, Dirección General de Tierras: Geodesia. "Archivo de mensuras." Folders No. 49, Buenos Aires, 1902; No. 51, Buenos Aires, 1903; No. 56, Buenos Aires, 1906; No. 120, Buenos Aires, 1930; No. 170, Buenos Aires, 1939; Mapoteca C, No. 86, Buenos Aires, 1915; Acta 102, Posadas, 1923. Reports on file at Oficina de Tierras y Bosques, Posadas, Misiones.

Republic of Argentina, Departamento de Tierras, Colonias y Agricultura. "Mesa de entradas y salidas, expediente No. 2,438, P." 1895. Unpublished archival report on file at Oficina de Tierras y Bosques, Posadas.

Republic of Argentina, Ministerio de Agricultura. *Ley de bosques y yerbales.* Buenos Aires, 1915.

Republic of Peru. *Inventario, evaluación e integración de los recursos naturales de la zona del Río Pachitea.* Lima, 1966.

Richter, Werner. "Der Moshav Ovdim. Entwicklung und Probleme einer typischen kooperativen ländlichen Siedlungsform in Israel." *Geographische Rundschau* 22 (1970):175–85.

Rocha, Augusto da. *Colección completa de leyes nacionales sancionadas por el Honorable Congreso durante los años 1852 a 1917.* Vols. 4 and 5. Buenos Aires, 1918.

———. *Decretos reglamentarios de leyes nacionales clasificadas.* 4 vols. Buenos Aires, 1935.

Roche, Jean. "Alguns aspectos da vida rural nas colônias alemãs do Rio Grande do Sul." *Boletim Geográfico* 18 (1960):378–94.

———. *La Colonisation Allemand et le Rio Grande do Sul.* Paris, 1959.

———. *A colonização alemã no Espírito Santo.* São Paulo, 1968.

Rogelio Alvarez, José, ed. *Noticia de Jalisco: 1953–1959.* Guadalajara, 1959.

———, ed. *Nueva imagen de Jalisco: 1953–1959.* Guadalajara, 1959.

Roig, Virgilio G., and Cei, José M. "Relaciones biogeográficas entre

Misiones y el sistema de la Serra Geral." *Boletín de Estudios Geográficos* 8 (1961):35–85.

Rothwell, Stuart Clark. *The Old Italian Colonial Zone of Rio Grande do Sul, Brazil.* Pôrto Alegre, 1959.

Ruiz de Montoya, Antonio. *Conquista espiritual hecha por los religiosos de la Compañía de Jesús en las provincias del Paraguay, Paraná, Uruguay y Tape.* Bilbao, 1892.

Salomone, G. A. *Disertaciones sobre Misiones, Chaco, Formosa, Chubut y otras regiones de la Patagonia por la Conferencia de Agrónomos.* Buenos Aires, 1920.

Samhaber, Ernst. *Südamerika. Gesicht-Geist-Geschichte.* Hamburg, 1939.

Santillán, Diego A. de. *Gran Enciclopedia Argentina.* Vol. 5. Buenos Aires, 1959.

Sapper, Karl. *Natur und Lebensbedingungen in tropischen und tropennaher Gebieten. Ein praktischer Ratgeber.* Hamburg, 1920.

Saravia, Belisario. *Memoria sobre los límites entre la República Argentina y el Paraguay, 1867.* Buenos Aires, 1867.

Scharrer, F. *Die Kolonisation in der Subtropischen Urwaldzone des Noerdlichen Argentiniens: Das Territorium von Misiones als Einwanderungsziel: Die Yerbamate-kultur.* Buenos Aires, ca. 1928.

Schauff, Johannes, ed. *Landerschließung und Kolonisation in Lateinamerika.* Berlin, 1959.

Schempp, Hermann. *Gemeinschaftssiedlungen auf religiösen und weltanschaulicher Grundlage.* Tübingen, 1969.

Schlüter, Otto. *Die Siedlungen im nordöstlichen Thüringen. Ein Beispiel für die Behandlung siedlungsgeographischen Fragen.* Berlin, 1903.

Schmidl, Ulrich. *Derrotero y viaje a España y las Indias.* Translated by Edmundo Wernicke. 2nd ed. Buenos Aires, 1947.

———. *Reise nach Südamerika in den Jahren 1534 bis 1554.* Stuttgart, 1889.

Schmieder, Oskar. *Die neue Welt.* Teil 1. *Mittel- und Südamerika.* Heidelberg, 1962.

Schmieder, Oskar, and Wilhelmy, Herbert. *Deutsche Ackerbausiedlung im südamerikanischen Grasland, Pampa und Gran Chaco.* Leipzig, 1938.

Schopflocher, Roberto. *Historia de la colonización agrícola en Argentina.* Buenos Aires, 1955.

Schröder, Karl Heinz, and Schwarz, Gabriele. *Die ländlichen Siedlungsformen in Mitteleuropa.* Bad Godesberg, 1969.

Schulz, Wilhelm. *Aimé Bonpland. Alexander von Humboldts Begleiter auf der Amerikareise 1799–1804. Sein Leben und Wirken, besonders nach 1817 in Argentinien.* Wiesbaden, 1960.

————. "Deutsche Geschicke und Leistungen in Argentinien." *Mitteilungen, Institut für Auslandsbeziehungen* 11 (1961):117–25.

Schuster, Adolph N. *Argentinien. Land, Volk, Wirtschaftsleben und Kolonisation.* 2 vols. Diessen vor München, 1913.

————. *Paraguay. Land, Volk, Geschichte, Wirtschaftsleben und Kolonisation.* Stuttgart, 1929.

Schwarz, Gabriele. *Allgemeine Siedlungsgeographie.* 3rd ed. Berlin, 1966.

Schweinitz, H. U. von. "Die heutigen Zentren für deutsche Einwanderung in Südamerika: Chaco, Paraguay, Misiones (Arg.)." *Phoenix* 17 (1931):263–67.

Schwelm, Adolph Julius. *Some Thoughts on Colonization: An Address Delivered at the Royal Empire Society.* London, 1932.

Scrosati, Emilio. *La tierra prometida Misiones.* Buenos Aires, 1944.

Sepp, Anton. *Viagem as missões jesuíticas e trabalhos apostólicos.* São Paulo, 1943.

Sepp, Anton, and Böhm, Anton. *Reisebeschreibung: Wie nemlichen dieselbe auss Hispanien in Paraquariam kommen; und kurzer Bericht der denckwürdigsten Sachen selbiger Landschafft/Völkern und Arbeitung der sich alldort befinden.* Ingolstatt, 1712.

Siewers, Enrique. "Openings for Settlers in Argentina." *International Labor Review* 39 (1934):457–91.

Smith, T. Lynn. *Brazil: People and Institutions.* 2nd ed. Baton Rouge, 1963.

Solari, Juan Antonio. *Miseria de la riqueza argentina.* Buenos Aires, 1932.

Sölch, Johann. *Die Auffassung der "natürlichen Grenzen" in der wissenschaftlichen Geographie.* Innsbruck, 1924.

Stanislowski, Dan. "Early Spanish Town Planning in the New World." *Geographical Review* 37 (1947):94–105.

————. "The Origin and Spread of the Grid Pattern Town." *Geographical Review* 36 (1946):105–120.

Sternberg, Hilgard O'Reilly. "Die Formen der Bodennutzung der europäischen Siedlungen in Südbrasilien." *Erdkunde* 12 (1958):141–43.

————. "Man and Environmental Change in South America." In *Monographeae Biologicae: Biogeography and Ecology of South America,* vol. 1. The Hague, 1968, pp. 413–45.

————. "A propósito da colonizãçao germânica em terras de mata da América do Sul." *Revista Brasileira de Geografía* 11 (1949):123–44.

Stewart, Norman R. "Cultural Conservation and the Farm Dwelling. The Mark of the Pioneer." *Landscape* 15 (1965):26–28.

———. *Japanese Colonization in Eastern Paraguay.* Washington, D.C., 1967.

———. "Migration and Settlement in the Peruvian Montaña: The Apurímac Valley." *Geographical Review* 55 (1965):143–57.

———. "Tea – A New Agricultural Industry for Argentina." *Economic Geography* 36 (1960):267–76.

Suaiter Martínez, Francisco. *Problemas sociales y económicos de Misiones.* Buenos Aires, 1928.

"Suplemento especial de Misiones." *Analysis* 4 (1965).

Tanzi, Héctor José. "Breve historia de la imprenta en el Río de la Plata, que trata de esclarecer el origen de la existente en el Museo Histórico Nacional." *Historia, Revista de Historia Argentina, Americana y Español* 25 (1961):22–33.

Taylor, Carl C. *Rural Life in Argentina.* Baton Rouge, 1948.

Techo, Nicolás del. *Historia de la Provincia del Paraguay de la Compañía de Jesús.* 5 vols. Madrid, 1897.

Thiesenhusen, William C. *Chile's Experiments in Agrarian Reform.* Madison, Wis., 1966.

Thompson, Reginald William. *Voice From the Wilderness.* 2nd ed. London, 1947.

Torre, Lisandro de la. *El territorio de Misiones: la industria yerbatera.* Buenos Aires. 1924.

Torre Revello, José. "Informe sobre Misiones de indios existentes en la segunda mitad del siglo 18, en las provincias del Paraguay (de los Padres Jesuitas) y de la Asunción (de los Padres Franciscanos)." *Boletín del Instituto de Investigaciones Históricas* 13 (1931):49–50.

Troll, Carl, and Paffen, Karl H. "Seasonal Climates of the Earth." In *Allgemeine Klimageographie,* edited by Joachim Blüthgen. 2nd ed. Berlin, 1966.

Turner, Frederick Jackson. *The Frontier in American History.* New York, 1920.

Uhlig, Harald. "Methodische Begriffe der Geographie besonders der Landschaftskunde." Offprint from Wolf Tietze, ed. *Westermanns Lexikon der Geographie.* Braunschweig, 1967.

Uhlig, Harald, and Lienau, Cay, eds. *Materialien zur Terminologie der Agrarlandschaft: Flur und Flurformen.* Gießen, 1967. Vol. 1.

Valverde, Orlando. "Excursão à região colonial antiga do Rio Grande do Sul." *Revista Brasileira de Geografía* 10 (1948):477–534.

Vasco, C. A. S. del. *Cultivos prácticos en los territorios del norte de la República Argentina.* Buenos Aires, 1870.

Verband deutscher Vereine. *Hundert Jahre Deutschtum in Rio Grande do Sul: 1824–1924.* Pôrto Alegre, 1924.

Victoria Colonization Company, The, Ltd. *Victoria: Colony for British Settlers on Paraná River.* London, 1934.

————. *Victoria: Colony for British Settlers on Paraná River, Argentine: Further Explanatory Notes.* London, 1935.

————. *Victoria, Paraná River Argentina: Some Extracts From the Press.* London, ca. 1933.

Vogt, Federico. *Estudios históricos: la civilización de los guaraníes en los siglos 17 y 18.* Buenos Aires, 1903.

Wagemann, Ernst. *Die deutschen Kolonisten im brasilianischen Staate Espírito Santo.* München, 1915.

Waibel, Leo. *Die europäische Kolonisation Südbrasiliens.* Bonn, 1955.

————. "European Colonization in Southern Brazil." *Geographical Review* 40 (1950):529–47.

————. "Princípios da colonização européia no sul do Brasil." *Revista Brasileira de Geografía* 11 (1949):159–222.

Walle, Paul. *L'Argentine: Telle Qu'elle Est.* Paris, 1912.

Warnecke, Edgar F. *Engter und seine Bauerschaften.* Hannover, 1958.

Wettstein, Karl Alexander. *Brasilien und die deutsch-brasilianische Kolonie Blumenau.* Leipzig, 1907.

Wilcken, Guillermo. *Las colonias. Informe sobre el estado actual de las colonias agrícolas de la República Argentina.* Buenos Aires, 1873.

Wilhelmy, Herbert. "Der Alto Paraná und die Fälle des Yguazú." *Zeitschrift für Erdkunde* 12 (1944):437–42.

————. "Aufbau und Landformen des Alto Paraná-Gebietes." *Petermanns Geographische Mitteilungen* 92 (1948):32–38.

————. "Die Besiedlung der Staatsländereien im argentinischen Territorium Misiones." *Petermanns Geographische Mitteilungen* 98 (1954):312–18.

————. "Bestandsaufbau und Wirtschaftswert des Urwaldes am Alto Paraná." *Zeitschrift für Weltforstwirtschaft* 13 (1949):61–67.

————. *Die deutschen Siedlungen in Mittelparaguay.* Kiel, 1941.

————. "Zur Klimatologie und Bioklimatologie des Alto Paraná-Gebietes in Südamerika." *Petermanns Geographische Mitteilungen* 94 (1950):130–39.

————. "Neu-Karlsruhe (Liebig): Ein warnendes Beispiel gescheiterter Genossenschaftssiedlung in nördlichen Argentinien." In *Festschrift für Karl Massmann.* Kiel, 1954, pp. 240–62.

————. "Probleme der Urwaldkolonisation in Südamerika." *Zeitschrift der Gesellschaft für Erdkunde zu Berlin* Nos. 7/8 (1940):303–314.

————. *Siedlung im südamerikanischen Urwald.* Hamburg, 1949.

————. "Wald und Grasland als Siedlungsraum in Südamerika." *Geographische Zeitschrift* 46 (1940):208–219.

Wilhelmy, Herbert, and Rohmeder, Wilhelm. *Die La Plata Länder: Argentinien, Paraguay, Uruguay.* Braunschweig, 1963.

Yssouribehere, Pedro J. *Investigación agrícola en el Territorio de Misiones.* Buenos Aires, 1904.

Zbinden, Karl. *Die schweizerische Auswanderung nach Argentinien, Uruguay, Chile und Paraguay.* Affoltern am Albis, 1931.

Zeballos, Estanislao S. *Arbitration Upon a Part of the National Territory of Misiones Disputed by the United States of Brazil.* New York, 1893.

————. *Descripción amena de la República Argentina.* 2 vols. Buenos Aires, 1881–83.

Zöller, Hugo. *Die Deutschen im brasilischen Urwald.* 2 vols. Berlin, 1883.

Zschocke, Herlig. *Die Waldhufensiedlung am linken deutschen Niederrhein.* Wiesbaden, 1963.

INDEX